# FAMILY DECLASSIFIED:

## UNCOVERING MY GRANDFATHER'S JOURNEY FROM SPY TO CHILDREN'S BOOK AUTHOR

KATHERINE FENNELLY

SUNBURY PRESS

Mechanicsburg, PA USA

Published by Sunbury Press, Inc.
Mechanicsburg, PA  USA

www.sunburypress.com

For information about special discounts for bulk purchases, please contact Sunbury Press Orders Dept. at (855) 338-8359 or orders@sunburypress.com.

To request one of our authors for speaking engagements or book signings, please contact Sunbury Press Publicity Dept. at publicity@sunburypress.com.

FIRST SUNBURY PRESS EDITION: August 2023

Set in Adobe Garamond Pro | Interior design by Crystal Devine | Cover by Sean Villafranca and Darleen Sedjro | Edited by Sarah Peachey.

Publisher's Cataloging-in-Publication Data
Names: Fennelly, Katherine, author.
Title: Family declassified : uncovering my grandfather's journey from spy to children's book author / Katherine Fennelly.
Description: First trade paperback edition. | Mechanicsburg, PA : Sunbury Press, 2023.
Summary: In *Family Declassified* the author delves into the family secrets of her grandfather Francis Kalnay, a high-level spy in WWII. In 1974 Francis fled to Mexico for twenty-five years where he reinvented himself as a children's book author and more. Until his death, he never spoke of his Jewish ancestry, work as a spy, or the Hungarian Fascists that murdered his sister and nephew.
Identifiers: ISBN : 979-8-88819-110-1 (paperback) | ISBN : 979-8-88819-111-8 (ePub).
Subjects: BIOGRAPHY & AUTOBIOGRAPHY / Jewish | HISTORY / Wars & Conflcts / World War II / European Theater | FAMILY & RELATIONSHIPS / Family History & Genealogy | BIOGRAPHY & AUTOBIOGRAPHY / Personal Memoirs.

Product of the United States of America
0  1  1  2  3  5  8  13  21  34  55

*For the Love of Books!*

This book is dedicated to the great-grandmother I never knew: Rózsa Margulit Kálnay, who was banished, and largely forgotten, until now.[*] The story describes the exploits of her youngest son, my grandfather Francis Kalnay—a focus that compels me to offer posthumous apologies to my own beloved mother, Elizabeth (Böske) Kalnay Fennelly, for writing about the father who abandoned her.

[*] Note on accent marks: In Hungarian Kálnay is spelled with an accent. I have employed this spelling when writing about my grandfather's childhood and the names of his relatives. However, Ferko was known as "Francis Kalnay," without an accent mark, in the United States. I have therefore used this spelling when writing about his life and career after leaving Hungary, and in any mention of his descendants.

# CONTENTS

*There are no secrets that time does not reveal.*

—Jean Racine

# FAMILY TREE A:
## FERKO'S PARENTS AND SIBLINGS

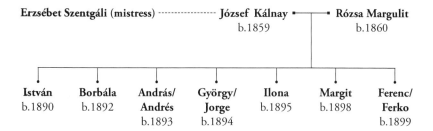

Erzsébet Szentgáli (mistress) ---------------- József Kálnay • ——— • Rózsa Margulit
b.1859    b.1860

| István | Borbála | András/ | György/ | Ilona | Margit | Ferenc/ |
|--------|---------|---------|---------|-------|--------|---------|
| b.1890 | b.1892  | Andrés  | Jorge   | b.1895| b.1898 | Ferko   |
|        |         | b.1893  | b.1894  |       |        | b.1899  |

# FAMILY TREE B:

## FERKO'S WIVES AND CHILDREN

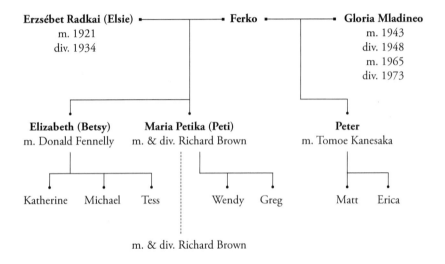

**Erzsébet Radkai (Elsie)** •————————• **Ferko** •————————• **Gloria Mladineo**
m. 1921                                    m. 1943
div. 1934                                div. 1948
                                                   m. 1965
                                                   div. 1973

**Elizabeth (Betsy)**     **Maria Petika (Peti)**                **Peter**
m. Donald Fennelly    m. & div. Richard Brown      m. Tomoe Kanesaka

Katherine    Michael    Tess        Wendy    Greg        Matt    Erica

m. & div. Richard Brown

# I

# INTRODUCTION

My Hungarian grandfather, Ferenc Kalnay, was born in 1899. He went by Francis in the United States and Francisco in Argentina and Mexico, but in each location people close to him called him Ferko (pronounced Fair-kō).

If you had told me when I was growing up that one day I would become fascinated—even obsessed—with researching Ferko's life, I would have been incredulous. I barely knew him, except as a man in a beret with a strong Hungarian accent who lived in Mexico and who sent us wooden marionettes and brightly embroidered blouses at Christmas. I also knew he was an award-winning children's book author whose books sat on our shelves in neat rows. However, my mother spoke of him rarely, and when she did, it was with thinly veiled resentment over his many girlfriends and his abandonment of her, her mother, and her sister when she was a child.

When I was in my early thirties, I learned that there was much more to our family history than I had known. First, a West Coast cousin informed me that our family was Jewish—something no one ever told me; then, a WWII historian contacted me and revealed that Ferko had been a spy for the Allies in World War II. Spies? Hidden Jewish ancestry? I decided to apply my academic research training to my own family and dig deeper into the life of this mysterious figure. What I learned had a profound impact on my life.

Francis Kalnay was articulate and well spoken and never hesitated or searched for words. He spoke seven languages and his narration was filled with literary puns, whether he was speaking English, Spanish, or Hungarian. Despite a childhood of disruption and tragedy, as an adult he excelled at multiple careers, working variously as an actor, journalist, architect, proprietor of a camp for writers and artists, a chef, an award-winning children's book author, and a high-level spy for the Allied Forces in Europe with the Office of Strategic Services (OSS). At the OSS he was one of the few foreign-born Americans informed and "indoctrinated" in what we now know as the ULTRA decrypts, the German Enigma messages used to capture or thwart almost all German offensive intelligence activity during the Second World War. These facts were not difficult to discern, but several questions required deeper investigation. How did a Hungarian refugee become a high-level government spy, working with top-secret information and recruiting covert operators to sneak behind enemy lines in Nazi-occupied Europe? What led Ferko to leave government service at the apex of his career and later flee to Mexico? Why did he never speak of our family's Jewish ancestry or the murders of his sister and nephew during World War II? My search for answers opened Pandora's box.

Family histories are like an intergenerational game of "Telephone," with fragments whispered from one relative to the next until a narrative finally emerges in an altered—and often unrecognizable—form. Some edits are accidental; others are intentional. We all think we know our family stories, but how can we sort fact from fiction, family lore from truth, when the principal characters are long gone? And what happens when some facts are intentionally distorted or obliterated? Can the truth be retrieved and distinguished from the myths? These are questions that I address in *Family Declassified*.

Should this book be classified as memoir or biography? I would call it a hybrid. It's a memoir in that it includes explanations of what drew me to the story of my grandfather's life, how I conducted the research, and reflections on his impact on me, my mother, her sister, and my maternal grandmother. It is a biography in that it records the history of Francis Kalnay, as revealed in hundreds of declassified government records.

I am not a trained historian, but my book fits into the academic category of family history, a domain that some historians characterize as one that is too subjective to conform to the norms of scholarly discourse. Although it is ironic that I should be the narrator of the life of a man I barely knew, the advantage of that distance is that it helped keep me objective in analyzing Ferko's character once I moved beyond my mother's contempt for her father.

*Family Declassified* also has elements of a mystery since so many aspects of Ferko's life presented as enigmas that I set out to decipher—much as Allied specialists deciphered the German Enigma code. After five years of research and scrutiny of declassified government files, I discovered facts that Ferko never mentioned in his lifetime. Others remain shrouded in mystery. In particular, family secrets are an underlying theme of the book as I sought to discover the origin of stories that nurtured our family's collective self-image.

If the truth can't be fully known, at least it can be put into context. Today, more than one hundred years after my grandfather left Hungary on a merchant ship bound for New York, I have attempted to do that by stitching together memories, archival data, and historical records to understand a man whose life was shaped by some of the most extraordinary events of the twentieth century.

## A MAN OF MANY FACES

People looked up when Ferko walked into a room. He had a twinkle in his eye, a lilting Hungarian accent, and a quiet, forceful presence that drew people in. He was charming and charismatic and fully aware of the effect of his aura. He used to say, "It's better to speak softly so that people have to lean in to listen to you." These qualities and his keen intelligence undoubtedly made him successful in his many ventures. And yet, he was also a philanderer who had multiple affairs and repeatedly abandoned his wives, children, and girlfriends.

My mother never forgave her father for abandoning her as a child in Hungary alone with her mother, Elsie, and her sister, Peti, leaving them destitute while he flaunted his girlfriends. Yet her sense of family duty was strong, and, despite the rift between them, Ferko visited our family every four or five years. My mother complained bitterly in advance of these visits but let him come nonetheless. Once, in New Jersey, he annoyed her by taking over the kitchen and rendering chicken schmalz. I wonder now if this essential ingredient of Ashkenazi cooking was a subtle clue to our hidden Jewish heritage. Another clue came in the form of a book we inherited from Ferko—traditional kosher recipes by Anne London and Bertha Kahn Bishov entitled, *The Complete American Jewish Cookbook*. Ironically one web reviewer described it as "the go-to cookbook when you can no longer ask your grandmother," which, of course, my relatives could not do. The book is filled with hand-written notes in which Ferko highlighted his favorite recipes.

My grandfather imbued everything he did with a storyteller's sensibility—if he was cooking, he would say, "Stir this until it feels stirred." This wasn't an affectation; it was his persona. On the other hand, although he wrote children's books, he wasn't adept at interacting with children. Given his abandonment of his own children, I was amazed when he unabashedly offered me parenting advice on how to get my four-year-old daughter Leila to eat healthy foods, or when he gave her a book on etiquette published in the 1950s. Ferko sent other eccentric gifts. On one occasion he gave my preteen brother a samurai sword.

In many ways, my mother was the opposite of her father. Although she too had bounced from continent to continent growing up, she had none of Ferko's outward romanticism or impracticality. Instead, she exhibited a fierce determination to address any problem—large or small—head-on, without relying on others. She was physically small but so strong and active that it was difficult to keep up with her. I used to joke that if my mother were waiting at a baggage carousel and a beefy man offered to pick up her suitcase, she would jump up to handle her luggage—and his too. Today I wonder if she acquired this fierce determination and pragmatism as a means of coping with her traumatic and chaotic childhood. In any case, they are characteristics that she passed on. Like my mother, I am more likely to search for "fixes" to immediate obstacles than to reflect on their underlying causes.

My sister, Tess, shared our mother's feelings toward Ferko. She recalls his visits with distaste because of the way he constantly petted her, or, as she put it, "stroked my head like a dog, saying 'beautiful, beautiful.'" This was particularly strange to her because my parents rarely demonstrated their love for us with overt verbal or physical signs of affection. I never doubted their love, but we were not a family that hugged frequently or said "I love you" aloud to one another. Ferko was an anomaly.

We all admired Ferko's children's books. He was proud of them and supplied us with copies in English and foreign translations. My cousin Wendy recalls one summer that she, her mother, and her brother spent with Ferko in Mexico when he read from drafts of *It Happened in Chichipica* (then named *The Seventh Tortilla*) each night after dinner. The adults gave him feedback, but he was especially interested in the children's reactions.

At first I didn't give Ferko much thought because I saw him rarely and, like my sister, I had absorbed my mother's disdain for him. Later, however, I became intrigued when I learned of his adventures. We lived in a conservative suburb of New York when I was in high school, but I dreamed of more exotic places. When I was sixteen I lived in Iran for a year with relatives who taught there. The trip opened my eyes to the world and left me feeling restless when I returned home. The more I learned about Ferko's life of languages, travel, and intrigue, the more interested I became.

A Google search for "Francis Kalnay" yields more than 54,000 results—the vast majority related to his work as the author of children's books, including *Chucaro: Wild Pony of the Pampa,* for which he won a Newbery Honor in 1959. Buried deep within the search results were a few references to his years at the OSS, the precursor to the CIA. However, none described how he became a high-ranking spy for the Allied Forces in Europe during World War II.

Nor is there any indication in those general web searches that my grandfather was Jewish. I learned of my Jewish ancestry in a roundabout way from one of my California cousins in 1979, when I was in my early thirties and had just given birth to my first child. He revealed the information in a conversation with my brother, who then passed it on to me. I found the revelation surprising.[2] As someone with an Irish-Catholic surname, raised in a secular household, it had never occurred to me that I might have Jewish roots—particularly because of my mother's vehement rejection of all religion. When I was growing up, my parents didn't attend church of any kind, and until I was old enough to know better, I thought this was normal for American families of my generation.

When I approached my mother to ask about our Jewish ancestry, her reaction was visceral. She was clearly annoyed and said firmly, "I'm an atheist—I'm not Jewish." To her, Judaism was something one subscribed to or rejected, like any other religion, rather than a marker of identity or ethnicity. Still, I had struck a nerve. The news of our Jewish ancestry caused me some cognitive dissonance, but in 1979 I was too busy raising a baby on my own and finishing my dissertation to dwell on its significance.

If there was ever any doubt about my Jewish ancestry, it was resolved four decades later in December 2018, when one of my daughters gifted me a 23andMe membership for Christmas and I saw our family history represented in graphs and statistics. Perhaps it should have been a Hanukkah gift since the DNA results revealed that—on my mother's side—my ancestry is 98.4% Ashkenazi Jewish. Why had this been kept a secret? Was it fear or shame that prevented my maternal grandparents or my mother from acknowledging our Jewish identity? At that point, hints of our family's hidden history awakened my curiosity and instincts as a researcher.

The intrigue was compounded in 2015 when I first learned that Ferko had been a spy for the Allied forces. This news came from a researcher at the University of Graz in Austria who wrote to me after reading a published family obituary that mentioned my grandfather.

*Dear Ms. Fennelly,*

*I am a researcher at the University of Graz in Austria and, in searching Google for information about one subject of my work, came across an obituary which you wrote in 2010 for your mother. Your grandfather (Francis Kalnay) is a central figure in research for my master's thesis and will play an even more important role in my PhD thesis for his involvement with American wartime (and postwar) intelligence organizations. If you, or any of your relatives would be willing to provide me with any information on him, I would be very grateful. Naturally, I can provide references to my research and*

*would be happy to share the documentation I have on him from the
National Archives in College Park, MD, should you be interested.*

*Thank you in advance,*

*Duncan Bare, BA
ACIPSS Executive Director
Karl-Franzens-University Graz, Austria*

Since our West Coast relatives had been both personally and geographically closer to my grandfather, I forwarded the query to my cousin Wendy Brown, who tended to Ferko during the last ten years of his life. She wrote back saying:

*In the early to mid-1940s, Ferko worked for the OSS, the precursor
to the CIA, and the main American intelligence (spy) operation of
WWII. The OSS was filled with recent immigrants from Hungary
and Yugoslavia, mostly because they tended to read and speak several
languages*

Wendy also mentioned that Ferko had fled to Mexico after the war. These tantalizing facts awakened my interest in the Kalnay family history.

## A PERSON AT THE EPICENTER OF MOMENTOUS WORLD EVENTS

Although he never went to university, Ferko was a polymath who held multiple jobs on three continents and a polyglot who spoke seven languages. Researching his life drew me to such wildly disparate topics as psychiatric hospitals in the Austro-Hungarian Empire, nudist camps in the rural US, the establishment of spy agencies during World War II, the history of Jews in central Europe, the McCarthy Era in the US, American expatriates in Mexico, and many others.

The sheer scope of my grandfather's adventures and the fact that he lived in an era of unparalleled upheaval and intrigue made an exploration of his life fascinating and daunting. He was like an incarnation of Woody Allen's film hero Zelig—a man who appeared at the epicenter of several momentous world events. I recap the events briefly here and describe them in detail later in the book. Ferko was born in 1899 in the Austro-Hungarian Empire and joined the Imperial Merchant Marines as the empire collapsed at the end of the First World War. At age twenty, he emigrated from Hungary to the United States during the "Red Scare," at a time when the Spanish Flu was still claiming millions of lives worldwide. He emigrated from Hungary to the US, where he married and moved to Argentina, then back to Hungary, where he abandoned his wife and daughters in 1933 during the Great Depression. At age forty, Ferko was working for the US government when the US joined World War II. By the time he was forty-five, he was directing espionage activities in strategic parts of Nazi-occupied Europe. Later, when the McCarthy hearings began in 1954, he fled to Mexico, where he lived for twenty years, returning to the US just as the Vietnam War was winding down.

As a social science researcher, I felt up to the challenge of investigating my grandfather's life. Fortunately, I was able to access his declassified OSS files and spend several days at the National Archives (NARA) in College Park, Maryland, before they closed during the COVID-19 pandemic. There, skilled archivists helped me locate hundreds of documents from among 400,000 pages of declassified OSS records released by the CIA in 2000. I also benefitted greatly from personal interviews with family members, such as my cousin Wendy Brown and Ferko's nephew Esteban Kálnay in Spain. Extensive reading and correspondence with specialists on the OSS, World War II, Hungarian history, the Holocaust, and many other topics were also invaluable. I describe this work in detail in the Research Methods and Acknowledgements section at the end of the book.

## BOYHOOD AND A MOTHER BANISHED

Early in my research, I was shocked to learn of the fate of my great-grandmother Rózsa Margulit, both because of the nature of her life and the fact that Ferko and several of his siblings tried to erase her from our family history.

Rózsa was born in 1860 in western Hungary near Lake Balatón. After marrying József Kálnay, she bore seven children. This was slightly more than typical for the era. The total fertility rate for women in Hungary in 1900 was 5.32.[1] The last of Rózsa's children was my grandfather Ferenc, born in 1899, whom everyone called "Ferko."

### Children Born to Rózsa Margulit and József Kálnay:[2]

- István Kálnay, b. 1890; d. 1980
- Borbála (Borbala/Barbara) Kálnay, b. 1892; d. Budapest, 1944
- András (Andrés) Kálnay, b. 1893; d. Buenos Aires, 1982
- György (Jorge) Kálnay, b. 1894; d. Buenos Aires, 1957
- Ilona (Ilonka) Kálnay, b. 1895; d. Budapest 1974
- Margit Kálnay, b 1898; d. Budapest, 1949
- Ferenc (Ferko) Kálnay, b. 1899; d. California, 1992

Although she looks youthful in photographs, Rózsa was considered elderly at the time of Ferko's birth—thirty-nine in an era when life expectancy in Hungary was only thirty-seven years. Her husband, József, was forty. The photo below was taken four years earlier, in 1895, when Rózsa was thirty-five.

*Rózsa Margulit Kalnay in 1895, age thirty-five, with her son, András.*
*(From the author's personal collection)*

I learned some of the details of my great grandparents' lives from my mother's cousin Esteban, the son of one of Ferko's brothers in Argentina. He recalls visits from Uncle Ferko and conversations with his father about their upbringing. In addition, Esteban's mother stayed in close touch with Ferko's sister Ilonka who filled in other details about the Kálnay family history. After her husband died, Esteban's mother told him more about the family, including our secret Jewish heritage.

Rózsa came from a wealthy family. After the Jewish emancipation law of 1867, her father, Leopold Margulit, purchased several properties in rural Hungary and managed others for local aristocrats. When he died, he left the family business to young Rózsa and her brother Gyula. In contrast, Ferko's father, József, came from a more modest background than Rózsa. In his youth, József was an aspiring actor and opera singer with a lovely baritone voice. However, he abandoned those dreams and accepted a job with the railroad to support his younger brother's desire to go to university. József built a career with the Royal Hungarian Railways of the Austro-Hungarian Imperial Rail Service, one of the largest state businesses in the empire. At the time, Jews rarely worked for prestigious ministries, but they were accepted in the lower-tier ministries governing railroads and post offices that had a need for technically skilled personnel.[3] To gain this employ, they were required to be Hungarian citizens and Magyar speakers.* By the time Ferko was born, József cut a dashing figure and Rózsa was a stylish beauty.

Ferko liked to say he was born in Budapest, but, in actuality, he was born in Koprivnica, northern Croatia, where József was a station master. Koprivnica had been devastated during the wars with the Turks but regained importance in 1871 when it became a stop on the new railway route from Budapest to Rijeka. The family lived in a flat at the train station and heard the whistles of trains day and night.

Ferko may have described Budapest as his birth city to sound more cosmopolitan (as someone from Jersey City might say they were from New York City). Or, he may have made these statements later in life when he wanted to be recognized as Hungarian in countries like the United States and Argentina, where citizenship is defined by place of birth. On the other hand, his birth certificate would have shown his true birthplace.

---

* Magyar is a term used to designate the Hungarian ethnic group and language.

*József Kálnay, circa 1898.*
*(From the author's personal collection)*

*Rózsa Margulit, circa 1898.*
*(From the author's personal collection)*

One year after giving birth to Ferko, Rózsa disappeared, and her fate was shrouded in secrecy to cover up the fact that she suffered a nervous breakdown and was sent to a mental hospital for over thirty years. Esteban attributes the crisis to her decision to undergo an abortion when she became pregnant again after bearing Ferko. However, given that Rózsa was confined for over three decades, it seems more likely that she had schizophrenia. Nevertheless, an additional pregnancy to an elderly mother who gave birth to seven live children in nine years may have caused sufficient strain on Rózsa to provoke a mental breakdown in 1900.

The symptoms of schizophrenia—withdrawal, depression, lack of affect, and strange behaviors—must have been devastating for József and the children. I wonder what symptoms she displayed during that first year of Ferko's life. Was she violent? Did she stop talking or have premature dementia after giving birth or having the abortion (as schizophrenia often first presented in women)?[4] Did she have any loving interactions with her youngest son before they were separated?

Ferko and his siblings did reside in Budapest at times. After marrying into the wealthy Margulit family, József was able to purchase an apartment in Budapest in the university quarter. It served as the Kálnay family home until he died in 1931. He also acquired a lodging house in Rijeka, called "Villa Elena," and a beautiful spa, Pension Villa Elsa, on the Adriatic Coast, where the family went for vacation until Ferko was eleven.

*Kálnay children at the family vacation villa, circa 1900. (From the author's personal collection)*

József didn't only benefit from his wife's wealth. He was a savvy businessman who invested in properties in Hungary (Budapest) and other parts of Europe—Italy (Trieste), the former Yugoslavia (Rijeka and Crikvenica), and Germany (a movie theater in Berlin). With the rents from these investments and his pension from the imperial railroad, he was able to support his children into adulthood. However, the majority of the holdings were lost during economic and political crises in Hungary. In the 1960s, on one of his last trips to Yugoslavia, Ferko tried unsuccessfully to recover family properties that the socialist government had expropriated.[5]

* * *

This is a book about my grandfather, but the fate of his mother, Rózsa, is a shadow that bears description because of its influence on Ferko and the entire family. Shame over Rózsa's hospitalization was so deep that József and his sons treated her as though she had died, which is what future generations believed had happened. When Ferko and his brothers were asked to list their mother's name on official documents, they entered the name of their Catholic stepmother. For the rest of his adult life, Ferko never acknowledged Rózsa Margulit as his mother, although he must have known of her existence since he was in touch with his sister Borbála who cared for their mother after she was eventually released from the psychiatric hospital.

Ferko's son, Peter, believes that Ferko was the son of his father's Catholic mistress, and that we dodged a bullet by not being related to a woman with schizophrenia. That theory was partially debunked when my own genetic ancestry test revealed that, on my mother's side, I am 98% Ashkenazi, leaving no doubt that both of my maternal great-grandparents were Jewish. On the other hand, it is possible that József's mistress was also a passing Jew. However, DNA data proves that my mother's cousins and I share the same great-grandparents—in other words, that Ferko was Rózsa's son.

In 1900, when Rózsa was institutionalized, the medical field viewed schizophrenia as a hereditary degenerative disorder that could not be treated with drugs or therapy. As a result, she was likely committed to the "national lunatic asylum" Lipótmezö Bedlam Hospital in Budapest and treated with electro-shock treatment, a practice that was only abandoned in the early 1950s.[6] The name "Bedlam" conjures up an image of a run-down, frightening facility. On the contrary, "Lipót" was a large and remarkably beautiful hospital that looked like a medieval abbey in a lush valley. It was built in 1868 in the Late Romantic architectural style, with a footprint larger than the Hungarian parliament. There were massive columns at the entrance, wide corridors, high walls along the perimeter, and a large Roman Catholic chapel with stained glass windows. The chapel included smaller worship spaces for adherents of other religions, including Jews, Greek Orthodox, Lutherans, and Calvinists. It was surrounded by a fifty-acre park designed by a well-known landscape designer and maintained by full-time gardeners.

*Lipótmező Hospital.*

Science historian Emese Lafferton tells me that, by the time Rózsa was admitted to Lipöt in 1900, the institution was overcrowded and somewhat run down. However, patients of means were put into rooms with fewer people and better food. No matter how halcyon the setting may seem from the outside, it must have been terrifying for Rózsa to have been wrenched from her family home in Budapest and forced into an overcrowded asylum. Although Lipót had a program of family care for calm patients, it seems unlikely that Rózsa's family participated, since her older sons were away at boarding school and a German nanny cared for the younger children in Budapest. At the same time, József was courting another woman. Later, Rózsa was moved to a private sanatorium operated by Dr. Jeno Ringer in Budapest. My mother's cousin Esteban found receipts for her care from April 1932, when Rózsa was still an in-patient there. It was an expensive sanatorium. The daily maintenance rate of 2,738 Hungarian pengö a year is the equivalent of $10,647 per year in 2022 dollars. The bills were paid by József and his eldest daughter, Borbála, who cared for Rózsa when she was finally released.* György and András also contributed to her upkeep.

## FAMILY HISTORY: HUNGARIAN NATIONALISM AND
## CHANGES IN OUR FAMILY SURNAME

Our original surname was Klein. In 1879, József changed his surname from Klein to Kalnai, according to a Hungarian database.[7] At that time Jews were not allowed to Hungarianize their names to end with a "y" because "y" was an aristocratic spelling. Kálna is the name of the village from which our ancestors hailed. In 1919, József changed the surname, again, to Kálnay.**

No one in my mother's family ever spoke of our German ancestry. The unquestioned assumption was that all Kálnays were Hungarian and that our ancestors had grown up speaking Hungarian. However, like most Jews in Hungary, Ferko's father and mother were more likely to have grown up speaking German than Hungarian. In 1878, the year the Kleins became the Kalnais, Hungary had the largest German-speaking population in Europe. Although three-quarters of Hungarian Jews officially declared Hungarian as their mother tongue, the vast majority spoke German—more than in any other European country. Furthermore, after Hungary became part of the Austro-Hungarian Empire, German became the dominant language of public administration, education, industry, and culture. When Ferko was growing up, his parents spoke both German and Hungarian to their children, and before Rózsa's institutionalization, she traveled to Germany with the express purpose of hiring a German-speaking nanny. An interesting anecdote demonstrates the extent to which Ferko identified with his German-Hungarian ancestry when he was an adult. When returning from Argentina to the United

---

* One pengö was worth US $0.18 in 1932. That is the equivalent of $3.90 in 2022 dollars. Source: Foreign Exchange Rates 1913–1941. Hungarian Pengö. New World Economics. https://newworldeconomics. com/foreign-exchange-rates-1913-1941-4-britain-leads-the-world-into-currency-chaos/. CPI Inflation calculator. US $0.18 1932 = $3.90 2022. https://www.in2013dollars.com/us/inflation/1932?amount=0.18

** Historically, "y" was just a variant of "ai" for Hungarian surnames, but by the early ninteenth century, names ending in "y" were more common among noble families. The change from "ai" to "y" was a common step taken by individuals who wanted to assume a more aristocratic spelling of their names.

States in 1927, he filled out a US customs declaration form as follows: "Nationality: Hungarian; Race: German."

During the Hapsburg Empire in Hungary, it was important to the government to emphasize Hungarian speakers, and counting them was as much a political exercise as a demographic question.

> Beginning in 1880, when citizens were first asked about their "language of daily use," the imperial census escalated into a high-stakes campaign for citizen allegiances, as the number of Czech speakers, German speakers, Polish speakers, or Ruthenian speakers came to be seen as a measure of national strength. Increasingly, numbers determined how state resources were allocated, where schools were built, and in which languages children could be educated. [. . .] A secret memorandum from the Hungarian undersecretary of state to the Hungarian Prime Minister explained, "for the institution of national statehood it is absolutely necessary that the ruling race . . . become the majority of the population."[8]

In 1903, the Hungarian government passed an extremely restrictive law *preventing* men aged seventeen and over from emigrating without the permission of the Defense and Interior ministries.[9] Perhaps Ferko evaded the restriction in 1919 because he was already in the Merchant Marines. But while the empire attempted to restrict emigration, the "pull factors" forcing people to leave to find a better life were stronger than ever. In World War I, Austria-Hungary lost 1.2 million soldiers and 120,000 civilians, and another half a million died of starvation or Spanish flu in 1918.[10] Despite attempts to restrict general emigration, the Hungarian government considered Jewish citizens like Ferko and his siblings "good riddance." According to historian Tara Zahra, long before the Nazi conquest, there was a broad consensus in eastern Europe and among many Western diplomats that mass emigration of Jews from the region was a desirable solution to the so-called "Jewish problem." As the Nazis gained power, "encouraging emigration" became a euphemism for deportation. Over a third of the migrants who came to the US from central Europe at the beginning of the twentieth century returned once, or even multiple times.[11] Ferko was among them, although, unlike many of his compatriots, he wasn't planning to stay in Hungary. Instead, he made multiple trips from New York to Hungary, New York to Argentina, and back.

Although he spoke many languages and grew up in a household where German was often spoken, Hungarian was Ferko's first language. In the 1910 Census, Hungarian was the most commonly cited mother tongue in Hungary proper, with ten million speakers, followed by German with close to two million. However, the statistics are questionable since a quarter of the population was illiterate, and officials of the Hungarian state were interested in inflating the number of Hungarian speakers to strengthen their political standing. In many cases, Hungarian employers provided census information for their mostly non-Hungarian employees.

Conversion to Christianity was another sign of assimilation. At the end of the nineteenth century, Simon Telkes, one of the most prominent and ardent proponents of name changes (and himself an assimilated Jew) wrote: "As one becomes Christian and is admitted into Christian society with the adoption of Christianity, one can gain full acceptance into Hungarian society, into the nation with a national baptism, by changing his foreign name to a Hungarian one."[12] Most converts came from assimilated upper-class families in Western Hungary and Budapest. Even those Jews who did not convert to Christianity often adopted "folk customs," such as coloring Easter eggs and decorating Christmas trees. This is how my mother's family and later my own were raised—attending neither church nor synagogue but exchanging Christmas gifts and hiding Easter baskets for the children.

### THE RICHEST BOY IN THE WORLD

Ferko and his siblings were not only separated from their mother at young ages. When Rózsa was hospitalized, József sent the four older children to live with an aunt in Zagreb while the three youngest, including Ferko, stayed in Budapest with the German nanny who had been with the family for several years. When Ferko was only seven years old, his father left Budapest for two years. Upon his return in 1910 József began living with Erzsébet Szentgáli, an aristocratic Christian Hungarian, although it is unlikely that he divorced Rózsa. Not only was divorce stigmatized, but it was only codified in civil law in Hungary in 1895, six years before Rózsa was institutionalized.[13]

In Budapest, Ferko attended the Horánszky Street Real School, where he edited a weekly humor magazine with his Jewish classmate Pál Királyhegyi until the teachers banned it. It was not unusual for Jewish students to attend public schools in Hungary. Beginning in the middle of the nineteenth century, some liberal ("neolog") Jewish communities regularly sent their male children to Christian primary schools to learn Hungarian and German, arithmetic, and Magyar history. A few such boys went on to Catholic or Protestant "Latin schools," where they acquired the then-current classical education in ancient languages, rhetoric, and philosophy. Jewish religion and history were learned through separate attendance at one of the private courses organized by the community's rabbi. While conservative Jews were opposed to non-Talmudic schools, the neologs welcomed the opportunity to assimilate into Hungarian society.[14]

From my mother's cousin Esteban I know that the older children did not get along with their stepmother, and they were miserable in Zagreb. As a result, József sent the eldest boys to a boarding school for the children of railroad employees in Kaposvár, Hungary, about 186 kilometers from Budapest. Ferko later attended the same school, but because Györgi and András were five and six years older, they didn't overlap. As an adult, András told his son Esteban of their sorrow at being torn from the family and arriving there.[15] As a result András began to suffer life-long migraines when he was only seven years old—the same year that Rózsa was institutionalized.

These were also unhappy years for Ferko, who was forcibly separated from his mother as a baby, shuttled between relatives' homes and his Catholic stepmother's house, and later sent to the same harsh boarding school his brothers had attended. Ferko later wrote a children's book about the school called *The Richest Boy in the World*. The riches refer to marbles that the children traded. The book jacket notes state:

> *When he was a small boy in his native Hungary, Francis attended a very rough boarding school where there was never enough to eat. Perhaps to smooth hunger pains, stories at bedtime were much in demand—at the beginning of the school year, all fifty of the boys in*

*each dormitory were tested for talent. After some angry disputes and free-for-all, three or four were chosen as "official" storytellers. "We were paid in both food and services," recalls Mr. Kalnay. "Five minutes before reveille my boots were delivered to my bed, polished strictly according to regulations. I could also count on an extra slice of bread which had to be at least as thick as a lead pencil and as large as the donor's palm. I put away my own bread for future reference and used the earned bread, dunking it into my plate of caraway seed soup, which for four immeasurably long years comprised my breakfast."*

In the book, the Royal Institute for Underprivileged Boys housed two hundred students who, like Ferko, were the children or orphans of railway men. The boys were "kept one notch above starvation level." The pantry of the headmaster faced the playground area, and in the window were "two rows of genuine Hungarian smoked sausages and hard salamis hung in generous lengths from plain wooden rods." When the school hired a new headmaster, he reduced the budget for food, and the savings were regarded as a sign of his true patriotism. Food was so scarce that the students became listless. When a locust tree bloomed in the spring, the boys vied for a chance to climb the tree and eat the sweet petals.

The novel focuses on high-stakes games of marbles in the schoolyard, the only type of recreation permitted for one hour each day. Marbles were a form of currency used by the boys to barter for food: a slice of bread was worth one marble, bean soup was worth two marbles of certain colorings, etc. A child with all the marbles was "the richest boy in the world." When the students hid marbles from the headmaster, he put their names on an official blacklist and scheduled them for corporal punishment administered with their pants pulled down.

How much of *The Richest Boy in the World* is autobiographical? What seems likely is that Ferko was describing harsh discipline and humiliations experienced in the boarding school he and his brothers attended in Kaposvár. However, beyond that, I am skeptical that a boy from a middle-class family like Ferko would have gone hungry, as described in the book. A friend who is a specialist in the history of food told me that in some societies, food deprivation was employed as a pedagogical technique.[16] This may have been the case in the Austro-Hungarian Empire. I found a description

The Richest Boy in the World.
*(Photograph of book illustration by author)*

of a 1906 study of the growth patterns of Austrian boarding school children that found that students aged seven to seventeen failed to grow during the regular school year but caught up in height during the summer months when they lived at home and were presumably better fed.[17]

In the boarding school depicted in my grandfather's book, there were two hundred "half-orphans"—peasant boys ranging in age from six to ten. Ferko could have qualified as a half-orphan since his mother was taken away when he was a year old. The main character in the book, Tony, has a best friend named Pali (a nickname for Pál). Ferko dedicated the book to his boyhood friend of the same name. He may have made other close friends at the school. Since Jews like Ferko's father were employed by the railroad in the Austro-Hungarian Empire, there would have been other Jewish children in the school. In any case, the story reveals several themes that resonated in Ferko's adult life—a keen interest in food and a thirst for adventure and subterfuge.

When Ferko was growing up, Magyarization meant being Christian, and there were penalties for being openly Jewish. András Kovacs writes that for a hundred and fifty years, the drive for assimilation was such that a "maxim of participation for the Jews living in Hungary in political life consisted of one basic rule: it was forbidden to appear as a Jew and represent particular Jewish interests in Hungarian politics."[18]

However, although our family's Jewish ancestry was a well-guarded family secret in later years, it was open knowledge when Ferko was young, and not something that could be hidden. During the Austro-Hungarian Empire, an individual's religion was as commonly known as their occupation. It was inscribed in most public records, such as deeds, school enrollment forms, and routine police files that recorded the number of residents in each dwelling. In fact, until 1896, religious officials at churches and synagogues maintained vital statistics (marriages, births, and deaths).[19] "Izr" (short for "Izraelite") was clearly marked on the school enrollment records of Ferko and his siblings. In official government statistics, the term was used to refer to individuals whose professed religion was Judaism, but not to many Hungarian Jews whose families had converted to Christianity. Furthermore, Jews remained identifiable as a group in the country because of their concentration in certain occupations and their endogamy. Kovacs argues that antisemitism also fostered a sense of group identity among Hungarian Jews who otherwise did not consider themselves Jewish.

By 1907, as an employee of the railway service, József was required to have Hungarian citizenship and speak Hungarian. As we have seen, he changed his surname in 1879 when he was nineteen years old, and again in 1919. He took the additional step of giving all his children typical Hungarian first names—István, Borbála, András, György, Ilona, Margit, and finally Ferenc (Ferko). As in Istvan Szabo's film *Sunshine*,[20] József first Magyarized the family name, took a Christian woman as his mistress, and—at least nominally—converted to Catholicism. However, his wife's surname, Margulit, is a variation of the identifiably Sephardic name, Margalit.

Although being Jewish wasn't a point of shame in Hungary at the end of the nineteenth century, there was intense nationalistic and political pressure to Magyarize German and Slavic names. The Nationalities Law of 1868 codified the notion of a "single nation, the indivisible unitary Hungarian nation." In 1881, a society to promote name changes was established, and all non-Hungarians were encouraged to Magyarize their surnames as a sign of "being accepted as a true son of the nation."*

Jews were especially likely to change their names to maintain their relatively solid economic and social status in the kingdom. Hungarian names were associated with modernization, secularization, and the desire to be identified as a member of the nation rather than as a "Jew." Between 1881 and 1919, some 45,000 Hungarian Jews—principally from Budapest—changed their surnames. During this period, name changes were so common among Jews in Hungary that—rather than masking Jewish identity—they made it more visible.[21] There was also an external political impetus for Jews to adopt Hungarian surnames since, without them, ethnic Hungarians constituted a minority of the population. Romanians, Slovaks, Croats, and Germans outnumbered Magyars.

According to Randolph Braham,

> no other minority or nationality in the Hungarian Kingdom adopted
> the Hungarian language and culture with the same spontaneous
> eagerness as the Jews . . . the overwhelming majority of Hungarian
> Jewry realized that complete assimilation and Magyarization was
> the price they had to pay for their emancipation. . . . adopting the
> Magyar language in their religious instruction and services and by as-
> similating the traditions, customs, and ideology of the Magyars.[22]

### COLLAPSE OF THE EMPIRE

After boarding school, Ferko moved to Budapest to attend high school ("gymnasium") when the Austro-Hungarian Empire was at the heart of the conflict that began World War I in 1914. As a result, all four Kálnay

---

* Studies of name changes within populations are the focus of an academic specialization called onomastics. From onomastic research, we know that Ashkenazic Jews in eastern Europe and Germany weren't
required to use surnames until the very end of the eighteenth century when Hapsburg Emperor Joseph II
issued a decree requiring Jews to adopt German surnames. Klein was one of the most common of these
names; in both German and Yiddish it means someone who is small or short in stature.

brothers were pressed into military service. At his father's urging, Ferko transferred to the Royal Hungarian Maritime Academy in Fiume (modern Rijeka, Croatia) at age fifteen, just as the war began. On his own personnel records Ferko states that he was a graduate of the academy, although a different source states that he left in his third year to volunteer with the Hungarian Merchant and Naval Reserve.[*]

*Ferko, Merchant Marine, age fifteen. (From the author's personal collection)*

All of József's sons served in WWI under the Austro-Hungarian Empire. The photograph below was taken in 1917 in Budapest when all four boys were on leave for a few days. In it, József appears to exude pride as he sits surrounded by his sharply uniformed sons.

*József Kálnay and his four sons, 1917. Ferko is on the left. (From the author's personal collection)*

---

[*] Ferko's application for military commission is dated February 13, 1943; however Esteban Kálnay cites records from a Captain Horvath suggesting that Ferko left the academy before graduating.

Remarkably all four brothers survived the First World War, although Ferko had a close call. In 1917 when he was on the Austro-Hungarian warship SMS *Wien*, it was torpedoed by the Italians. Forty-six crew members died in the blast, but Ferko had the good fortune to have left for home leave the previous day. At the end of the war, his older brother András survived a risk of a different kind. He contracted the Spanish flu as a second wave of the deadly virus traversed the world, but he was able to take leave from the military to recuperate at home for a few weeks. During the war, Ferko's sisters remained in Budapest. They are shown in the photo below, from left to right: Margit, Borbála and Ilona Kálnay, and a visiting cousin.

*Ferko's sisters and a cousin circa 1917.*
*(From the author's personal collection)*

In the photograph below, József and his mistress are shown with two of their daughters and four of their sons. This is likely the last time the family was together before the boys all left Hungary.

*József and Erzsébet Szentgáli with six of their seven children, July 1917.*
*(From the author's personal collection)*

World War I ended in the fall of 1918 and the Austro-Hungarian Empire was dismantled. Before that, "Greater Hungary" was comprised of the predominantly Hungarian-speaking areas in all of present-day Hungary and Slovakia, and territory now within Romania, Ukraine, Austria, Croatia, Bosnia, and Serbia. With the 1920 Treaty of Trianon, Hungary was dismembered. She lost over half of her population, almost three-quarters of her territory, and access to the sea as borders were reconfigured. As a result, millions of Magyar-speaking Hungarians were transferred to the surrounding states of Czechoslovakia, Romania, Yugoslavia, and Austria. To this day, many Hungarians harbor anger over the treaty and refer to "Greater Hungary," as if the prewar borders still pertained. As fervent Hungarian nationalists, Ferko and his brothers shared their compatriots' sorrow over the loss of the country's stature.

Questions of where people are from can be similarly complex for individuals whose ancestors emigrated from Austro-Hungary. During the empire, the realm consisted of the Kingdom of Hungary and Imperial Austria. In 1867, the Kingdom of Hungary covered seventy-one counties and had a population of about twenty-one million people. After ignominious losses under the 1920 Treaty of Trianon, the kingdom was broken into lands in the states of Czechoslovakia, Romania, Yugoslavia, and a small part of Austria. At the end of the Second World War, Hungary invaded Yugoslavia and occupied a region of northern Serbia.[23]

## Antisemitism in Hungary between the Wars

After the war, Hungary was beset by political turmoil, unemployment, high inflation, and shortages of food and coal. Jews were blamed for much of the trouble and, in October 1918, there was a revolution during which soldiers and civilians looted Jewish shops and homes and beat up Jewish civilians. In March 1919, antisemitic policies were hardened under the short-lived communist dictatorship of Béla Kun in spite of the fact that the leader's father was a Jew. Kun's family background served to reinforce the views of many Hungarians that communism and Judaisim were inextricably linked.[24]

A month after Kun's rise to power, Ferko became the first of the Kálnay children to immigrate to the United States, arriving three months before his twentieth birthday. He was fortunate to sail on a marine vessel because transatlantic passenger travel had been all but halted during the war. Only one year later, Ferko's older brothers, András and György were denied visas by the American Consul in Milan because the Austro-Hungarian Empire had been a central power allied with Germany in the First World War.

It is unlikely that Ferko left Hungary as a direct result of antisemitism. In the larger context his departure followed the dismantling of the enormous Austro-Hungarian Empire in 1919 and the exodus of hordes of his brethren in earlier decades. Between 1880 and 1914, about 1.7 million migrants from the Habsburg Empire came to the US, constituting over a quarter of all immigrants during that period.[25]

Nevertheless, Ferko's departure was none too soon. Conditions in Hungary worsened after Kun nationalized all industry and paid workers in worthless currency. After he was overthrown and fled to Austria in August of 1919, Christian nationalists used the occasion to blame "Judeo-Bolsheviks" for conditions in the country.[26] Many Jews were murdered outright and others brutally beaten. Although most Hungarians regarded the Soviet Republic as Jewish and continued to hold this view for many decades after its fall, the overwhelming majority of Jews neither identified with nor supported the Soviet regime. Moreover, as staunch Hungarian patriots, many believed that Hungarian Jewry and the ruling feudal elites shared a commonality of interests. Some Jews continued to clutch at this idea throughout the interwar period and beyond.[27] The year that Ferko immigrated to the US, a prominent Jewish organization issued a statement emphasizing that "the Hungarian Jews consider themselves the children of the Hungarian nation. It is in this spirit that we shall continue our work on behalf of our denomination and country."[28]

After Kun's fall, Admiral Miklós Horthy was named Minister of War, and then commander-in-chief of the armed forces. By August 1919, he had initiated a program of "White Terror" that led to the murder of thousands of liberals, communists, and Jews. A decade and a half before Hitler became Chancellor of Germany, Horthy's army units encouraged people to "smoke the Jews out" of their communities in some parts of the region. In this, they were aided by some ten thousand right-wing Christian and paramilitary societies created to "defend the Magyar cause" with impunity. Historian Randolph Braham states that with these actions, "the Hungarian government emerged as the first one in postwar Europe to begin tackling the 'Jewish question.'"[29]

In 1920 the National Assembly elected Horthy to serve as regent of the postwar Kingdom of Hungary, the same year that the Treaty of Trianon resulted in enormous territorial and population losses. The complexity of life for Hungarians during the period between the two world wars is described by Eleanor Perényi in her memoir, *More Was Lost*. Perényi married a Christian Hungarian aristocrat who owned a chateau on land that was ceded to Czechoslovakia with the Treaty of Trianon. Suddenly refugees streamed in from Transylvania, northern Hungary, and Croatia, and her husband needed a passport and government permission to be on his own property. Resentment of the Treaty of Trianon was so pervasive and all-consuming in Hungary that "revisionism" became the theme of Hungarian politics from the end of World War I to current times.[30]

The loss of territory made Hungary much more ethnically and linguistically homogeneous. This change had negative repercussions for Jews who had been valued under the Habsburgs for their intense loyalty to the monarchy and their role in helping to glue together an enormously diverse, multinational state.[31] After Trianon, Jews had to reconstruct new identities in more homogeneous nation-states that were hostile to them.

During World War I Budapest had one of the largest Jewish populations in the world, and Jews were heavily represented among professionals and in universities. Suddenly there were quotas on Jewish university students and attacks on Jewish university students with demands for the expulsion of "all Jews and Bolsheviks." Jewish officials were dismissed from military and government positions and forbidden to work in certain trades. Enforced Magyarization was about giving up "the Jewish nation" in order to establish one's fealty to the nation-state where one lived. In the debates about "the Jewish question" at the time, one of the key issues was how a Jew could be loyal to two sets of laws, two sovereigns, two nations. To resolve this, the state endorsed a privatized form of Judaism in which Jews expressed civil-political fealty to the Hungarian state rather than the Jewish nation. There were simultaneous attempts to paint Jews as disloyal citizens. When Admiral Horthy became regent and head of state of Hungary in 1920, he began a campaign to rid the country of suspected communists, and Jews were the principal victims of the purge. Economic hardship in the country led to overt antisemitism, and Horthy took advantage of the situation to dismiss Jewish army officials and restrict the involvement of Jews in scientific institutions, universities, and certain businesses. In 1922, fifteen thousand Jewish residents were said to be non-citizens and were expelled from the capital.

Among the wave of Hungarians rushing to leave the defeated Austro-Hungarian Empire was Ferko's old classmate and fellow student journalist from middle school in Budapest, Pál Királyhegyi, the person to whom Ferko dedicated *The Richest Boy in the World*. Like Ferko, Pál arrived in the US in 1919 and freelanced with Hungarian papers. Unlike Ferko, he returned to Hungary in 1938, and in 1941, he was deported to Auschwitz.

## IMMIGRANT IN AMERICA

In 1919 Ferko asked each of his brothers to give him an article of clothing—a jacket, pants, hat. He then left town without saying where he was going. Two months later he sent his father a postcard saying that he was in America.

What happened when Ferko arrived in the US as a twenty-year-old sailor? How did he manage to stay and gain a foothold in the country? As a scholar of contemporary immigration, I was especially interested in these questions.

Ferko sailed into the Port of Philadelphia on April 18, 1919, on the SS *Magyarorszag*, a Hungarian merchant ship flying the Italian flag. Fortunately for him, when he entered the US, the screening of people with alien seaman's permits (and holders of second- and first-class travel tickets too) was very lax. Unlike passengers who landed at Ellis Island and underwent thorough screening, seamen were only subject to a health screening onboard ship, after which they were admitted to the US if they didn't have a communicable disease or meet other grounds for exclusion. As a result, Ferko was able to leave his vessel and remain in the US—like scores of thousands of other merchant seamen.

*SS Magyarorszag*

He arrived in the nick of time—five months after the end of World War I but before the November 7 Bolshevik Revolution that unleashed a Red Scare in the US and led to mass deportations of individuals arriving at Ellis Island, particularly Jewish immigrants who were suspected of being "socialist terrorists." When Ferko landed, no more than a handful of immigrants were prosecuted and deported from the US each year, but a few years later, restrictionist policies brought immigration from the "enemy states" of central and eastern Europe to a near halt.

Although Ferko arrived at a time when anti-immigrant sentiments were at a fever pitch, it was before the implementation of restrictions that would have denied him entry or government employment. Large numbers of people who entered the country before 1924 did not have sufficient records of their arrival to be able to naturalize. When Ferko eventually applied for US citizenship in 1936, he most likely appeared before a judge who simply accepted his witness statement with the name of his ship and the date of his arrival. In fact, so many immigrants had incomplete admissions records for the years before 1924 that very simple mechanisms were later created to "fast-track" them through the naturalization process. The Registry Act of 1929 allowed immigrants who arrived before 1921 but had no record of their admission to register retroactively for a twenty-dollar fee.

Despite his easy entry to the US, Ferko may have faced some anti-immigrant sentiments fueled by charges that foreign European workers were taking American jobs or because Austro-Hungarians in the US were suspected of being pro-Bolshevik or even enemy aliens during WWI.[32] Within a few months of his arrival, no fewer than six bills to suspend immigration were introduced in Congress. Public anger was reflected in the cartoon on the next page.

By 1920, the US Census recorded almost a million self-designated Hungarians in the US, half of whom were Magyar-speaking.[33] Fear of Bolshevism and the growth of the eugenics movement paved the way for further immigration restrictions from eastern Europe. In May 1921, the first quotas were established under a bill signed into law by President Harding, and in 1924, the Johnson-Reed Act barred immigrants from Asia and set quotas for immigrants from the Eastern Hemisphere. Assertions that immigrants were un-American and couldn't assimilate

*Cartoon printed with permission from "Ding" Darling Wildlife Society. "Ding" Darling Wildlife Society owns the copyright of "Ding" Darling cartoons.*

were common, and calls for restrictions multiplied. On the other hand, Ferko may have been less likely to face discrimination because he was middle class and not readily identifiable as a "Hunkie" laborer who worked in the mines or for a large American steel or automobile corporation.

Ferko was also eager to assimilate. In Hungary many Hungarians, including the Kálnays, participated openly in displays of patriotism. When he arrived in New York at age twenty, the common displays of American nationalism and pressures to assimilate must have felt familiar to Ferko. He not only participated in those displays but became a representative of the system, writing a manual for new Americans and collaborating with ethnic organizations that promoted naturalization and voting.

## A Surprising Immigrant Enclave: New Brunswick, New Jersey

To find housing, jobs, and a common language, immigrants everywhere flocked to areas with concentrations of their countrymen, and Hungarians were no different. After landing in Philadelphia, Ferko immediately moved to what was unofficially known as "the most Hungarian city in the United States"—New Brunswick, New Jersey. The first wave of Hungarians had come to the city in the late nineteenth century when American employers placed advertisements in newspapers in rural Hungarian townships and others recruited workers in the New York harbors. By 1910, there were 2,463 Hungarian immigrants in New Brunswick, accounting for 41% of the foreign-born and 11% of all residents, and by 1920, there were 5,278. Hungarians became the largest ethnic group in the city, which led to clashes with the Irish, who were part of a smaller but more powerful and prosperous ethnic community. In response Hungarians joined political clubs to turn out the ethnic vote for Democratic candidates, ensuring their ward leaders a share of public jobs and services.

In her book about the history of Hungarians in the United States, Julianna Puskas writes that almost everyone in her Hungarian village in the 1930s was either already in the US or planning to go there, and that the place they dreamt of settling was New Brunswick, New Jersey. The pharmaceutical company Johnson & Johnson was the major employer in the city when Ferko arrived. Two-thirds of the employees were Magyars—so many that J&J became known as "Hungarian University," and speaking Hungarian was required to be promoted to superintendent. Other major employers in the city included a tannery and factories producing cigars, tin, rubber, buttons, and paper.

Although Ferko didn't work at Johnson & Johnson, its presence ensured a thriving and welcoming community of Hungarians. As a result, much about life in the US must have felt familiar to him. New immigrants promoted the Hungarian language, culture, identity, and even a sense of Magyar superiority. There were Hungarian restaurants, churches, bakeries and cafes, bilingual schools, and print shops, as well as a loan association, a mutual aid society, and numerous social clubs. There was even a baseball team called the New Brunswick Young Hungarians and a Magyar theater troupe. In addition to many Christian churches, there were four synagogues in New Brunswick when Ferko arrived, including a Hungarian congregation established in 1918.[34]

It wasn't difficult for Ferko to find odd jobs in the US. He had an affinity for journalism and the arts influenced by his early years in Budapest, where Jews made up half of the Hungarian journalists and an even larger proportion of editors, publishers, critics, and cabaret directors.[23] In New Brunswick he worked occasionally as an actor and wrote poetry and articles for one of the five Hungarian language daily papers in the city and for some publications in other cities. He also began to move freely between New Jersey and New York City, where he found a job for a year in a gallery showing the work of a Hungarian painter. In New York City there were as many as sixty-eight Hungarian papers focusing variously on religion, politics, literature, humor, and fraternal and political organizations.[35] The publications helped Ferko develop a large network of compatriots in New York.

Ferko loved poetry even more than prose, read it in several different languages, and wrote his own verses in Hungarian. An audience for nostalgic poetry flourished in the United States, with expressions of alienation and anguish over discrimination against "Hunkies." He also maintained strong ties to Hungary, and in 1920, he wrote a melodrama to raise funds for Hungarian prisoners of war in Siberia. *Towards Translyvania* was presented in Budapest at the Great Hall at Parliament Square with piano and horn accompaniment.[36] In 1922 an anthology of his poems and ballads, *Feltámadás elött* (*Before the Resurrection*), was published in Budapest.

Ferko was fortunate to have arrived in the US before the implementation of harsh anti-immigrant policies. The economic consequences of the war made it difficult or even impossible for many Hungarians to return, and he had little incentive to move back. Instead, his older brothers György and András stowed away on a Hungarian ship to join Ferko in New York in 1920. However, the ship was denied entry and diverted to South America, leading them to settle in Argentina instead—a move that altered the course of their lives and forged a Latin connection for Ferko as well.

It wasn't surprising that the Kálnay brothers were able to remain in Argentina. At the end of the nineteenth century, leaders in both western and east-central Europe promoted immigration to South America as a means of national expansion and a kind of peaceful colonization. The idea was to maintain close economic and political ties with groups of resettled compatriots. For its part, Argentina welcomed the immigrants as a means of promoting progress and economic ties with Europe. On the other hand, with the exception of groups of Zionist emigrants, the vast majority preferred Europe or North America, but at the beginning of the twentieth century, many—like Ferko's brothers—were thwarted in their goals by restrictive immigration policies.

András and György settled in Buenos Aires, and, by 1923, they had become successful architects known as Andrés and Jorge Kálnay.* Their training for the profession had begun years before. Andrés, for example, began studying at the Royal State Hungarian Architecture School of Budapest at age fourteen and graduated in 1911. He also took a carpentry workshop at age twelve and, in 1907, began a two-year stint as an apprentice mason. In 1909, he began working with the architect Pollak Mano.[37] The brothers opened an architectural studio there but had to close the business with the onset of the First World War in 1914 when both were conscripted into the Hungarian military.

The photograph below shows one of the Kálnay brothers' most famous buildings in Buenos Aires: the Munich Restaurant and Beer Brewery, which today houses government offices.

*Cervecería Múnich (Restaurant and Beer Brewery), Buenos Aires designed by Andrés Kálnay, 1927. (From the author's personal collection)*

---

* As immigrants to Argentina, they were advised to assume Spanish names.

## Marriage

At 5'9" and 145 pounds, Ferko was an attractive man of slight build, with chiseled features, brown, curly hair, and—even as a young man—a slightly receding hairline. Women were attracted by his intelligence, his European manners, and his ability to recite poetry in a soft Hungarian accent that was carefully preserved, even after decades of living outside of Europe. In short, he was a charmer who never lacked girlfriends before, during, or after his marriages.

Ferko's first marriage was to my grandmother Erzsébet Radkai when he was twenty-two and she was nineteen. An old photo of Erzsébet, whom we all called Elsie, leaves little doubt about how she and Ferko ended up together. Ferko loved beautiful women and he was immediately attracted to this petite, blue-eyed Jewish Hungarian from Budapest who loved to dance. In the photograph, a teenage Elsie is a femme fatale with a coy smile and a plunging neckline.

*Erzsébet "Elsie" Radkai.*
*(From the author's personal collection)*

Elsie immigrated to the US from Hungary in 1906 when she was four years old. She lived with her parents and younger brother in Chicago—a popular destination for Hungarian immigrants before the First World War. As a young woman she worked as a stenographer. Although the Radkai family was not wealthy, Elsie dressed in the latest fashions created for her in her father's tailor shop and later by her sister-in-law Rose, who was a talented couturier.

While Ferko had many girlfriends of varied backgrounds, as a first-generation Hungarian immigrant, it would have been unthinkable to marry a non-Hungarian—at least in his first union at a time when rates of Jewish-Christian intermarriage in the United States were so low that he would surely have felt pressure to take a Jewish Hungarian wife.[38]

In some ways, learning about Ferko's Jewish parents was an academic exercise for me—fascinating, but not something that deeply affected me since I didn't grow up with my grandfather. Learning about Elsie's Jewish ancestry was another matter altogether since she was a constant presence during my childhood. I knew that my mother's maiden name was Ratkay* but had no idea that her grandmother's maiden name was Katz or that her paternal grandfather, Benjamin, changed the family surname from Rosenbluh to Ratkay in Hungary in the nineteenth century.

Clearly Elsie's parents' Judaism was known within the Jewish community in Chicago and South Bend. One web source lists her father Samuel Ratkay's establishment as a "Jewish tailor shop" in Chicago. Nevertheless, a coverup, or at least a silence about our ancestry, took hold while Samuel and Hanna were still alive, and they sent all their children to Catholic Schools in South Bend. In 2022, I began online conversations with one of my mother's cousins through 23andMe. She told me that her mother— Elsie's niece Pat—was a teenager when Hanna Katz Ratkay died in 1957 and that she was forbidden from attending her grandmother's service because it was held in a Jewish funeral parlor. I was ten that year, and I don't recall anything about Elsie or my mother going to South Bend to attend Hanna's funeral. However, I do know that my mother spoke lovingly of her grandmother, whom she knew well when she was young.

Fortunately for the Ratkay family, Elsie and her parents and siblings emigrated from Hungary to the US in 1906—long before both world

---

* Ratkay was a variation of Radkai.

wars. As a result, the closest that Elsie came to Holocaust-related trag-edies in the family were Ferko's relatives and the experiences of her best friend, Rose Weiss. Elsie and Rose met in Hungary when Elsie was an adult. Elsie introduced Rose to her brother Lester and they married in Hungary. Rose and several of her siblings stayed in Europe even after Hitler conquered Poland. Like many Hungarians, they believed they were safe from Nazi reach there. One of Rose's brothers converted to Catholicism but was deported to Germany and murdered in the Bergen-Belsen concentration camp. Rose never learned English, and she resisted moving to the US for a long time. When she finally came, she continued to hide her Jewish identity. Once, when a long-lost Hungarian cousin showed up at her house in the US, she rushed to the door to implore him not to tell her children that the family was Jewish. Rose and Lester's daughter Pat had suspected as much. Pat wasn't secretive about the family ancestry to the same degree as her mother, but she believed that it was "past history" better left unspoken.

In the thirty-two years I knew my grandmother Elsie, I cannot re-call her ever talking about religion. In this, she was like my mother. Elsie was similarly hard-working and resilient, but she could also be frivolous and a bit vain. She insisted that we call her Elsie rather than "Grandma," and although she was plump, she was very proud of her small feet, which she showed off with fancy heeled pumps. Her hair was always well coiffed, and she wore strands of costume jewelry to adorn the silk dresses created for her by her sister-in-law in Indiana. Elsie loved a party and would become tipsy after a few glasses of wine. In her later years in Brewster, New York, her best friends were a gay male couple who took her out to dinner and looked in on her as she became older and frail. She could be critical of others and frequently made com-ments to my mother in Hungarian about strangers. In one infamous incident at Bonwit Teller Department Store in New York, she ridiculed a person's hat in the restroom only to have the woman turn to wish her "good afternoon" in Hungarian as she exited.

Like my mother, Elsie rarely spoke of Ferko and never talked about her marriage or her experiences in Europe in the early 1930s before es-caping to the US. I don't know how the couple first met, but on August

6, 1921, two years after his arrival in the US, Ferko and Elsie were married at her parents' home in Chicago. They were twenty-five and twenty-one years old, respectively, which was young for a Hungarian couple. In Hungary, the average age at marriage in 1920 was twenty-five-and-a-half for women and twenty-nine-and-a-half for men.[39]

*Ferko and Elsie, 1921.*
*(From the author's personal collection)*

In 1922, Ferko and Elsie moved to Argentina to join his older brothers, Andrés and Jorge. In the next few years they traveled back and forth between the two countries multiple times by freighter. With his linguistic accomplishments and study of Latin in boarding school, it didn't take Ferko long to master Spanish. In Buenos Aires he set up a up a small business in an office next to his brothers' architectural studio. Compañía Cultural de Films distributed educational films to schools and universities across South America. To promote it Ferko edited a film magazine called *Educación Visual.* One such film, called *La Mosca,* was screened in Buenos Aires in 1923 for an audience of "Young and Old," "Parents and

Children," and "Teachers and Students." Ferko supplemented this with
some import-export work and occasional jobs as a Spanish-Hungarian
interpreter for which he co-authored a Hungarian-Spanish dictionary.[40]
In a summary of his work experience during this period, he wrote that
he worked with a wide range of people, including government officials,
industrialists, merchants, and educators.

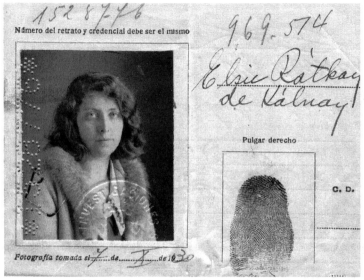

*Elsie's Argentine visa, 1930. (Photograph by author.)*

Not long after their move to Buenos Aires, Elsie became pregnant,
and in November 1924, she gave birth to my mother, Böske (Elizabeth)
Herminia Ratkay de Kálnay. Having a wife and a newborn didn't stop
Ferko from making frequent trips back to New York and Europe. Each
trip meant a long separation from Elsie and Elizabeth since transatlantic
voyages took a week or two in either direction. Elsie confided to her
daughter Peti that Andrés and Jorge would chase after her relentlessly
whenever Ferko was out of town. She begged Ferko not to leave her alone
in the apartment in Buenos Aires, but he ignored her entreaties.

By 1926, Elsie was pregnant again. This time, she and Elizabeth returned to the US alone and went to South Bend, Indiana, where Elsie's
parents were living in a small Hungarian community. Their second

daughter, Maria Petika Kálnay, was born there at her grandmother's home. Ferko had wanted a boy and gave his daughter the nickname Peti, a Hungarian diminutive for Peter. Later, Elsie and the children joined Ferko in New York, where he had relocated and was working at several jobs—always with Hungarian connections. In 1927, they purchased land in rural Brewster, New York, Putnam County, the town in which they had married six years earlier.

### Finding Family in Politics and Mysticism

Ferko had no models for attachment and romantic love in his own child-hood. He was ripped from his mother's arms when he was one year old, after which he was left with a nanny while four of the older siblings who might have nurtured him were sent to live in another city. I wonder what he was told about his mother's fate when he was old enough to talk about her absence or what he felt when he was abandoned a second time by his father, who left Budapest for two years when Ferko was seven. A few years later, Ferko was sent to a harsh boarding school without his siblings, and when he was eleven, his father took up with a mistress whom none of the children liked. In 1914, when World War I broke out, Jószef encour-aged fifteen-year-old Ferko to join the Merchant Marines.

The Kálnay family had no cultural or religious traditions that might have given young Ferko a sense of security and community. He is unlikely to have participated in a family seder or Shabbat or to have attended re-ligious services. Although it is possible that Rózsa fostered some religious practices before she was torn from the family, Ferko was too young to have been influenced by them. And when Jószef brought his Catholic mistress to the family, any Jewish traditions that may have existed would have been ignored, at best. More likely they would have been obliterated since, according to Catholic teachings, the children would go to Hell if they were not baptized and raised in the Catholic church.

Ferko was lonely and tormented during his first two years in the United States. In his early twenties he published a book of Hungarian po-ems in Budapest that describe despair and religious conflict. *Feltámadás elött* (*Before Resurrection*) is a book of twenty-seven poems and ballads divided into four chapters entitled "Before Resurrection," "On the Road," "Encounter with Love," and "I Greet You."[41] The overall tone is sorrowful and downbeat, with recurring themes of remorse, regret, and loss. One particularly striking poem is about living in the present and looking ahead to the future rather than revisiting the past.[42]

In the foreword, Ferko describes the book as being borne out of "the horrific battle of the soul between faith and unfaithfulness." A Swedish Hungarian friend who read it notes that many of the poems contain overtly Christian themes, especially the first section that deals with resurrection.[43]

These themes include faith, God, sin, forgiveness, confession, death, burial, and the soul. Ferko appeals to what he terms the "sinfully blind" and "self-important holy people" who were "late with their tears" and who brought on his weeping. "It is with divine humility that I open my heart, so that you may feel my amity and know that I will be with you on your journey as you seek solace and resurrection."

What should we make of these overtly religious themes on the part of a man we knew as a nonbeliever? Perhaps as a Jewish boy who was raised Catholic, he struggled with beliefs that were exacerbated by loneliness in a new and seemingly godless country. The themes of remorse, regret, loss, and apology may reflect despair over abandoning family and homeland. Or perhaps Ferko was trying to reconcile his religious upbringing with the agnosticism of his older brothers Andrés and Jorge or to what Andrés's son Esteban describes as their philosophy of Christian anarchism. Ferko's Hungarian inscription in the book of poems was to Andrés, whom he called Bandi: "To my dear Bandi, with the deepest understanding and holy brotherhood."

My cousin Wendy adds that it makes sense to her that Ferko would use poetry to allegorize his personal struggles and his deepest values. She notes that he had read Dostoevsky and may have been acting out themes from *The Grand Inquisitor*.

Ferko's social isolation seems to have ended in 1921—not as a result of his marriage to Elsie that year but because he became part of a Greenwich Village coterie of artists and socialists and a devotee of the Russian mystic Gurdjieff. Ferko's close Hungarian friends, Julian

DeMiskey and Ilonka Karasz, were members of both of these circles. Julian emigrated from Hungary five years before Ferko and settled in Ohio at the start of the First World War. In 1917 he moved to New York to study at the Art Students League. He was a talented illustrator who drew over sixty-two covers for *The New Yorker Magazine* and exhibited paintings in the Museum of Modern Art, The Guggenheim, and numerous New York galleries.

Ilonka Karasz came to the US the same year as Julian. She opened a studio in Greenwich Village where she did graphic design and illustration and created textiles and furniture for top fashion houses and department stores. Ilonka founded the Society of Modern Art, which attracted writers and actors with Hungarian connections and other illustrious figures, such as Willa Cather, Edna St. Vincent Millay, and Wassily Kandinsky. Like Julian, Ilonka designed covers for *The New Yorker*, and, in time, she became one of the foremost artists of the era. She also established a Hungarian theater troupe in the Village, which may be where she first met Ferko, given his interest in acting. When he spoke of it, Ferko called it a "socialist theater troupe."

Ilonka and her husband, Willem Nyland, purchased property in Brewster, New York, where Ferko and Elsie were married in 1921 and where they bought a small dairy farm. Willem (or Wim, as he was called) was a disciple of the mystic Gurdjieff, who founded the Institute for the Harmonious Development of Man in 1918. Ferko and Nyland became such close friends that Nyland wrote a letter of reference for Ferko several years later when he first applied to work for the federal government.

Gurdjieff's Institute began in the Caucasus and then moved to Constantinople, Berlin, and Fontainebleau, near Paris. Gurdjieff made six or seven fundraising visits to the United States, but he spent most of his adult life in France, where he wrote four books and instructed disciples in his philosophy of transformation through intensive manual work, dance, cooking, eating, drinking, reading, and music. He maintained that these efforts would force students to break loose from their mechanical, somnambulistic states and achieve "harmony"—a level of consciousness that he believed followers of other religions failed to achieve.

Julian DeMiskey was also a disciple of Gurdjieff, and Wim Nyland became a leader in the Gurdjieff movement in the US. Ilonka and Wim created a commune on their Brewster property where they held discussions of Gurdjieff's book *The Fourth Way* four or five nights a week, year-round. Both were trustees of the Gurdjieff Foundation and they visited Gurdjieff in Europe before and after the First World War.[44] Visitors to their meetings in Brewster included Alexander Calder and Frank Lloyd Wright.

There were two aspects of Gurdjieff's teachings that were particularly important to Ferko: first, the idea that we are always observing ourselves, and that this keeps us from becoming subjective or falling into deep wells of depression. Ironically, Ferko was also drawn to Gurdjieff's hyper-rationalism, although he himself was a romantic. Perhaps he cast off his youthful, conventional beliefs about God after "discovering" Gurdjieff.

In addition to being devotees of Gurdjieff, Julian and Ilonka contributed illustrations to *The Liberator*, an organ of the American Communist Party. It was a successor to *The Masses*, which the Justice Department shut down during World War I when Max Eastman and his sister Crystal were the editors. The illustrations that Julian and Ilonka drew for *The New Masses* and *The Liberator* were integral to the publications' models of visual art in support of the Soviet Communist Party. Contributing artists were expected to create illustrations that reflected class struggles.[45] One example is DeMiskey's cover illustration for *The Liberator*, entitled "Peace and There is No Peace," situated above a lead article by Eastman on "The Wisdom of Lenin."

*Cover illustration by Julian DeMiskey. http://www.papillongallery.com/julian_de_miskey.html for* The Liberator. *(The images on the marxists.org website are in the Public Domain under the Creative Commons Commons Deed.)*

As a young adult, the friendship of artists and followers of Gurdjieff provided Ferko with a close-knit community and something akin to a religious experience for the first time in his life. Is it any wonder that he was in thrall to them? He was also deeply involved with the Bohemian Socialists in Greenwich Village, a group that included many artists and writers, as well as an infusion of newly-arrived immigrant Jews like Ferko. Their ranks included journalists, novelists, artists, trade unionists, actors, poets, and feminists whose views of modern life emphasized free speech, free expression, and free love with class equality.[46] As a journalist and actor who wrote poetry and bonded with fellow immigrants, Ferko fit in perfectly.

Secular Jewish immigrants composed a second wing of American socialists, and Eastman's publication, *The Masses*, was an outlet for their views on cultural revolution, including a rejection of Christianity as a guide to moral behavior. The publication included many articles on women's rights to suffrage, equal treatment in the workplace, marriage and divorce, access to birth control, and expressions of sexual desire. In addition Max wrote about his personal free love experiences with multiple lovers.[47]

### Camp Artemis

Ferko and Julian were influenced by the sexual mores of Gurdjieff followers and the Bohemian Socialists of Greenwich Village. Gurdjieff discussed sex openly with his pupils in public lectures and private conversations. In addition to the objective of procreation, he taught that sex produced an energy that nourished spiritual development. He had a reputation for alternating periods of celibacy with open sexual liaisons. As a result, he fathered the children of several of his younger female disciples, including one who was married to someone else.[48]

The Bohemians saw sex, both inside and outside of marriage, as a political matter and a means toward a better life. They elevated principles of honesty about sexual desire among freely participating partners above marriage and argued that women had erotic needs comparable to those of men.[49]

In the late 1920s, Ferko and Julian leased property together in Brewster and opened Camp Artemis, a libertine adult camp for other artists and writers. Ferko was attracted by the opportunity to create a community of individuals who shared his political and artistic sensibilities and his interest in naturism. Nudism was a key element in youthful "body culture" among left-wing young people in the 1930s, and many naturist communities were established in rural parts of the US where their founders promoted an idealized image of opportunities for healthy communing with nature in tranquil, secluded communities.

Max Eastman, a self-professed advocate of free love and nudism, was a frequent visitor to Camp Artemis. He was a friend of Ernest Hemingway, Charlie Chaplin, Carl Sandburg, Edna Millay, and E. E. Cummings. Eastman's third wife, Hungarian Yvette Szekely, was the paramour of the famous American author Theodore Dreiser for many years. Dreiser shared the group's leftist views. He lectured for the Committee for Soviet Friendship and American Peace, although he only formally joined the American Communist Party in 1945 to protest US involvement in the war.

Dreiser and Szekely met at Ferko's camp in 1930 and began a love affair when Yvette was seventeen and Dreiser was in his fifties. It was Yvette's stepmother, a magazine journalist, who introduced her to Dreiser at Camp Artemis, and later to Max Eastman, whom Yvette married after her long affair with Dreiser. In her biography of Dreiser, Yvette described her month-long stay at the camp and the libertine environment there:

*Come summer and my mother decided Sue and I should spend the month of August at an adult summer camp named Artemis near Brewster, New York, that had been founded by the Hungarian New Yorker artist Julian DeMiskey with his Hungarian friend Francis Kalnay, a writer. It accommodated not more than about twenty people and had few facilities and equipment except for ping pong and pool in the dining hall and two old mares who shared a woodshed. Those who came, mostly artists, writers, photographers, concert musicians, and now and then a doctor or philosopher— predominantly Hungarians—already knew each other or, if not, promptly became acquainted and often amorously involved for they were dependent on each other for every diversion.*

*Julian, then in his mid-to late thirties, was "tall, dark and handsome," with the Slavic feature of almost slanty eyes. He had a sweet, kindly, personal way with the young, such as we were, but was reputed to be less chivalrous with the score of women who became infatuated with him. His wit and sense of humor were reflected in his many New Yorker covers and drawings, but I was more impressed with him as a spiritual thinker, a disciple of Gurdjieff. Julian was not one to set the table laughing, but Francis—whom everyone called "Ferko," with his lean face, slender pointing nose, thin pursed lips, and wiry blond hair—was.*

In the same book, Yvette described her eighteenth birthday party to which her mother invited several of her own close friends, including Ferko, Julian, and Theodore Dreiser.

When I was growing up, my mother didn't mention her father often, but, when she did, she provided brief anecdotes about his many girl-friends, the times that he abandoned her and her mother and sister, and her embarrassment over the "nudist camp" that he ran on their property when she was growing up. Those comments were all I knew of Ferko's misadventures until I began to research his life.

I can only imagine how difficult it must have been for my grandmother Elsie to have been associated with Camp Artemis. Then—as later—Ferko didn't hide his attraction to other women. However, neither she nor my mother ever mentioned the camp other than my mother's acknowledgment of her embarrassment. The fact that the only surviving photographs from the camp are of very young women seems especially sordid in light of Yvette Szekely's report of her seduction there by Theodore Dreiser when she was a teenager. I don't know how long the naturist camp continued, but Ferko and Julian continued to lease the property for Camp Artemis until at least the early 1940s, several years after Ferko and Elsie divorced.

Ferko's proclivity for naturism is also illustrated by a photographic postcard that he produced in 1930 when my mother and her sister Peti were four and six years old.

*Camp Artemis. (From the author's personal collection)*

*Elizabeth, Peti, and Ferko at the lake.*
*(From the author's personal collection)*

---

* The photo may not be salacious; nude swimming was common for boys during the era, though less so for girls. In 1926 the American Public Health Association issued the first swimming pool guidelines with a recommendation that boys swim separately and in the nude, while girls should wear simple tank suits.

## Crisis in Hungary and in Ferko and Elsie's Marriage

Elsie and Ferko divorced in 1934 after thirteen years of marriage. The 1930s were a rocky time for many Hungarian couples because of the political and economic problems of the interwar period.[50] On the other hand, Elsie and Ferko had a particularly tumultuous relationship characterized by many separations. Here is a dizzying, partial record of Ferko, Elsie, and the children's trips to Buenos Aires, New York, and Hungary between 1923 and 1933:

> 1923: BA – NY – BA; Ferko, Elsie
> 1924: BA – NY – BA; Ferko, Elsie, and infant Elizabeth
> 1925: BA – NY – BA; Ferko only
> 1925: BA – NY; Ferko, Elsie, and Elizabeth
> 1926: Chile – NY: Ferko only
> 1927: BA – NY; Ferko, Elsie, and toddlers Elizabeth and Peti moved
>    to Brewster
> 1928: BA – NY; Elsie and the children
> 1929: NY – Hungary; Ferko, Elsie, and the children
> 1930: Hungary – NY; Elsie and the children
> 1930: NY – BA – NY; Ferko, Elsie, and the children
> 1931: NY – Hungary; Ferko, Elsie, and the children
> 1931: Hungary – NY; Ferko only
> 1932: Hungary – NY – Indiana; Elsie and the children
> 1932: NY – Hungary; Elsie and the children
> 1933: Ferko abandons Elsie and the children in Hungary
> 1934: Ferko divorces Elsie and accuses her of abandonment

What must it have been like for Elsie and the children to be dragged across the ocean every year—sometimes with Ferko, and sometimes by themselves? I don't know what drove Ferko to make these frequent moves, but I do know that they took their toll on his family. In 1930, when Elizabeth and Peti first enrolled in school in Putnam County at ages six and four, they only spoke Hungarian and Spanish, and the other children laughed at them for their limited English. The following year, at the height of the Depression, the family was back in Hungary, where they stayed with relatives who clearly didn't want "guests." Of all the moves, this one seems to have left the deepest imprint on my mother. In her later years, when dementia began to take her memory, she repeated the story of starting school in Hungary when neither she nor Peti spoke Hungarian well.

By the time my mother was nine years old, she had made at least twelve Atlantic sea voyages between New York, Buenos Aires, and Europe. In each city they stayed with relatives, with the result that for the rest of her life, my mother was deeply reluctant to spend even one night at the homes of friends or family because she feared "being a burden." To a lesser degree, Peti too was hesitant to impose on family or friends.

In 1933 Ferko permanently abandoned Elsie and the children when she was thirty-one and the girls were ages seven and nine. They were left at the home of relatives in Hungary at the height of the worldwide Depression in a year marked by antisemitic rioting and manifestos at Hungarian universities. Tensions were further exacerbated by the collapse of the Hungarian grain export market, and by 1933, unemployment in Hungary was close to 36%. The incipient Nazi regime dominated Hungarian politics, and the country moved increasingly to the right, with leaders extolling a "nationalist Christian" policy.[51] An earlier photograph of Elsie and the children in ethnic Hungarian dress (see next page) belies the stress of moving back and forth between the US, Hungary, and Argentina and the undercurrents of antisemitism in Magyar nationalism.

Suddenly Elsie was stranded in Budapest with two children, no money, and no way to get back to the US. Out of desperation she wrote to an older American farmer, Dan Steinbeck, who owned property next to the Kalnay farm in Brewster. She entreated him to pay their passage back to New York. According to a Putnam County newspaper article, just before receiving Elsie's letter, Dan had considered leaving New York and "becoming a citizen of Nebraska." Perhaps he saw Elsie's plea as a change in his fortunes; he quickly wired her the money, hired her as his housekeeper, and took her in as his mistress. For Elsie it was hardly a love match; she was thirty-one, and Dan was fifty-one. Still, she had no recourse when Ferko abandoned her and left her penniless in the midst of the Great Depression

*Elsie, Elizabeth, and Peti in Buenos Aires, wearing Hungarian ethnic dress.*
*(From the author's personal collection)*

just as Hungary was turning to the Fascist right. The year that Elsie fled to
the US with Elizabeth and Peti, Gyula Gömbos, a National Socialist and
radical antisemite, had been appointed premier. Gömbos had been in contact with the German Nazi Party since its creation in 1921, and he viewed
Hungarian Jews as anti-nationalists whose numbers needed to be reduced.
He was the first head of state to visit Hitler when he became chancellor in

1933.[52] Elsie's departure was none too soon. In September 1935, Gömbos returned to Berlin to sign a secret accord with Hitler's deputy Hermann Göring. The agreement was to transform the Hungarian government into a system resembling the Third Reich within two years. During that period, German economic interests increased greatly in Hungary, and the number of agencies connected to the Nazi Party proliferated, as did Nazi representation among the higher echelons of civil service.[53]

\* \* \*

Permit me to temporarily divert attention from Ferko to Dan Steinbeck, the man to whom Elsie wrote requesting help, and someone who had a profound effect on the lives of my mother, aunt, and grandmother during the time they lived on the Steinbeck farm in Brewster.

Dan Steinbeck's ancestry couldn't have been more different from Elsie's Jewish immigrant background. He was descended from a long line of farmers in Putnam County who emigrated from Holland and Scotland to the United States before the Revolutionary War.

However, like Ferko, Dan had a history that was hidden from his descendants. From my mother's terse descriptions of him as a hardscrabble dairy farmer, I imagined he came from an impoverished background. To my surprise I learned from newspaper archives and court records that he was a wealthy eccentric.

In 1914, long before meeting Elsie, Dan convinced his paralytic and possibly demented father to disinherit his two sisters—one of whom had been summoned by the old man to nurse him when he became ill. When John Steinbeck died in 1915, his son inherited $60,000—the equivalent of $1.5 million in today's dollars. The fight with his sisters made national headlines when Dan took Louise and Elizabeth to court over custody of their father's corpse after the old man died.[54] Dan lost that bizarre case, but he became the sole heir to the 176-acre family farm, one of the largest in Putnam County. It included a ten-room house, a grist mill, a cow barn for sixty dairy cows, a two-story horse barn, a carriage house, a tenant house, and two large private lakes.

Even more astounding were newspaper accounts describing Dan's arrest for bootlegging during Prohibition. In November 1930, Dan and two employees were arrested and then indicted for violating the National Prohibition Act. According to the indictment, "Danny Steinbeck" (as he is called in the indictment) produced thousands of gallons of grain alcohol in a two-thousand-gallon, $25,000 copper still hidden in the barn. Late each night, several truckloads of grain alcohol were moved off the farm by stealth. A county newspaper reporter called it "one of the finest and largest alcohol producing plants ever discovered in this section." Federal authorities said it had the capacity to produce enough alcohol to net the owners $1,000 a day—the equivalent of over $300,000 a year or almost $5 million in today's dollars. According to the local papers, "Danny Steinbeck" pled not guilty but was arraigned and indicted. The other three defendants pled guilty and were sentenced to three months each. Fortunately for Dan, he was let out on bail, and the case was postponed and finally dismissed at the end of 1933 when Prohibition was repealed.

### Excerpt: Putnam County Courier, December 5, 1930, page 1

### Three Employees and Daniel Steinbeck, Property Owner, Each Held in $2,500 Bail

*An alcohol manufacturing still operating at full capacity of several hundred gallons daily was discovered Sunday morning by State Troopers Galvin and Quinn in the old mill on the Daniel Steinbeck farm, located about a mile south of Towners. The three men of foreign birth who were operating the apparatus were arrested and one of the troopers with deputy sheriffs guarded the equipment and alcohol until federal agents arrived Tuesday and destroyed the apparatus.*

*The three men, who comprised the day shift and were arrested, gave their names and addresses as follows: Joe Sisno, aged 45, Italian, 387 Grost St., New York City; Julius Rudy, 38, Austrian, 940 East 173rd St., New York City; Bennie Yararo, 29, Italian, 138th St. and 3rd Ave., New York City; were arraigned before Justice of the Peace Junla W. Dykeman in Patterson and remained in the county jail until Monday when Sheriff Secord took them to New York where they were given into the custody of the Federal Prohibition Enforcement*

*officers and on being arraigned before a Commissioner were admitted
to bail of $2,500 each for a hearing on Dec. 16th. The Federal
authorities directed Sheriff Secord to bring the owner of the property
on which the still was operating and on Wednesday he took Daniel
Steinbeck to New York where upon being arraigned he was likewise
admitted to $2,500 bail for a hearing on Dec. 16th.*

Before Elsie and her daughrters moved in, Dan lost his fortune, as was typical of even the most successful bootleggers after the repeal of Prohibition. What happened to the money? Perhaps the process of civil forfeiture was used to seize Dan's vehicles and the still. Convicted bootleggers rarely, if ever, reclaimed seized property. The government often used their assets to settle fines and the money couldn't be reclaimed without self-incrimination.[55] Bootleggers frequently paid off local law enforcement, politicians, and judges for protection, and Dan may have bought his way to freedom after his indictment to avoid conviction on concomitant charges, such as tax evasion or smuggling across state lines.

According to Anne Funderburg, author of *Bootleggers and Beer Barons of the Prohibition Era*, the IRS often went after high-profile bootleggers. She told me, "It's amazing how the bootlegging fortunes just seemed to evaporate. Even Dutch Schultz, who made millions . . . had money problems after repeal. The bootleggers claimed they had little money left after they paid off the crooked cops and the lawyers."[56]

Dan may also have purchased gold coins. Bootleggers eschewed banks for obvious reasons and preferred gold coins that could be hidden. If so, the government may have confiscated them after President Franklin D. Roosevelt issued a decree forbidding the hoarding of gold coins by private citizens.[57] Or, perhaps there is a treasure trove of coins still buried on the Brewster property.

Prohibition was repealed in 1933, the same year Dan paid Elsie and the children's passage from Europe to the US. When they first moved back to Brewster in 1933, Elsie, Elizabeth, and Peti lived in a separate building on Dan's farm where the three of them worked, cooking, cleaning, and performing other chores. Dan was a taciturn man who preferred the company of animals to people and had little time for children, except as workers. To him, reading was a frivolous waste of time. Elizabeth and Peti hid their novels behind the radiators in the farmhouse, daring to pull them out only when Dan was out of sight.

Life on the farm was hard—even Dickensian. From a young age my mother, Elizabeth, rose every day at 5 A.M. to light the wood stove and prepare a large breakfast for the dairy hands before she left for school—a one-room schoolhouse in Brewster, where she taught the younger children. The family took in a Hungarian boarder to make ends meet, and the girls had only basic clothes and very little money. My mother told stories of saving pennies assiduously, and of her own mother's fury on a day when she lost twenty-five cents on the way to the market.

Despite their austere life, Elsie managed to imbue her daughters with a love of "culture." She would take them shopping in Manhattan department stores, where they bought nothing but enjoyed trying on clothes. Elsie's sister-in-law, Rosie, was a talented seamstress in South Bend, Indiana, who copied patterns and sent her fashionable clothes. Elsie also took Elizabeth and Peti to the theater in New York City from time to time. They would buy the cheapest seats and then move to empty ones closer to the stage during intermission.

Life took a turn for the worse after Dan suffered a near-fatal accident in December 1934 and was hospitalized for two months. He had been trapped in a small stall and badly kicked by one of his horses. The story's headline in the local paper read, "Dan Steinbeck Narrowly Escapes Death." His injuries included a compound fracture of the right leg and a case of double pneumonia. Just as he was about to be released from the hospital, he had a setback when it was discovered that his leg had healed badly and had to be broken again and reset. As a result of the accident, a year after moving to the farm Elsie was forced into the role of personal caretaker. She, Elizabeth, and Peti moved from the residents' building into the main house—a large, drafty building that got so cold in the winter that the water in the indoor toilets would freeze.

In 1940, seven years after the end of Prohibition, Dan sold almost all of his property in what was described as one of the largest sales in Putnam County. In that year's census Elsie listed her occupation as "housekeeper," working ninety hours a week for an annual income of $800. The stress was too much for her. She suffered a nervous breakdown and Elizabeth suddenly became responsible for her mother and Peti while just a teenager herself. Many years later she confided to my sister, Tess, that Dan sexually molested her during that period. We don't know whether Elsie knew of the molestation or whether her breakdown was related to the event, but she married Dan Steinbeck in 1943. For her, the marriage was likely a strategy for survival. As for Dan, his motive for the marriage may have been to ensure continued help with the farm and his own care. In 1941, two years before they married, he stipulated in his will, "should Elsie Kalnay and I become married, she is then to have the life use of the same if she remains my widow or during her lifetime, should she remarry after her marriage to me. This I do in appreciation of her many acts of kindness to me."

Despite the hardships in her life at home, my mother excelled at school, skipping two grades. Books were an escape for both Elizabeth and Peti, and some of their achievements are likely to have been motivated by desperation to leave Brewster. Elizabeth graduated at age fifteen and was accepted by NYU. Although Ferko had an apartment in the city, he refused to let my mother live with him in New York—most likely because it would have limited his ability to pursue his current girlfriends. Instead, he encouraged Elizabeth to accept work as a live-in helper at the home of a friend of his. There too she was sexually molested—something she revealed to me half a century later during the Anita Hill hearings in 1991, when women all over the country felt emboldened to share their stories of sexual exploitation.

To distance herself from her mother, father, and stepfather, Elizabeth applied to and was accepted by the Home Economics School at Cornell University, where tuition was free for New York State residents. Peti followed her to Cornell two years later and studied arts and sciences. Peti described arriving at Cornell with two skirts, two blouses, a sweater, a jacket, and a single pair of shoes. She did not perceive the family as poor until she got there and saw the wardrobes of other students. Both Peti and Elizabeth had paid jobs every semester of college, but they reveled in their freedom at Cornell. On the other hand, Dan was sorry to lose the children as help on the farm. A few years later, in 1945, when my mother married Donald Fennelly—the brother of her Cornell roommate—Dan refused to attend the wedding.

Dan and Elsie remained married until he died in 1951. Dan had a realtor's license and introduced Elsie to the business. After his death he left her the main house and a large barn filled with antique furniture, but little else. Elsie was overwhelmed with bills and debts. She was forced to sell the farmhouse and move to a one-bedroom apartment in Heidi's Motel in Brewster, where she supported herself with her modest earnings as a realtor and with some help from her grown daughters. She lived at the motel until her death in 1979.

# II

# HOW TO BECOME A SPY

How did a Jewish refugee from a war-torn country work his way up to become a highly ranked agent in the Office of Strategic Services during World War II? Using declassified materials that I found at the National Archives and copies of his personnel file obtained from the CIA, I was able to piece together the trajectory of my grandfather's career.

In his early years in New York, Ferko held various jobs, helping Hungarian friends as a salesperson at an art gallery, working for Greenberg Press, and performing translations, market research, and outreach to immigrant communities for Newell-Emmett Advertising. While working at the Hagstrom Map Company in Manhattan, he compiled an atlas called *Market Atlas of the United States,* and in 1936 he published *Transatlantic Steamship Arrivals.*

My grandfather maintained close ties to the expatriate community. He directed Hungarian language programming on WWRL, a radio station that broadcast from Woodside, Queens, to Italian, German, French, Hungarian, Slovak, Czech, and Yiddish communities. Later he published a book of stories for second-generation Hungarian children in the US called *Foglalj helyet Péter* (*Take a Seat, Peter*).[1] It is a fantastical and whimsically written tale about St. Peter, who accidentally loses his beloved pipe and leaves Heaven to retrieve it on Earth. While there, he researches the aspirations of young humans and has many misadventures. The book ends with St. Peter writing to the highest authority in Heaven to say he is having such a good time that he won't be returning.[2]

During his lifetime, my grandfather maintained a transatlantic Hungarian-American identity. He was devoted to many aspects of Hungarian culture—language, literature, music, theater, and food. During his many years living outside of Europe, Ferko retained ties to Hungary through his connections to expat communities in the US and Argentina and with frequent return trips. In his final decade he yearned to travel to Budapest and revisit Budapest's famous mineral baths.

Although he lived in Hungary at a time of political oppression, Ferko never spoke of that. At the same time, he was a deeply loyal and patriotic American. As xenophobia increased in the US, he realized that rapid assimilation was the key to success in the US, much as Magyarization had once been essential to Jews in Hungary. In 1931, upon his return to the US from a trip to Hungary, he filed a Declaration of Intention, and six years later, on April 5, 1937, he became a naturalized citizen.

From his first steps on American soil, Ferko's facility for languages, his background, and the connections he forged prepared him for government work and, ultimately, for espionage. He was multilingual—by his own account on OSS forms, he was fluent in English, knew "fair" Russian and Croatian, and spoke "good" Spanish, German, and Italian.

Hungarians have always had to learn other languages because so few people outside Hungary speak theirs. During the Austro-Hungarian Empire, German was the language of public administration. According to his nephew Esteban, Ferko's father and stepmother spoke Hungarian and German at home and contracted a German-speaking nanny when the children were young. József and other Kálnay family members may also have spoken Yiddish, although we have no record of that. In the Austro-Hungarian Empire, when József was a young man, Yiddish was significantly undercounted. The Austrians recorded it as a dialect of German rather than a distinct language in order to prevent Jews from being considered a separate nationality. Since Hebrew was mostly spoken in synagogues, it too was not recorded as a spoken language by the Habsburgs. Nevertheless, unlike Jews in some other parts of central

Europe, Hungarian Jews more often spoke Hungarian than Yiddish, except on the borders.[3]

In the US, by 1930 over a quarter of Hungarian Jews reported speaking some Yiddish, although this was masked by the much larger percentage who claimed Hungarian as their primary language. When Ferko was born three decades earlier, the percentage of Yiddish speakers was likely to have been even higher, but Yiddish proficiency was often intentionally hidden during anti-Jewish periods in Hungary.

The Kálnay children learned Serbo-Croatian from their time in Jasenovac, where Ferko was born. Proficiency in Spanish was the result of Ferko's many trips to Argentina, where his brothers Andrés and Jorge settled. He may have learned English in the Navy School in Fiume and perfected it when he arrived in New York at age twenty. However, his mother tongue, Hungarian, remained Ferko's first love and his entrée into immigrant life in New York.

Ferko's attraction to journalism was likely influenced by his early years in Budapest. Once in New York, Hungarian publications were a way for him to quickly integrate into Magyar expatriate culture. In 1920 there were as many as seventy semi-weekly Hungarian papers in the US, focusing variously on religion, politics, literature, humor, and fraternal and political organizations, as well as three national dailies: the *American-Hungarian People's Voice* in New York, the Ohio-based daily *Liberty*, and the socialist-internationalist *Forward*. Ferko wrote for Hungarian language newspapers, including a socialist weekly. He was able to use his radio and print connections with fellow immigrants in New York to get work in market research and advertising outreach with the Newell-Emmet Advertising agency and Greenberg Press and to secure part-time translation and editorial work.

Ironically, the increase in anti-immigrant sentiments in the US in the early 1920s helped Ferko get his first quasi-governmental work. He had already moved in artistic and journalistic circles in the New York area and regularly met with newly arrived émigrés from eastern Europe. Beginning in 1922, these networks positioned him to secure work with the Foreign Language Information Service (FLIS), a division of the US Committee on Public Information that was created to promote the assimilation of immigrants during WWI and to temper anti-immigrant attitudes.

The FLIS had offices in New York and Washington and programs for individuals representing eighteen foreign language groups and the Jewish diaspora. The programming involved disseminating materials to non-English speakers in their native languages and submitting articles to some of the eight hundred US-based foreign-language publications on topics related to US government structure, laws, and obligations, such as registering for the draft, paying taxes, and securing Liberty Loans. Information came from the War Department, State Department, Navy Department, Treasury Department, Labor Department, Food Administration, Fuel Administration, Shipping Board, Railroad Administration, and Council of National Defense. After the First World War, the FLIS became an independent organization until it was abandoned in 1939.

Ferko worked with the FLIS off and on during its entire duration, in between his trips to Argentina and Hungary, as well as later when it became the Common Council for American Unity. The CCAU released information to foreign language presses, operated a radio service, published *Common Ground*, and assisted the government with alien registration and English language classes. On his resumé Ferko described the FLIS/CCAU objectives:

> One of the functions of the Common Council is the syndication of articles interpreting American life and institutions to over 1,000 foreign language newspapers printed in this country. It also helps the immigrant to become a citizen of the US. It interprets the immigrant to older Americans and works to eliminate discrimination against the foreign-born and his children. It strives to promote American unity among all the diverse elements of the population. Its activities are carried out chiefly through the social and fraternal organizations of the foreign-born and the Nation's foreign language press.

The Hungarian section of the FLIS also helped individuals locate relatives, send money or packages to Hungary, and understand the bureaucratic requirements of US agencies, such as war-risk allotments, passport and land regulations, employment, and income taxes. In 1941, Ferko compiled related information in a book he co-wrote with Richard Collins called *The New American*. A reviewer in *The New York Times* wrote:

*Timeliness as well as comprehensiveness marks this new "Handbook
of Necessary information for Aliens, Refugees and New Citizens."
Naturalization procedures and educational requirements are set forth
in helpful detail, but immediately pressing problems in the newcomer's
life are given equal emphasis. As the editor explains in his preface,
whatever the immigrant's motive in selecting the United States as his
**permanent** home, he must earn a living before anything else . . . Some
of this valuable information is presented in question-and-answer
form, and personal usefulness is the book's well-met criterion.*

A brief but equally favorable review of the book appeared in *The New
Masses*, a publication of the US Communist Party. The reviewer said that
the editors had done a useful and intelligent job addressing almost every
question that might be relevant to refugees or immigrants.

The handbook has nothing of the lyrical quality of Ferko's later books
for children or even his articles on cooking. Instead, it is a dry compen-
dium of information on topics such as social security regulations, how
to become a citizen, and how to search for employment in each state,
find immigrant-serving organizations, or locate relatives in the US and
abroad. A few years earlier Ferko co-wrote another prosaic publication
with Richard Collins: *The Handbook of Seasickness.*[4]

### JOINING THE GOVERNMENT AS HITLER INVADES EUROPE

Ferko was not the only writer to make a career of espionage—Graham
Green, Somerset Maugham, and other renowned writers of the twentieth
century were also spies. Perhaps this is not surprising, since both professions involve luring others to enter a fictional world. In my grandfather's
case, the onset of World War II led to the creation of agencies that ultimately recruited him into government service.

On the first day of September 1939, Adolf Hitler's armies invaded
Poland and overwhelmed the Polish forces with a blitzkrieg of bombs
targeting communication lines, railroads, and munitions dumps. Within
slightly more than a year, German troops moved further into Europe,
trampling Denmark, Norway, Belgium, the Netherlands, and France in
rapid succession.

Churchill and Roosevelt were convinced that Hitler's use of propaganda and espionage was instrumental to his European conquests, and they began to meet to plan coordinated intelligence campaigns even before the US entered the war at the end of 1941. As a result of their conversations, Roosevelt sent his old Columbia law school classmate Bill Donovan to London to study espionage tactics from the British. "Wild Bill," as he was named during the First World War, was appointed head of the first American intelligence agency in July 1941. He modeled it after the British Special Operations Executive (SOE).

As head of the Office of the Coordinator of Information (COI)—later to become the Office of Strategic Services, or OSS—Donovan reported to the White House rather than to the Joint Chiefs of Staff, who looked askance at the unconventional forms of warfare and Donovan's intention to play what he referred to as "a bush league game, stealing the ball, and killing the umpire." The Chiefs made sure that the title of the new agency didn't include terms like "strategic" or "defense," but they tolerated its creation since they were reluctant to engage in espionage themselves.[5] Everything changed after the attack on Pearl Harbor on December 7, 1941, when the COI was authorized to collect intelligence and conduct sabotage behind enemy lines in North Africa.

Donovan appointed his friend Ned Buxton as assistant director of the COI, and the two of them created an Oral Intelligence Division to capture information by debriefing refugees from Europe as they arrived in New York. It was Col. Buxton who recruited Ferko to work in the division, tasking him with developing a network of spies who would gather economic, political, social, and military information about enemy activities and networks in Europe, North Africa, and the Middle East. Ferko's years of work in the Foreign Language Information Service, his extensive network of European expatriates, and his command of multiple languages made him a natural choice. Although antisemitism was still rampant in the United States, many of the most valuable recruits to the COI, and later the OSS, were naturalized European Jews like Ferko, who had broad language skills and deep-seated motivation to assist in the war against the Nazis.

My grandfather joined Oral Intelligence the week before the bombing of Pearl Harbor, an event that convinced President Roosevelt to heed Bill Donovan's recommendations to commit to guerilla warfare.

In June 1942, the COI was disbanded, and covert activities were assigned to the OSS under the Joint Chiefs of Staff. Although Donovan was eventually given the rank of major general, he remained relatively independent of military control. According to Peter Finn, national security editor at the *Washington Post*, the OSS buildings were soon teeming with recruits:

> *Donovan hired what he called his "league of gentlemen"—the*
> *wealthy, the blue-blooded, and the well-connected, including*
> *President Roosevelt's son—but he would also consider anyone with*
> *a skill he coveted, regardless of background, which gave the OSS*
> *much of its daring and creative energy. Safecrackers, burglars, forgers,*
> *Mafia enforcers, and madcap inventors were as welcome as scientists,*
> *linguists, chemists, historians, and mapmakers. Those who failed*
> *to get into the military and those who didn't want to get into the*
> *military also turned to the OSS. "We get all the crocks working for*
> *us eventually, high blood pressure boys, grey bearded professors, young*
> *draft dodgers, and tired business men."*[6]

Donovan employed a diverse network of spies to collect economic, political, social, and military information about enemy activities and networks in Europe, North Africa, and the Middle East. The intelligence was included in detailed reports to President Roosevelt.

A key player in building the OSS was Donovan's influential friend, Allen Dulles, an OSS agent posted to Bern, Switzerland, whose close connections to Donovan and President Roosevelt afforded him a great deal of influence and a generous budget.[7] Both Dulles and Donovan knew they needed spies in the field to back up the intelligence information gathered from émigrés. With his extensive network of European émigrés, Ferko was a natural choice. In fact, an advertisement for the recruitment of OSS agents foreshadowed his assignments.

> *We are looking for officers who want to volunteer . . . overseas*
> *duty of a secret and highly hazardous nature and close combat . . .*
> *excellent physical shape and a high degree of endurance are*
> *necessary . . . background with field training . . . work that is similar*

*to commando operations . . . fill out the enclosed forms if you are*
*interested.*[8]

Ferko's first OSS work was in New York. Although Donovan had a hundred analysts working out of cramped offices in Washington, he had few spies or saboteurs in the field and none in Germany or Japan. His head of OSS operations in Europe, David Bruce, directed Dulles to organize a major outpost in New York to collect and analyze overseas intelligence as well as to hatch covert operations that might destabilize Germany or Japan. As a world center of business, banking, and legal affairs, and home to Ellis Island, New York was the logical site for this enterprise.

On February 16, 1942, Dulles signed a lease for a suite of offices in the International Building at 630 Fifth Avenue in Rockefeller Center, which became home to several top-secret intelligence programs, some of which rivaled Donovan's work at the COI in Washington. In June 1942, the COI became the OSS, and by the end of 1942, the New York office had sixty-nine employees, more than half of whom reported directly to Dulles in his section of the OSS Secret Intelligence Branch. One of them was Francis Kalnay.

The offices included space on the thirty-eighth floor for a laboratory, where spy devices were engineered, and a production plant on the thirty-first and thirty-sixth floors for printing falsified documents for agents. Ferko worked on the thirty-fifth floor in the Oral Intelligence Unit. He rose quickly within the OSS, becoming a central source of intelligence for Allied war strategies in the Balkans and the Middle East. In four years, he moved from overseeing the collection of strategic data in the United States to assiduously directing and carrying out important clandestine operations behind enemy lines.

It is possible that Ferko also worked on a highly secret project to collect information on German companies operating in South America.[9] Given his ties to the region and knowledge of Spanish, this would have been a logical assignment, although I didn't find corroboration in his declassified files. However, Ferko did list "intelligence work in Argentina" on one of his OSS personnel summaries. At the time, Nelson Rockefeller headed the US Office of Inter-American Affairs, whose goal was to heighten American influence in the region and combat Axis incursion. In Argentina, the coordination committee distributed documentaries and produced propagandistic Spanish language radio shows—something Ferko would have understood well from his work there producing educational films and materials.

### THE SURVEY OF FOREIGN EXPERTS

In February 1942, Col. Donovan disbanded the Oral Intelligence Unit of the COI, where Ferko began his government work. When the OSS was established, he and Allen Dulles made plans to create a Survey of Foreign Experts office in New York. Dulles's close connections to Donovan and President Roosevelt afforded him a great deal of influence and a generous budget. Both he and Donovan understood the value of intelligence information gathered from émigrés, as did David Bruce, the OSS chief in Europe.

The survey was established as a unit of the Secret Intelligence (SI) Branch of the OSS in collaboration with the Board of Economic Warfare (BEW), serving the objectives of the two organizations—that of the SI to train locally recruited spies to gather intelligence in enemy territory, and BEW work on plans for bombing economic assets in Axis-occupied countries and procuring foreign materials for the war.

To set up the office, Dulles hired several attorneys and businessmen, including Murray Gurfein, a lieutenant colonel in the Psychological Warfare Division of the army and an expert on intelligence in the Balkans—Ferko's region of expertise. Gurfein charged Ferko with designing the Survey of Foreign Experts and then running its day-to-day operations. In a memo he wrote in December 1942, Ferko defined the purpose of the survey as "identifying individuals who can assist in problems affecting certain theaters, playing an active role in the prosecution of the war, and reoccupation and reconstruction programs."[10]

Once the Survey Office was established, the Navy transmitted lists of passengers on all incoming ships docking at New York, Baltimore, and New Orleans. Ferko hired and trained interviewers who were fluent in relevant languages and knowledgeable of country conditions because they were refugees or had business contacts, relatives, or friends in enemy-occupied countries. In this way new immigrants constituted a vital source of information on German chemical and weapons production, transportation systems, and economic and political successes and vulnerabilities in occupied countries.

Ferko and his staff vetted the passenger lists to target passengers deemed likely informants with knowledge about manufacturing, mining, transportation, infrastructure, political organizations, and opposition groups in each of these countries. They asked selected respondents to contribute to the war effort by filling out a written questionnaire and agreeing to an oral interview. These initial contacts were carefully designed so as not to alarm the participants, many of whom had only recently left Fascist-controlled areas and feared official questions. Interviewers needed to convince them that they were selected because of their potential to contribute to the Allied war effort, not because the FBI or the Department of Immigration was investigating them.

After the interviews, the subjects' records were supplemented with assessments of their moral character, stature, and potential for recruitment as spies. In some cases, interviewers were sent to their homes to retrieve relevant photographs, maps, and charts that could be indexed, reproduced, and shared in top secret reports.

Ferko designed and directed a comprehensive database of refugees derived from the interviews, after which the data were indexed and sent to Washington and local offices of the OSS and BEW. In both Washington and New York, he conducted special investigations and oversaw interviews of recent arrivals to the United States. In a 1942 report, Col. Buxton referred to 1,500 names Kalnay indexed for the Survey of Foreign Experts. In effect, my grandfather used the surveys and his existing networks to create an extensive spy database. In an era with no internet or high-speed communications other than operator-to-operator radio signals, these interviews constituted the best source of strategic information to aid the war effort.

Ferko was appointed director of the Survey of Foreign Experts in January 1943. In his own words, his assignment was to collect "confidential and vital information from private individuals, which is of strategic value to the government" and to determine the credibility of the information. The following memorandum from Ferko to his staff illustrates the kind of information sought by the survey.

**Memorandum**

From:       Francis Kalnay
To:         Interviewers
Date:       December 3, 1942
URGENT:     Please furnish best available sources for information on
            the following subjects:

A.  Summary of General Conditions of the Italian railroad system
    resulting from consideration of:
    1.  Traffic
    2.  Supply conditions of freight cars, tank cars, and locomotives
    3.  Labor situation
    4.  Fuel and lubricant position
    5.  Indications of what effect any unusual traffic, such as heavy
        troop movements would have on the railway system

B.  Bottlenecks to the flow of traffic:
    1.  Location and capacity of marshaling yards
    2.  Location and capacity of rolling stock repair shops
    3.  Lines without bypasses that are essential to North - South
        movement of goods. It would be particularly useful if any
        information about tunnels and bridges on these lines were
        made available.
    4.  Electric power plants vital to operation of electric line

C.  Ameliorating the railroad situation as shown in A&B by:
    1.  Construction of locomotives and freight cars by (company,
        location, and capacity)
    2.  Construction of bypasses for vital lines, especially any new
        developments in the lines leading from the Alpine region
    3.  Conversion from coal- and oil-burning locomotives to electric
        power.
    4.  What non-Italian steamrolling stock could be made available
        to Italy if electric motor power sources were destroyed?

Some individuals were first approached in person; other contacts were initiated in writing, as in this excerpt from a letter Ferko sent to a Mr. Simon Baer in New York:

> *Our attention has been called to your knowledge of German transportation. We would appreciate it if you would, at your earliest convenience, fill out and return to this office the enclosed questionnaire, after which a representative of the Board of Economic Warfare will probably get in touch with you.*

An interview with a Mrs. Hacker, who had recently returned from Hungary, revealed that when she left Hungary in August 1941, the Germans had two new airfields within a few kilometers of Budapest and a third under construction. Mrs. Hacker also had detailed information on the Adolph Emerging Fireworks company of Budapest, which had been owned by the mother-in-law of her former employer. She reported that the Nazis took over the company and began to produce rockets, explosives, and aerial bombs for the Signal Corps.

Another recent arrival from Hungary—Mr. Gomperz—provided detailed information on two companies in Budapest—Hirtenberg Works, a branch of an Austrian firm specializing in percussion caps and ammunition for small weapons, and machine gun production by the Manfred Weiss Company.

Foreigners at Ellis Island were another source of potential survey informants. In one instance, conditions in Yugoslavia were derived from interviews with young seamen held at Ellis Island in June 1942 for overstaying their visas. "Friendly conversations with these boys" revealed that they were motivated to desert their posts because of an attraction to the American way of life and resentment toward shipowners for low pay, insufficient food, and poor sanitary conditions on their freighters.

What follows are examples of two of the scores of declassified, confidential reports on Fascist-occupied countries in Europe that Ferko sent to OSS Assistant Director Edward Buxton.

Date:        07/20/1942
To:          Col. Buxton
From:        Francis Kalnay
Subject:     Joseph Samuel Fuchs, Cannes Airfield

Mr. Fuchs, 40 years of age, a Polish citizen, was an antique dealer in
Czechoslovakia, where he lived until March 1939. At that time, he left
for Paris, remaining there until June 1940. After the German occupation
he settled at Nice. He arrived in the USA on the SS Guine, June 30,
1942.

At Nice, approximately 4 km from the heart of the city, a large airfield
is being built. Work is going on day and night. Subject passed by
several times and saw German officers there. The Promenade des
Anglais leading to the field is being widened.

Subject learned that most of the locksmith and machine shops at Nice
are busy repairing and cleaning cylinders for airplane motors.

There is a severe food shortage in Nice and the cost of food rations and
items in the Black Market, as well as the effects of Nazi propaganda.
Subject stated that most Frenchmen with whom he had contact were
on the side of the Free French. From his own observations, Nazi
propaganda made no impression at all upon the French except on
the very young, who are gradually being drawn into various Youth
Movements of a Fascist character.

A report on conditions in Italy under Mussolini came from a mark-
edly different informant—the former wife of an Italian prince.

October 13, 14, 1942

To:        Col. Buxton
From:      Francis Kalnay
Subject:   Anne Marie Wallace del Drago, Italy

Subject, residing at the Hotel Delmonico, New York, arrived on the
SS *Drottningholm* on June 30th. She is 33, was born in Viterbo, Italy, of
American parents, and has retained her American citizenship as well as
that of her two children, aged seven and eight, despite her marriage to
an Italian prince from whom she is now separated. Her boy is now in a
Jesuit school in Italy; her daughter is in a convent in Rome.

Subject emphasized that she and her husband are not on speaking
terms. She has spent most of her life in Italy, particularly Rome, but
has traveled extensively. Ever since she was a child, she has made
almost yearly visits to the United States. Apparently, subject has a wide
acquaintance in Italian Court circles and stated she was "close to the
Vatican." She expressed a desire to aid the United Nations cause in
any way she could, preferably by doing "canteen work" and added that
towards Italy, she felt "as one does towards a sick child."

Subject appeared to be anti-Fascist, and close to the Royal Family. She
claims friendship with the Patino family of Bolivia.

Nazi Penetration:

According to subject, Rome is full of Germans, "although one does
not meet them socially." They dress as civilians but fool nobody. She
was told by a German officer that they are not supposed to wear their
uniforms except when on active duty. They fill all the hotels. Naples
especially is crowded with Germans. She has heard that in Naples,
street signs are printed in German.

In November 1942 Ferko sent a memo to his superior, Murray
Gurfein, acknowledging matters that Gurfein had suggested as the subject
of future interviews under the headings "Germany," "France," "Bombing
Objectives," and "Markings of Military Planes." Ferko also summarized
some survey topics of interest to the US Bureau of Economic Warfare and
the British Ministry of Economic Warfare as they related to Hungary:

- Contribution of Hungary to the Axis war effort
- Transportation in and through Hungary
- Danubian shipbuilding
- Congestion on the Danube
- Expansion of Bauxite production in Hungary and its shipment from and to Hungary for processing
- Aluminum plants in Hungary
- Electrical power facilities in European aluminum industry

Soon thereafter, Ferko sent a memo to John McGrail of the OSS Pictorial Records Office regarding his "urgent need for pictures of Danube bridges, harbors, and some cities."

Initially, data from completed interviews were incorporated into detailed intelligence reports for the Allied leaders regarding prewar and current economic, political, and military conditions in Europe. However, in November 1942, Ferko reported to Gurfein that Judge Norwood Allman, head of Far East Counterintelligence for the OSS, had expressed interest in "gradually taking over all Far East interviews" and that Sherman Kent, chief of the OSS Europe-Africa Division, had suggested establishing a close collaboration between the survey and the African desk, with a possible arrangement whereby Ferko's office would send out questionnaires and interview people regarding conditions in Africa. The scope of the survey was expanded to include countries in Africa and the Far East, including Morocco, China, Syria, Lebanon, and Iraq.

An example of the value of survey work in North Africa is illustrated by this excerpt from a letter Kent received from another OSS officer:

> *Two recent people interviewed by the Survey of Foreign Experts, Francis Kalnay's unit, may be of great value to us in the Who's Who Project. One is the son of the owner of Banque Hassan, Tangier, who was last in Tangier sometime late in 1941. The second is an interesting sounding-source of information on Morocco . . . Francis promised to have the two sources re-interviewed immediately so that reports will reach us in Washington Wednesday morning.*

In January 1943, Ferko was promoted from the position of OSS field representative to chief of the Survey of Foreign Experts, a position he held until May of that year. On his OSS resume, he described the position as follows:

> *Under the general supervision of the Chief of Strategic Intelligence is responsible for the direction of a survey of foreign economic experts now resident in the United States, in order to obtain strategic economic information and data relative to foreign countries; directs personal contacts with economic theorists, writers, teachers, and technicians in universities, schools, business, and private life in order to obtain inflation of value to the work of the Office of Strategic Services and the Board of Economic Warfare; directs the activities of special Field Investigators in order that specific data on designated subjects may be obtained; directs the maintenance of a register of foreign economic experts in the United States, including current arrivals, in order that all personal sources of foreign economic information may be available to the OSS; performs similar duties as required.*

Ferko excelled as chief of the survey. An official "Report of Efficiency Rating" for his work for December 13, 1942, to March 31, 1943, assessed him as + (outstanding) on 26 of 29 items, including "skill in the application of techniques and procedures, attention to pertinent detail, accuracy of operations and final results, ability to make decisions," and several others. Three of the "outstanding items" were underscored for special emphasis: "effectiveness in planning board programs, laying out work and directing the work of subordinates, and promoting high working morale." He received a check (adequate) on 3 of the 29 items: physical fitness for the work, effectiveness in determining space, personnel and equipment needs, and effectiveness in setting and obtaining adherence to time limits and deadlines.

After the three-month evaluation, Ferko received another promotion in rank and a pay increase. General Donovan's close advisor, Ellery Huntington, OSS Deputy Director for Psychological Warfare, proposed

Ferko to be commissioned as a major in the army and began to pay him at that level while the paperwork was submitted.* In April, P.W. Loomis, the principal intelligence officer representing the Board of Economic Welfare's connection to the Survey of Foreign Experts, also recommended Kalnay for an army commission. He wrote: "Mr. Kalnay's performance has been nothing short of brilliant and has been a source of great satisfaction to all the officials concerned. [He] is conspicuous for his administrative ability, enterprise, quickness of mind, tact discretion, and ability to cope with difficult personal situations. He inspires the confidence and draws out the best efforts of his subordinates and is universally well liked by those who work with him."

*Ferko in OSS uniform. (From author's personal collection)*

---

* By mid-1943 the OSS was able to give military commissions to and draft deferments for its recruits.

## THE KAY PROJECT

In April 1943, Ferko's OSS work changed from research to action, in the form of direct sabotage of enemy targets and training local resistance forces in guerrilla warfare. The change began with his transfer to Special Operations (SO)—the branch of the OSS responsible for mounting sustained insurgencies against the Fascists.

The SO Branch had been created as part of the COI after the December 1941 attack on Pearl Harbor and modeled after the British Special Operations Executive. COI Director Donovan wrote to President Roosevelt, arguing that the United States needed an organization staffed with "men calculatingly reckless with disciplined daring, who are trained for aggressive action . . . it will mean a return to our old tradition of the scouts, the raiders, and the rangers." Roosevelt agreed, and the branch continued when the COI became the OSS in June 1942.

Ten months later Ferko began to work with small SO teams sent behind enemy lines to hit factories, railway tunnels, bridges, and supply dumps. They trained local resistance groups and supplied them with weapons. Once dropped into occupied territory, SO agents linked up with the resistance groups, mapped zones, and then radioed for parachuted drops of supplies. They also helped rescue downed Allied airmen.

In an April 22, 1943, memo, Col. Huntington authorized Ferko to "recruit agents for Areas D, T-I, BRH & G." Not all of those abbreviations are decipherable, but I do know that Area D was part of a training camp established by the OSS in 1942 to train underwater demolition units and other OSS personnel being sent to make seaborne landings in rubber boats and other small crafts.[11]

The OSS/SOE supply effort for Europe was massive. One resupply center in England packed more than 3,335 tons of supplies, including 75,000 small arms and 35,000 grenades, into aerial delivery containers for resistance groups in Belgium, Denmark, France, Poland, and Norway. In France alone, SO airdrops armed over 300,000 resistance fighters before D-Day.

In his new assignment, Ferko reported to the chief of the SO division for a position that he described as highly confidential, involving responsibility for "planning, organizing, and directing intelligence missions in the United States and foreign countries; selecting and assigning field staff engaged in the collection, analysis, and evaluation of economic, military, geographic and psychological information, and data of strategic importance; and personally completing difficult and confidential project assignments." To begin, he developed a top-secret plan for the SO that became known as the "KAY Project"—shorthand for Kalnay.

To carry out the plan, Ferko was given access to high-level training and high-level classified information—something unusual for a foreign-born American. However, his appointment was not without controversy because of his foreign birth and the fact that he still had siblings in Nazi-occupied Hungary. He was ultimately approved, as shown by an unsigned personnel form from OSS files in Washington.[12]

> *10/23/1943. MINUTE SHEET*[13]
> *Re: Francis Kalnay about whose case you spoke.*
>
> *In view of the difficulties which you have about obtaining the services of suitable American officers with knowledge of the Balkan languages and people, I am prepared to agree to Kalnay being indoctrinated in most secret matters despite the fact that he has a brother and two sisters in Hungary.*
>
> *I should wish, however, to reserve my opinion about allowing him, once he has obtained knowledge of most secret matters, to operate so near to Hungary as in Istanbul. If you decide to bring him to London, therefore, may his subsequent posting be the subject of further consultation between us?*

The OSS deputy director and General Donovan's close advisor, Ellery Huntington, described the KAY project in a letter to R. Davis Halliwell, chief of Special Operations: "This is a group being organized by Francis Kalnay to operate from the Mid-East into Serbia, Northern Italy, Bulgaria, and Hungary . . . Kalnay is one of the most intelligent chaps I have ever seen and I think his crowd offer the greatest possibilities of any groups we have. I have asked that Francis be commissioned as a major, have arranged for an office set-up for him at the New Weston Hotel in New York, and believe that he should be allowed to do his own recruiting. His contacts are the best in the country."* In response, Director Donovan wrote to the head of the Selective Service Manpower Division, saying, "I am planning to send Mr. Kalnay on a confidential mission for this organization, and I would appreciate your taking such steps as may be necessary to have a permit issued for him to leave the country for an indefinite period."

A KAY Project recruiting office was set up at 640 Fifth Avenue in New York, and Ferko was tasked with establishing offices for the project at OSS Headquarters in DC and the OSS Mid-East Office in Cairo. He began by recruiting chief operations officers and support personnel for both sites and assembling field groups that would receive training from both the Special Operations and Secret Intelligence Branches of the OSS. After training, the recruits would be given supplies, maps, clothing, and equipment and transported to the Middle East. Each of the foreign field base units was to be staffed with a leader, radio operators, and assistants for "primary induction on Coast D"—the Dalmatian coast. R. Davis Halliwell, chief of the SO Branch, approved all the plans.

Huntington was duly impressed with Ferko's plan. On April 29, 1943, he wrote to Ulius Amoss, head of OSS Middle East operations:

> *The more I see of Kalnay (The "KAY" Group) and his work, the*
> *more confident I am that he is even better than I thought. He would*
> *like to send out soon one officer, who will bring you the details of*
> *his plans and who can be the contact in Cairo for the KAY Group.*
> *Kalnay himself and his personnel would follow shortly thereafter. His*
> *program generally would involve the induction of a small group along*
> *the Dalmation coast for the purpose of establishing a base. Either*
> *with this group or a second group should be one or two people already*
> *recruited, who know Italy and the area along Trieste. With the next*

---

* Letter from Ellery Huntington to Ulius Amoss, "KAY Group," April 29, 1943, declassified 17950, National Archives at College Park, College Park, MD. After reading these comments about Ferko, OSS expert and author Kirk Ford wrote: "I noted the very favorable comments Huntington gave about your grandfather. By all accounts Huntington was not one to give praise easily, so those were compliments well earned." (Personal communication with the author, March 03, 2022.)

*group would be included one or two people familiar with Hungary, Bulgaria, and Romania.*[14]

### LIFE AS A SPY

Ferko never spoke of his OSS assignments to family or friends. As a result, we must turn to other sources to imagine his incursions into enemy territory to organize commando attacks. One source is the diary of Wayne Nelson, who also served as an OSS spy in Italy in 1943.[15] Nelson described a typical day, including work on radio communications, code books, and semaphore towers. On one day, he recorded an afternoon working on preparing fake German insignia and devising field strategies, followed by drinks, dinner, and an evening game of chess at the Officer's Club. On another day in Sardinia at 9 A.M., he met with an Italian officer to plan future work, and then returned to his hotel at 10 to confer with team members. At 10:30, he went to the patrol torpedo base and talked to officers there. After lunch, he attended intelligence training and pistol practice.

On another day, Nelson described a close call when German planes bombed a site a mile from his station in the middle of the night. He couldn't distinguish the number of planes but heard their motors and the sporadic lines of fire that followed. Most of his team went to a local shelter—some because prostitutes would be there—but he and his partner stayed in the hotel lobby. The raid finally ended at 3:30 A.M.

Ferko's area of incursion was the Balkan Peninsula rather than Italy.* Although Roosevelt didn't consider the region a primary theater, Donovan saw Yugoslavia and Greece as sites where guerrilla uprisings and attacks on key rail lines, bridges, and telephone exchanges used by the Germans would draw their soldiers from France and the Eastern Front.

Yugoslavia had two main resistance movements: the Chetniks, headed by Draza Mihailović, who supported the royalists, and the independent communist leader, Josip Broz, known as "Tito." Tito's rise to power as the head of the National Liberation Army came about because of the

---

* Croatia, Bosnia and Herzegovina, Slovenia, Serbia, Montenegro, Kosovo, Macedonia, Romania, Bulgaria, Albania, Greece, and the European part of Turkey.

devastation wrought by the Nazis when they invaded Yugoslavia in 1941. Some areas of the country were annexed by neighboring states, while Germany occupied others. Hitler stripped the country of valuable raw materials and forced thousands into labor. Conflicts over scarce resources led to violent fights between Serbs and Croats.

## TOP-SECRET WORK WITH X-2: AN ELITE WITHIN AN ELITE

In the summer of 1943, Ferko began espionage work that resembled the covert operations depicted in spy films—employing agents and double agents to infiltrate enemy camps and sabotage communications. Underlying the work was one of the best-kept secrets of the war: ULTRA—the cache of intelligence gathered when the British deciphered German radio and teleprinter communications with their Enigma machine. Information gathered using ULTRA was passed on to a few British leaders and the president of the United States. At the height of the war, 40% of British intelligence and 65% of their best information came from their ULTRA intercepts of German radio transmissions. It was so successful that British security services captured every German agent in the UK and turned some into double agents who passed on bogus reports to Berlin.

At first, intelligence from ULTRA was the exclusive purview of the British SOE. However, SOE officials asked FBI Director J. Edgar Hoover to create a new counterintelligence organization in the OSS to share the intelligence gathered by ULTRA. Hoover rejected the request, but OSS Director Donovan used the opportunity to set up the counterintelligence (CI) section of his organization for just that purpose. On March 1, 1943, he created a CI section known as X-2, with James R. Murphy in charge. X-2 had its own overseas stations and communications channels and was the only branch of the OSS that had access to British ULTRA materials from intercepted Nazi radio intelligence communications of the German Abwehr. By the end of the war, X-2 had identified about three thousand Axis agents.

After the British trained the Americans in covert warfare, the X-2 office in London became a strategic center for sending spies behind enemy lines to lead resistance groups, destroy Axis transportation and communication centers, and accompany Allied invading forces. Their objective was to penetrate the Axis intelligence systems while preventing Axis infiltration of OSS operations. The central registry on enemy operations based in New York was transferred to X-2 London. Ferko's role in compiling much of that information was key, as was his extensive network of contacts and his linguistic mastery of Italian, German, Russian, and Croatian.

In July 1943 Ferko was promoted to senior field representative, given another salary increase, and sent to DC to begin an assignment described cryptically as "work of a special nature in Washington." OSS Assistant Director Buxton told Ferko that "this transfer is not for your convenience, but is in the best interests of the Government." He was ordered to apply for a new passport and to update immunizations against smallpox, diphtheria, pertussis, tetanus, yellow fever, typhus, and cholera. Ferko summarized his duties in a classified OSS document as follows:

> *Under general supervision, is responsible for the local organization*
> *of specific activities and projects; works out detailed operations of a*
> *specific undertaking devised to aid and encourage friendly groups*
> *in foreign countries; compiles information and data relative to*
> *the progress of subversive undertakings for transmittal to the OSS*
> *operating offices in Washington; performs similar duties as assigned.*

In August 1943, the OSS ended counter-espionage research in New York and transferred responsibilities to X-2 London, the new headquarters of X-2. Ferko began his work in London and then was posted to the OSS communications headquarter for the Mediterranean Theater in Caserta, Italy, a strategic location for pushing the Germans back up the Italian peninsula.

In the fall of 1943, British intelligence helped X-2 create Special Counterintelligence (SCI) detachments that would accompany the Allied invading forces in continental Europe and perform counterintelligence operations using ULTRA intercepts. That was the key juncture at which Ferko was transferred to the European Theater of Operations. On November 5, James Murphy, chief of X-2, sent a cable stating that there had been a revision of plans for Ferko—his transfer to Cairo was canceled so that he could assume a confidential assignment at the European head-quarters of X-2 in London. A postwar CIA report to the assistant direc-tor of Special Operations described this appointment as a "remarkable exception" since Ferko was "one of the only X-2 officers with access to top-secret sources even though he was of foreign birth."

In mid-November, Ferko received security clearance from the theater commander and "British vetting" for work in London and Cairo. His expense report for the period refers to preparation time in Washington "establishing contacts and interviewing prospects." The president of the OSS Draft Deferment Committee sent a confidential letter to the chair of the New York City Local Selective Service System asking for draft deferment for Kalnay so that he could get a passport and "follow prear-ranged schedules for departure."

At the end of November, after receiving security clearances from the Americans and the Brits for work in London and Cairo, Ferko was of-ficially transferred from SO to X-2 and put onto the OSS special funds payroll for work in the Balkans, infiltrating German Abwehr communi-cations. Before his departure, however, he was sent for specialized train-ing in counter-espionage methods.

## COUNTER-ESPIONAGE TRAINING AT 'THE FARM'

In the fall of 1943, Ferko was about to be trained in photography, cipher, driving, and weapons, and to go on an undercover mission posing as a government official when the plan was canceled. Instead, on November 23, 1943, the deputy director of X-2 in Washington arranged for Ferko to attend three weeks of training at a top-secret dynamite and demolition school in Virginia. Camp Peary was a 9,000-acre OSS training area that had been opened the previous year. From November 1942 until June 1944, some 100,000 men were trained there at what had previously been luxurious country estates surrounded by horse farms. Because hogs were raised on the property, it was given the colloquial name, "The Farm." During the war, The Farm also served as a detention site for German POWs who the Germans believed had been killed in combat. Shrouding the camp in secrecy was essential to prevent the Nazis from realizing that there were POWs there, something that would surely have compromised the Enigma machines and convinced the Nazis to change encrypted codes that the OSS had broken.

Although thousands of individuals were in the OSS, Ferko was part of a small, elite group that included many European Jews with foreign language skills. Of the roughly 20,000 OSS members who served in the OSS during the war, about 7,500 served overseas, and only about 2,500 received parachute training to infiltrate enemy-held territory as spies, saboteurs, guerrilla leaders, or clandestine radio operators. All trainees were sworn to secrecy and given pseudonyms and uniforms without rank or insignia.[16]

The training was physically and psychologically demanding. Recruits had to scale a forty-foot jungle gym apparatus, swing from platforms, and run across narrow planks. They traversed a demolition trail, wiring small explosive charges, and were sent through what many referred to informally as a "House of Horrors," where they shot at shadowy mannequin targets (including one dressed as Hitler) who jumped out at them from the shadows. Ferko must have found the training physically challenging. At 5'9" and 145 pounds, he was a man of slight build. In one of his OSS job evaluations, the only checklist item for which he didn't receive a plus was "physical fitness for the work."

At the completion of their training, agents were required to practice their skills by infiltrating actual war production facilities in Baltimore and taking mock actions to blow up the plants. They carried shortwave radios and demonstrated skills in encryption, decryption, and International Morse code. A National Park Service report describes the instruction in detail.

> *Trainees were taught lock-picking and burglary techniques, how to parachute behind enemy lines, how to use weapons and plastic explosives, and conduct hand-to-hand combat with a stiletto, including dislocating a person's arm while holding a knife to the ribs, and how to go limp before grabbing a man's testicles. They also were shown how to operate and destroy locomotives and power plants, and how to take the controls to turn a train into a runaway weapon.[17]*

A final test for the newly trained agents was an assignment to break into an American defense plant or other sensitive target and to steal classified documents without being detected.[18]

Before being sent into Axis-controlled territory, OSS agents were given a codebook with an elaborate five-digit system for encrypted communications. They were instructed to destroy each page of original coding after using it once and to start with a new set of codes for the next. Agents were also given a suicide pill to ingest in case of capture by the enemy.

In his lifetime, Ferko never mentioned any of this. The one exception was an offhand comment to a granddaughter that, during the war, he had learned to kill a man with a rolled-up newspaper. He spent the duration of the war at a high level of tension, chain-smoking two to three packs of cigarettes every day and never taking a single day off.

Many German espionage tactics were almost identical to those of the Allies. In *Agent ZigZag*, Ben Macintyre tells the story of a British criminal who was trained as a spy for the German Abwehr and then became a double agent working for the Brits. It is based on numerous declassified records describing the training of the protagonist, Eddie Chapman. What caught my attention was the startling similarity between Nazi espionage training for Chapman and Ferko's training as a spy for the Allies. Chapman parachuted into Britain with British identification cards and objects, a wireless radio, money, and explosives. His charge was to sabotage an aircraft factory, gather information on Allied troop movements and convoys, and find intelligence on railway movements and shipbuilding.

Violence took a toll on Ferko. After the war, he was a pacifist who was terrified of fireworks and explosions of any kind and avoided conflict at all costs. It is possible that he suffered from what would today be diagnosed as post-traumatic stress.

## COUNTER-ESPIONAGE IN YUGOSLAVIA AND THE BALKANS

With the defeat of the Austro-Hungarian Empire at the end of the First World War, the Kingdom of Yugoslavia was carved out of several countries in southeastern Europe. In 1941 Germany, Italy, and their ally,

Hungary, invaded and quickly conquered the kingdom. The Germans occupied Serbia, while Italian fascists occupied Montenegro and parts of Croatia and Slovenia, but Hitler was unable to defeat the Yugoslav nationalists and resistance fighters.

In June 1943, Donovan convinced the Joint Chiefs to authorize the creation of operational groups of US Army soldiers trained to wage clandestine warfare in enemy territories by training guerrillas and collecting intelligence. His plan was to integrate espionage, sabotage, guerrilla operations, and demoralizing propaganda to subvert enemy control and weaken their rear lines of communications and supplies before and during an assault at the front by conventional Allied forces.

The collapse of Mussolini in July 1943 heightened the importance of the Balkans to the Allies as Tito's Partisans waged anti-German guerrilla campaigns. Petroleum refineries in Romania were the driving force of Hitler's war machine, and partisan guerilla groups in Yugoslavia constantly threatened this supply and his armies. After the fall of Mussolini, the Balkan Peninsula grew in strategic importance as a site for diverting Hitler from the Eastern Front.

The Allies hoped to convince Hitler of something he had long feared—that they were planning an offensive through the Balkans. The region was of particular importance to Donovan for another reason. He was strongly anti-Soviet and feared Soviet armies might advance through southeastern Europe without Allied deterrence. Furthermore, a few months before Stalin's defeat of the Germans in February 1943, Ulius Amoss (OSS chief of southeast Europe operations) argued that the US should build a spy network in Axis-occupied countries of eastern Europe, the Balkans, and Turkey to provide intelligence on Stalin after the war.[19]

The first two US forces parachuted into Yugoslavia in August 1943: one to support Mihailović and the other to support Tito.[20] OSS Balkan operations were directed from Cairo, Egypt; Caserta, Italy; and then from Bari, an Italian port strategically located on the Italian side of the Adriatic, across from Yugoslavia. Soon after the Allied invasion of Italy in September, the OSS established a base there. The Bari base remained under the control of OSS Cairo, but it became the center for operations in the Balkans and hazardous air operations aimed at the penetration of central Europe. It was also the base for Balkan air and ship support of the Yugoslav Partisans, and thus the site for large shipments of supplies to Tito and for the evacuation of thousands of refugees from internment camps in Italy. The existence of the base was top secret, and the OSS told agents that none of their family or friends could know where they were. The agency censored their letters home, and anyone who disregarded regulations faced immediate discharge with serious consequences.

When Ferko left Washington, his staff were instructed not to mention his name or that he was outside the US. Callers were to be told, "He cannot be reached just now, but we will be glad to take any message." He further instructed them that "no information whatsoever concerning my connection with OSS should be given to an outsider, even though he or she may be, or claim to be, a member of my own family or friend."

Throughout the war, Donovan saw the Balkan peninsula as an important locus for OSS espionage, but he was limited by the 1942 "London Agreement," in which the US had agreed to take a subservient role to Britain in the region. Instead, he set up the OSS regional office in Istanbul, Turkey, a central hub for railways connecting Asia and Europe, and a neutral country with proximity to the Balkans. When Ferko's official appointment with X-2 began at the end of November 1943, his first action was developing a plan supporting Donovan's strategy. On November 26, 1943, just before going to The Farm for training, he sent it to Lt. Col. Carroll Gray, chief of the Administrative Branch of the War Department.* In the memo, Ferko proposed taking advantage of a steady stream of disaffected Balkan emigrants in Istanbul and strengthening the Balkan Division of X-2 METO (Middle East Theater of Operations) there to recruit undercover agents to spy on Nazi organizations, collect intelligence, and protect American government agencies in Turkey from enemy penetration. To do that, they would need to assign six officers, eighteen field operatives, and additional support staff to be divided among Bulgaria, Romania, and Hungary. All would operate under the cover of existing banks, import-export agencies, or an embassy.

One of the officers in each country would recruit and train local nationals to become agents; the other would develop files on suspected Nazi agents who had entered Istanbul from their countries. Two groups

---

* The full proposal is shown in Appendix A.

*Map of Italy and the Dalmatian Coast produced by CIA. Public Domain.*
*https://www.loc.gov/resource/g6710.ct001501  NOTE: The Central Intelligence*
*Agency has not approved or endorsed the contents of this publication.*

of agents were to be sent to the field: some to carry out specific sabotage missions, and the other to track down enemy spies. Ferko recommended that the Washington headquarters of X-2 METO collect, analyze, classify, and channel material on contacts in the Middle East using his Survey of Foreign Experts database of thousands of profiles of foreign nationals residing in the United States. Relevant individuals would include representatives of established industrial firms, engineers, government officials, officials of transportation companies, commercial travelers, scientists, press representatives, or church dignitaries. Others would be political dissidents who might have contacts with parallel groups in neighboring countries. The rest of Ferko's proposal covered recommendations for staffing the expanded Istanbul office, divisions of responsibilities, and coordination of training and recruitment with British intelligence and intelligence units of other Allies.

On November 29, 1943—the day Ferko reported to "The Farm" for training—the OSS authorized him and six other men to travel by ship from New York to London to Cairo.* The order was stamped "SECRET" and specified that "the travel directed is necessary in the public service for the accomplishment of an emergency war mission." There was no change in Ferko's OSS title (principal field representative), but in London, he served as desk head for the Middle East section of X-2. Furthermore, his appointment was changed to an exempt, non-civil-service position based in the field, instead of a "departmental position," and the OSS agreed to reimburse the War Department for his expenses that were charged to a special funds payroll.

On December 11, 1943, Ferko sent a memo to Lt. Col. Gray indicating he wasn't sure how long he would be in London before going to the Balkans to infiltrate the German Abwehr communications. He asked Lt. Col. Gray to "expedite transportation for my assistant, Sylvia Press, to London—unless my stay in London is of short duration, in which case she would go directly to my station . . . As you know, she has been working with me for a long time and has considerable knowledge of the regions and individuals in those regions which are my concern. She will be of great help to me . . . I suggest that she use her spare time before departure in concentrating on Abwehr and cipher, and following closely the latest reports concerning the Balkans."

On December 13, Ferko's declassified OSS records show that he was "sent to ETO [European Theater Operations], London and transferred to Special Funds Payroll for work in Balkans infiltrating German Abwehr communications." After Ferko died, his granddaughter Wendy found a copy of a manual that he had annotated entitled *Counter-Intelligence Handbook for Germany: General Guide to Machinery of the Nazi State.*

---

* The six other men were Gerald E. Miller, Walter Dorn, Horace Abram Rigg, Jr., Roger Bourdin, Rene Charpentier, and Roger Renquet. Miller was appointed chief of the OSS Special Operations Branch in London at the end of 1944.

After receiving final instructions and a physical examination, Ferko boarded a ship to Europe on December 18, 1943, with other OSS agents, including Horace Abram Rigg. They were told to bring their orders, inoculation certificates, and passports. Ferko's hand-filled checklist was labeled "January 1944: Destination: Istanbul, Turkey."

As the hub for railways connecting Asia and Europe and the largest city of a neutral country with proximity to the Balkans, Istanbul had strategic importance for the OSS. It was a central site for the receipt of information from sixty-seven OSS agents who operated from spy cells across southeastern Europe, feeding information on German troop movements and local politics and conditions to the Allies. Other classified information from these agents included country reports on Yugoslavia, Hungary, and Romania, lists of members of the Italian Fascist Party, a registry of products, and detailed maps of Yugoslavia showing the location of mines, factories, mills, and leading food industries. Istanbul is also the city where the Hungarians had been meeting with representatives of the Allies to discuss the possible defection of Hungary from the Axis. The Germans knew of these meetings and became increasingly convinced of the need to rein in Hungary.[21]

Reports on Ferko's incursions into Yugoslavia are not among his declassified OSS papers that I examined at the National Archives. However, we can infer what they were through reports from another agent, Franklin Lindsay, who wrote a book about his experiences with the OSS in Yugoslavia. Like Ferko's men, Lindsay parachuted into Slovenia to bring supplies to the Yugoslav Partisans. Once they spotted a campfire on the ground and an agreed-upon Morse code signal, the cargo chutes were dropped to lighten the load, and then the three men jumped. Their parachuted containers held guns, explosives, radios with batteries, backpacks, and medical supplies. Lindsay also described reconnaissance raids in which men would go to different Dalmatian islands in fishing boats provided by the Partisans. They brought an interpreter and radio operator to establish continuous coverage and contacts on each island. After meeting with Partisans, the men would observe as much as possible and send back reports of any intelligence of interest.[22]

The preparation of foreign agents to work for the Allies entailed meticulous training. Most were foreign men or women who spoke the language of their assigned destinations. The Documents and Camouflage Division of the Research and Development Branch of the OSS prepared clothing and documents and provided training to promote the subterfuge. Personnel scoured local newspapers and recorded conversations with prisoners of war to educate the agents on the smallest details of their false identities. These included slang vocabulary, the history of the towns from which they pretended to hail, where their fictitious parents were buried, and how to swear, walk, eat, drink, urinate, and smoke cigarettes like a local. According to John Lisle:

> *American agents in Europe learned to identify these minute cultural distinctions, such as whether to pour tea or milk first, smoking cigarettes down to the stub as the French did, walking with hands dangling instead of in pockets, and "eating continental," keeping a knife and fork in their respective hands instead of shifting them after each mouthful of food.*[23]

Ferko's role in overseeing the recruitment and training of foreign agents grew in importance in the spring of 1944 when the the Allies mounted a successful propaganda campaign to convince Germany that Allied troops in Egypt would invade Greece and Yugoslavia in March, leading Hitler to keep tens of thousands of troops in the Balkans instead of sending them to southern Europe. At the same time, the Russians advanced on the Germans from the east, putting them in an increasingly desperate situation.

In June 1944, shortly after D-Day, OSS Director Donovan appointed Ferko chief of the Balkans Field Station of the X-2 Division.* He was based in Bari, Italy, gathering information in the heart of Axis territory—the Balkans, Yugoslavia, Bulgaria, Romania, and later Hungary. His unit had a great deal of autonomy. On paper, the X-2 office for the Mediterranean Theater of Operations was directed by Captain Graham Erdwurm, but the units operated independently.

---

* In government documents the unit was variously called X-2 Balkans, SAINT Bari, and later SCI/Z Venice. Duncan Bare, "Hungarian Affairs of the US-Office of Strategic Services in the Mediterranean Theater of Operations from June 1944 until September 1945" (master's thesis, Universität Graz, 2015) 47.

In Italy Ferko was in a strategic location to benefit from recent changes in Donovan's authority and the importance of the OSS and X-2. The departure of key figures heading the OSS sister branch of Secret Intelligence in February 1944 left Angleton in charge of the Italian section for X-2 when the OSS presence in theaters of war was expanding.[24]

By the fall, Ferko's authority expanded further. In a September 1944 report, the chief of X-2 Cairo wrote:

> *Francis Kalnay, chief of X-2, Bari, who came to this theater with Capt. Graham Erdwurm, chief of X-2, Caserta, and deputy chief of X-2 in the MEDTO Theater, has returned to Bari after consultation here with Maxson and this office with respect to operational plans being now carried forth in the Balkans. It now appears that the missions in Romania and Bulgaria will clear through Bari rather than Istanbul. Another member of this office, Miss Nichol, has gone to Bari, to assist the X-2 office there, which is rapidly becoming more important.[25]*

Norman Holmes Pearson, head of European X-2 operations, later lauded Ferko's accomplishments as chief of X-2 Balkans. In a nomination for a Certificate of Merit, he cited "Kalnay's very considerable knowledge of Balkan diplomatic and political intrigue."*

> *Through his efforts the desk established elaborate files of Balkan materials, and built up a reservoir of information so impressively useful that many enemy espionage activities were localized, and through being identified, neutralized, and important links between Balkan personalities and the German intelligence service in other countries were established. On numerous occasions Mr. Kalnay's careful piecing together of fragmentary evidence revealed facts about Abwehr and* Reichssicherheitshauptamt *functioning in central and western Europe, which the activities of agents and controlled enemy agents in those regions had failed to uncover. He was never at a loss for a helpful suggestion or a new insight into some aspect of the enemy's espionage system.*

---

\* The full memorandum is in Appendix B.

*With intense devotion to duty and a keen sense of urgency, he kept himself thoroughly informed on complicated political, national, diplomatic, and military problems, and his work made X-2 inroads upon the German Intelligence Service easier and more deliberate.*

Ferko traveled back to Washington regularly for training and briefings in preparation for top-secret assignments. Another report in his OSS files, dated February 12, 1945, stated that he was about to depart from the US for six months for confidential OSS business.

# III

# FAMILY SECRETS

### FAMILY TRAGEDY

What was happening to the Kalnay family in Budapest at the end of the war while Ferko directed X-2 operations in the region? Many of his siblings had emigrated years earlier, but István, Borbála, and Ilona were living in Hungary in 1944. Ferko's youngest sister, Margit, immigrated to England before WWII, and Borbála studied in Bratislava and Munich before returning to Budapest.

Ferko's eldest brother, István, had left Hungary for several years, but he was back in Budapest during the war. As an adult, István married and had two children. In 1923 he left his family and moved to Buenos Aires for two years while Ferko and Elsie lived there. In Argentina, István suffered a terrible accident when his leg got caught between a train car and the platform at the Olivos Station. After his leg was amputated, he returned to Budapest, where he was cared for by his wife and children. István also suffered from diabetes and was forced to have his second leg amputated due to the disease. Because he could no longer work, the family lived on his military pension and money from his father, József. He also earned a small amount selling crossword puzzles to newspapers published in one of the seven languages he spoke. I do not know how István and his family survived the Holocaust in Hungary, but despite his health challenges, he lived a long life and died in Budapest in 1980 at age ninety. After the Second World War, his two children worked for the Stalinist Hungarian government.

As we have seen, Jewish ancestry wasn't the only shared family secret. The fact that Ferko's mother, Rózsa, didn't die when he was an infant is another. After her release from the sanatorium, Rózsa moved in with her daughter Borbála and her young grandson Denes in an apartment in Budapest. This photograph of the two of them shows the transformation of a young and wide-eyed bride into a wizened old woman.

*Rózsa and Borbála.*
*(From the author's personal collection)*

How long had Rózsa been confined in Lipótmezö and the Jeno Ringer sanatorium? It was at least twenty-five years. She was institutionalized in 1900 at age forty, when Ferko was one year old, and was still interned when her son Andrés visited Budapest in 1925.[1] We will never be certain of the exact date of her release because patient records from both institutions have been destroyed.

Although Ferko didn't formally acknowledge Rózsa as his mother, he would have known of her institutionalization and release from his siblings, particularly from his eldest sister, Borbála, who cared for her mother. Esteban found a copy of a poignant letter written by Rózsa to her children in 1939 that shows that she was not entirely estranged from them.

> *My dearest, unforgettable and dear children, my beloveds. Your good mother wishes you a Happy New Year and Happy Holidays at the close of the year. Any news from you makes me happy. I send you my greetings by way of your sister, Borbála.*
>
> *Your mother, Rózsa Margalit Kalnai*[*]

When she was released, Rózsa returned to a society racked with turmoil and growing antisemitism. From 1920 to 1946, Hungarian Regent Miklos Horthy ruled what he called a "Christian and national" government, the ideals of which were symbolized in this poster.

*Christian National Union Party poster by Bela Sandor. (In public domain. https://budapestposter.com)*

---

[*] Rózsa used the old family spelling of her married name although it had been legally changed to Kalnay.

Hitler didn't invade Hungary until 1944, but pro-Fascist sentiments in the region were prevalent well before then and were strengthened after he became chancellor of Germany in 1933. Most officers in the Hungarian Army were of German heritage, and most were pro-German. The public was highly polarized, but pro-German nationalism was bolstered by continued resentment over the country's losses after the First World War.[2]

Prime Minister Horthy was servile in the face of German pressures, but he retained some public support because of Hitler's promises to return some of Hungary's lost territory. Between 1938 and 1941, Hungary regained portions of Slovakia and Romania. In the same period, Horthy acceded to Nazi pressures to pass a series of antisemitic laws that emulated the Nuremberg Laws in Germany. The laws reversed the equal citizenship status of Jews, forbade marriage to Christians, and excluded Jews from civil service and many professions.[3] Judaism was equated with communism in order to justify antisemitic laws, as shown in the 1944 poster below.

*Hammer & Sickle=Jewish Star. (Public domain image.*
*Source: Fortepan.hu #72657 by Lissák Tivadar, 1944)*

When Hitler finally invaded Hungary in March 1944, the Germans pressured Horthy to appoint Döme Sztójay as prime minister—a former Hungarian ambassador to Germany with strong ties to the Third Reich. Once in office, Sztójay legalized the fascist Arrow Cross Party and, with the help of Hitler's SS officer Adolf Eichmann, 437,000 Hungarian Jews were deported to Auschwitz where most were gassed on arrival.[4] According to scholars at the US Holocaust Memorial Museum (USHMM), even the Germans were surprised by the cruel efficiency of the Hungarian authorities.

> *Hungary implemented the wearing of the yellow star on April 5, 1944. The Hungarian government decided on the ghettoization on April 7 and began implementing the edict just nine days later, on April 16. By the end of May, ghettos and camps had been created in more than 200 localities. Deportations took place at a torrid pace. In a sordidly cynical rivalry, Eichmann wanted to beat the "record" set by SS-Sturmbannführer Hermann Höfle, who had deported the 275,000 residents of the Warsaw ghetto in Treblinka—a distance of 100 kilometers—over a span of 53 days between July 22 and September 12, 1942. Despite the approaching front lines, the deteriorating infrastructure, and the fact that deportation trains from Hungary to Auschwitz had to travel an average of 400 to 500 kilometers, Eichmann was successful thanks to the work of his Hungarian accomplices. Hungarian authorities deported 437,402 Hungarian Jews on 147 trains in just 56 days between May 15 and July 9, 1944; apart from 15,000, all of these deportees were sent to Auschwitz-Birkenau.[5]*

There was no easy way to hide Jewish ancestry in Hungary since it was inscribed on most public records. Although they may have practiced Catholicism after József's remarriage, Kálnay family members were considered Jews under the Horthy regime. The Nazis defined a Jew as "anyone with three Jewish grandparents; someone with two Jewish grandparents who belonged to the Jewish community on September 15, 1935, or joined thereafter; was married to a Jew or Jewess on September 15, 1935, or married one thereafter; was the offspring of a marriage or extramarital liaison with a Jew on or after September 15, 1935." This definition led to the reclassification of thousands of Christian Hungarians as Jews.

After the German occupation of Hungary in March 1944, the Fascist Arrow Cross Party helped identify Jews in the country. I corresponded with Peter Black, a historian at the Center for Holocaust Studies, who told me that:

Undoubtedly the Hungarian Gendarmerie, the Budapest police,
and the German occupiers after March 1944 had access to lists of
Jewish community members. These would have been available to the
Arrow Cross after the coup d'état in October 1944. Even in the case
of conversions to Catholicism, depending on the relationship of the
individual parish priest with the Arrow Cross authorities between
October 1944 and February 1945, these records would have been
made available upon demand.

Furthermore, protective passes had to be reported to the government
after they were first issued in March and April 1944. As a result, when
they came to power, the Arrow Cross had lists of individuals like my great-
grandmother and great-aunt who had been issued protective passes by the
Swedish government. I say more about this later in the chapter.

In April 1944, all Hungarian Jews were required to wear yellow stars
on their clothing. By mid-May, 800,000 Hungarian Jews had been forced
into ghettos or prison camps nationwide. A month later, all 220,000
Hungarian citizens in Budapest who were legally defined as Jews were
forced to move into some 2,000 "Yellow-star Houses" in the city—a move
designed to facilitate their deportation. The decree, which was confirmed
by the mayor of Budapest, was unique in Europe.

The large ghetto in Budapest was created later in the war, in November
1944. Many assimilated Jews thought that they had been corralled by
mistake when they were identified by the Hungarian Arrow Cross, the
Budapest police, and the German occupiers, forced into a locked ghetto,
and only allowed out on the streets at prescribed hours.[6] A yellow-star
door and a forced march of Jewish women and children in Budapest are
shown in the following photographs. My great-aunt and great-grandmother could have been among the women with their hands in the air.

Inside the ghetto, a leader appointed by the Jewish Council was responsible for providing residents with food and organizing fire brigades
and the care of children without parents. Ghetto police were charged with
preventing the theft of food or heating supplies. Initially, residents were
allowed to bring in personal property, but much was forcibly confiscated.
Soon there was severe overcrowding and shortages of food and basic ne-
cessities. Outside the ghettos, the non-Jewish population benefitted from

*Building in Budapest with yellow star.*
*(Public Domain Photo, Budapest, 1944. Source:*
*Fortepan.Hu)*

*March of Jewish women and children.*
*(Public Domain Photo, Budapest, 1944. Source: Fortepan.Hu)*

the division of confiscated property. The ghetto police were notorious for their cruel responses to even minor infractions, such as not having the yellow star sewn on properly. Local officials and police who did not follow these policies were denounced and suspended.

To keep them busy, residents were forced to do meaningless work, such as digging pits that were later filled in. Jews who were considered "well off" were subjected to violent interrogations and torture to force them to reveal information about hidden valuables. Women were forced to strip and were subjected to brutal exams to see if they were concealing money or jewelry in their bodies. Many were sexually assaulted.[7]

The testimonies of Hungarian Holocaust survivors give us insight into what Ferko's family lived through in Budapest in 1943 and 1944. Eva Brust Cooper grew up in a well-to-do, secular Jewish family in Budapest.[8] In March 1943, German troops marched into Budapest and her whole world fell apart.

Eva's apartment building was designated a Jewish house with a yellow star. Their staff—a governess, a cook, and a maid—were dismissed and the family was forced to live in one room. Eva remembers her close Christian friend telling her that they could no longer play together, and soon thereafter, Jews were forbidden from going to school and were only allowed outdoors to shop for a limited period, late in the afternoon. Eva and all Jews were forced to wear yellow stars on their coats. In her words, if someone wanted to spit on you, kick you, shoot you, or take you away, they could. She recalls many false conversions to Catholicism because people thought being half-Jewish would prevent their deportation to a concentration camp and because the priests were happy to have converts.

Like Ferko's mother and sister, Eva's parents secured Wallenberg passes. However there were hundreds of Jews crowded into their "safe house," and they decided it was better to leave. There was nowhere to bathe or wash clothes, and Eva was often cold. They moved from one friend's house to another, enduring Allied bombing raids on the city, sleeping on floors, and eating little. Eva remembers seeing people steal possessions from the body of a person who had been shot and left in the street.

Food was scarce and most of the children ate whatever they could find, including meat from dead horses. Ultimately, a number of Eva's relatives were deported to Auschwitz and gassed. When the Russians liberated Budapest in February 1945, she saw dead bodies hanging in the trees and recalled feeling happy if they turned out to be German soldiers.

Gibor Weinberger was another Holocaust survivor whose testimony is recorded by the USHMM.[9] Like Eva, Gibor came from a secular family and attended public school. His father was called into conscripted labor in 1943, but as a doctor, he was sent to work in a health service outside of Budapest and could come home for a weekend every six to eight weeks.

After the German occupation in March 1944, there was increased Allied bombing. The Nazis began deporting Jews from the countryside, but Jews in Budapest were left alone. In December, Gibor's uncle, an electrician in a hospital, was deported to the Mauthausen concentration camp. Another uncle came to live with Gibor's family after his apartment was ransacked by Germans who beat him up looking for gold and jewelry.

> *The Germans immediately imposed many restrictions on the Hungarian Jews. Wearing the Jewish star was obligatory except for children under five. The laws did not allow the Jews to practice law or journalism, attend motion pictures or the theater. They could no longer ride in cars, taxis, trains, buses, and ships; the only mode of transportation left to them was the streetcar. Eventually, even telephones and radios disappeared from Jewish households. Because the government froze or restricted their bank accounts, the Jews could only have a nominal amount of money, which made even buying a meal nearly impossible. . . .*
>
> *On October 15, 1944, Admiral Horthy, who had been the governor of Hungary since 1920, announced that he would surrender and withdraw from the Axis. That night the leader of the Hungarian Arrow Cross, Ferenc Szálasi, and his troops took power and a horrific period began for Hungarian Jews.*
>
> *About ten days after the takeover, Hungarian soldiers with Arrow Cross armbands showed up at five o'clock in the morning and ordered all Jewish men between sixteen and sixty years of age to report downstairs and to pack warm clothing and food for three days. When everybody was downstairs, they marched them away, my father among them.*

Gibor never saw his father again. After a forced separation from his mother, Gibor was able to find her again. They hid from the Arrow Cross and ultimately survived the war.

Both Eva's and Gibor's fathers were conscripted into forced labor, as was Borbála Kálnay's son, Denes. He was one of thousands of men between sixteen and sixty and women between sixteen and forty who were sent to the borders of the Reich to ease severe labor shortages in Austria and to construct a wall along the border with Hungary.[10] Since there were not enough trains to carry the workers, many were marched by foot to the Austrian border.

Shoah records document that Denes and 1,600 other coercively conscripted Jewish laborers were marched to Balf, a Hungarian village on the Austrian border, in November 1944. It was known as the "March of the Poets" because it included so many Hungarian writers and poets. From Balf, Denes was marched to Turja-Remete, Czechoslovakia (now in Ukraine), where he endured hard physical labor without adequate clothing or food. Those who dropped from fatigue and hunger were summarily shot and buried in mass graves. I don't have photographs of conscripts on the Austrian border. The following are of Hungarian laborers sent to Poland.

*Hungarian Labor Service conscripts serving a meal. ushmm.org*
Hungary Before the German Occupation
*Permission to reproduce the photo granted by USHMM*

*Hungarian Labor Service conscripts laying rails. ushmm.org Hungary*
Before the German Occupation
*Permission to reproduce the photo granted by USHMM*

Back in Budapest, my great-grandmother, Rózsa, was still living with
Borbála and Denes at Szent Domonkos Avenue, number eighteen, when
Denes was forcibly removed. I learned from Professor Tim Cole at the
University of Bristol that my relatives' address was one of the yellow-star
houses designated by the Budapest mayor's office on June 16, 1944, before the Arrow Cross period. It was close to the Danube and Szent Istvan
Park but not part of the international ghetto, which was created after
many Jews received protective passes and permission to emigrate from
foreign governments.

Life in Budapest became extraordinarily difficult for Jews in the fall
of 1944. Although Rózsa and Borbála were not confined to the Jewish
ghetto, they wore yellow armbands and lived in a yellow-star house from
which they would have seen other Jewish men, women, and children
evicted from their homes, beaten, and sometimes forcibly marched to the
train station for deportation as non-Jewish Hungarians cheered, hurled
insults, and threw things or shut their windows and drew the curtains.[11]

Mária Mádi was a Christian Hungarian who kept a detailed diary of
her life in Budapest under the Nazi occupation.[12] The transcription of

these pages reveals what Rózsa and Borbála were living through in their last months of life. By the end of March 1944, Jews were forbidden to leave Budapest or to drive cars. They had to surrender radios to the police and to register all their property with the Jewish Council including all clothing save one change of clothes. By April, Jews were barred from employing or receiving visits from non-Jews, and Jews were required to wear yellow stars on their clothing. Mária wrote that the stars made her Jewish friends sick with shame and fear. In June, she learned of the treatment of Jews in the western Hungarian city of Györ where they were "searched naked before a military commissioner for jewels, women and girls even by midwifes. Then they were driven out of their houses, over the streets of the town, like cattle into an empty brick kiln, waiting for deportation."

Beginning in early June the Allies were bombing Budapest several times a day, and for the rest of 1944 the city was under regular air raid alert. Jews were forced out of their apartments into ever more crowded units and forbidden to leave. By October, no non-Jewish visitors were allowed in. They became the frequent victims of raids by Hungarian police looking for money and jewels or for men to be forced into labor battalions. Their food rations were cut to starvation levels. By November, all Jewish property was turned over to the state, and Mária worried that forced evacuations were part of a plan to annihilate all Jews.

In a note of sad irony, Borbála was almost spared execution when she and her mother were issued protection documents by Raoul Wallenberg, the Swedish diplomat whose efforts prevented the deportation and murder of many Hungarian Jews. Wallenberg issued a passport (called a *Schutz-Pass* in German) to Rózsa and Borbála, which identified them as Swedish subjects waiting for repatriation. Wallenberg's documents looked official and were generally accepted by German and Hungarian authorities. He used funds from the US War Refugee Board to rent thirty-two buildings protected by diplomatic immunity in Budapest. The buildings housed close to 10,000 people and were adorned with Swedish flags and signs, such as "The Swedish Research Institute." The following image is an example of a protective pass issued to another Hungarian woman (not part of the Kálnay family).

*Schutzpass for Erika Vermes.*
*(Permission to reproduce the photo granted by USHMM)*

It is possible that Ferko had a role in securing passes for his family members, but such extra-official efforts are unlikely to have been documented. Regardless of the source, Borbála refused to use the Swedish pass to leave Hungary while her son, Denes, was still in a labor camp. As a result of this tragic but understandable decision, she and my great-grandmother remained in Budapest.

Borhi describes the atmosphere there at the end of 1944:

> *[Budapest] was divided between hunters and hunted: armed Nazi*
> *thugs were seeking out Jews, left-wingers, and deserters some of them*
> *hiding out in hospitals, convents, or private homes and other hiding*
> *places. Extreme violence, the constant sight of death in a city that*
> *became a battlefield, mass starvation, and breakdown of public*
> *services and utilities served as the backdrop . . . The murders were not*
> *decreed by the upper echelons of the Arrow Cross Party, most leaders*
> *of which fled the city before the Soviet encirclement was completed in*
> *December. Previously low-level functionaries and others who joined*
> *their ranks took events into their own hands and perpetrated a series*
> *of crimes unprecedented in Hungary's history.[13]*

Borbála was taking a package to mail to her son when she was arrested and taken to the Arrow Cross headquarters at 60 Andrássy Boulevard.

The building has since been converted into a museum and named "The House of Terror" because the large cellar was converted into a torture chamber that became the site of forced confessions and murders. There Borbála was beaten and murdered on December 2 when the Red Army that had encircled the city was only a few kilometers away.[14]

As many as 20,000 Hungarian Jews in the capital were executed like Borbála, from the middle of November until the end of the siege on February 13, 1945, when the Soviet Army liberated Budapest. Many were taken to the banks of the Danube, shot, and thrown into the river like the victims in the photograph below. As the Red Army entered the city at the end of December, gangs of armed Arrow Cross roamed the streets, randomly attacking Jews.

*Arrow Cross Party members execute Jews along the banks of the Danube River. Budapest, Hungary, 1944. (USHMM National Archives and Records Administration, College Park, MD. In Public Domain.)*

Rózsa was not arrested with Borbála. She died of heart failure a month later, on January 3, 1945. Life in Budapest during those last four weeks must have been unbearable for her. At age eighty-one, after decades in asylums, she lost the daughter who was both her caretaker and companion at a time when Budapest was under siege.

Dr. Istvan Hollos, the chief medical doctor at Lipót during Rózsa's confinement, barely escaped Borbála's fate. Late in December 1944, he and his wife were forced from their home in Budapest and marched barefoot through the snow to the execution site on the banks of the Danube. He was saved at the last minute after a successful intervention by Wallenberg.

Four months after the murder of his mother, Denes Noti was shot to death in the Balf Sopron labor camp at age twenty-three. Conditions were so bad in the camp that about half of the prisoners died there, and many others died in death marches after it was shut down. Yad Vashem, the World Holocaust Remembrance Center, recorded Denes's death on March 31, 1945, just as the camp was being shut down in anticipation of the approaching Red Army.[15]

Ultimately, almost 600,000 Jews were murdered in Hungary—close to 75% of the Jewish population. The full horror of what happened to Borbála, Denes, and thousands of other Jews in Hungary at the end of 1944 was captured in a *New York Times* article published on July 7, 1945. The article stated that the Hungarian Arrow Cross "outdid the Nazis in the viciousness of its treatment of Jews," including outside the capital, where Hungarian police were feared more than the SS.

*The unvarnished story of the Arrow Cross organization's terrorism makes one of the bloodier pages in Hungary's history under the Nazis . . . Hungarian brickyards served as collection stations where railroad cars were packed with Jews being sent to death at Dachau and other German concentration camps. The loading was directed by an Austrian Nazi leader named Eichmann . . . Jews and other known anti-Nazis were shot in droves in October 1944 after the pro-Nazi Arrow Cross forces of Ferenc Szálasi had overthrown the Hungarian Government of Admiral Nicholas Horthy . . . Later, ghetto occupants were marched periodically to piers along the Danube, lined up in rows, and shot by Arrow Cross men.*

The devastation was so brutal that after the war, about 100,000 of 180,000 surviving Jews fled Hungary for Palestine or the West.[16]

Ferko had another sister who suffered terribly because of the war. In the 1930s, Ilona Kálnay lived in Paris, but when her father died in 1931, she returned to Budapest to assume responsibility for caring for her stepmother, Erszébet. She married a man named Deszö Bókor, who opened a prestigious bookstore in Budapest, selling Hungarian translations of British, French, Russian, and other classics. By the end of the 1930s, when the Hungarian government began to enact Fascist policies, Deszö and Ilona made several trips to the United States, hoping to establish an arm of the business there.

Some of these events were referenced in a letter that my mother's cousin Esteban found in the archives of the well-known Bauhaus architect and furniture designer Marcel Breuer. Like our family, Breuer was a Hungarian Jew. On September 5, 1938, Ferko wrote to him at the Harvard University Graduate School of Design. Esteban translated the letter into Spanish, and I have translated it from Spanish to English. In it, Ferko says that he recently spent two months in Hungary and received a tape that a friend of Breuer's asked him to pass on. He added:

> *I'm certain that you are following the dangerous gyrations of the political situation in Hungary and that your sister is trying to move to Yugoslavia at your suggestion. That would be an intelligent move, at least for now. I will do everything possible to sell my sister's things here as she has authorized me to do in order to save her work. On the other hand, we are also interested in popular Yugoslav art, and from now on we will collaborate closely with them. I wish that we could meet in person and that you could visit me in New York.*
>
> *Respectfully,*
> *Francis Kalnay*
>
> *P.S. They have beautiful ceramics, mosaics, and tiles that could be used in modern architectural design and that may be of interest to you. Or one might find a company in Boston that could produce them for you. Should we look for one?*

The letter to Breuer is of interest for two reasons. First, it demonstrates that Ferko was aware of the dangers facing Jews in Budapest and the wisdom of emigrating. Secondly, it suggests that he was pursuing personal business interests while he was still employed in the OSS.

Ilona and Deszö lived in New York at the end of the 1930s and later in Paris from 1939-1940. In 1940 they tried unsuccessfully to immigrate to the US, but the State Department had begun cracking down on visas for refugees from Europe out of the conviction that it would provide an opening for potential spies and saboteurs. Assistant Secretary of State Breckinridge Long advised American consuls to put every obstacle in the way of prospective immigrants.[17] In addition, isolationists succeeded in promoting a rule whereby anyone with a relative left behind in a totalitarian country was suspect and denied a visa.[18] These policies produced confusion, massive delays, and rejections such as those experienced by Ferko's sister and brother-in-law.

Ilona and Deszö's two daughters waited for them in Paris just as the Nazis arrived. Eventually, the four returned to Hungary with Wallenberg passports that protected them, although Deszö was conscripted into a labor camp until the Soviet Army liberated it several months later. According to my maternal grandmother, Elsie, the Nazis arrested and raped Ilona. My mother told me this too—it's the only comment I ever recall her making about violence against her family during the war, and she provided no other details. Like Rózsa, Ilona had mental health problems. When I visited him in Spain, Esteban told me that he spoke to Ilona's older daughter in London but that she didn't want to talk about family roots or history because it brought back terrible memories. My parents and my sister, Tess, visited Ilona and Katy in Budapest in the early 1970s and described a broken and destitute family to whom they sent money after the trip. Two years later Ilona died. Some family members said that she commited suicide, but Esteban believes that the cause of death was heart failure.

József's brother Adolf was another family member who died of war atrocities. He lived in the town of Szeged, Hungary, where he reportedly died of starvation right after the war. József's other brother Simón had a son named Jenö who died in the Dachau concentration camp in Germany. For Ferko's nephew Esteban, the death record came as a surprise because his mother had told him that Jenö died of tuberculosis after the war.

There were surely other Kalnay and Margulit relatives who died in the Holocaust. One was a pharmacist who may have been a relative of Ferko's mother. Milan Margulit was sent to Jasenovac Concentration Camp in Croatia. According to the Shoah Registry, he died there in 1942. Another was Ferenc Hecht, the son of one of József's second cousins. Like Ferko's nephew, Ferenc died in a forced labor battalion.

I feel tangible grief when I view photographs of men, women, and children who, like my great-aunt Borbála, were murdered during the war. A less painful way to commemorate her is this portrait from 1930, before the horrors of Fascism were apparent in Hungary. At the same time, the innocence depicted in the photograph begs the question of how the insane brutality of the 1940s could have occurred and reinforces the importance of acknowledging her brutal death as well as her former life. Daphne Kalotay said it well in an opinion piece in the *New York Times*:

> *As we move farther and farther from the event, these images are ever more divorced from the people who wore those shoes and lived in those bodies. A single person's or family's story rehumanizes and reinvigorates general-ized history. That is why our collective recollection and understanding of historical events relies on storytelling, past, present, and future, and why the next generations of writers haunted by the Holocaust now shoulder this responsibility.*[19]

*Borbála Kálnay Noti, 1930.*
*(From the author's personal collection)*

### How Ferko's Beloved Budapest Became a "Holocaust City"[20]

The history of the Holocaust in Hungary is confounding because it occurred so late in the war and took place in a country where Jews constituted a very large and often exalted population. Both Ferko and his parents were raised in an era many called the Golden Age for Hungarian Jews. The age began with the passage of the Jewish Emancipation Law in 1867, when József was ten years old, and continued until the end of WWI in 1918, the year before Ferko immigrated to the US. During that time, Judaism was designated a "received religion" in Hungary, on a par with Christianity, and Jewish business leaders rose to social and economic prominence, particularly if they had converted to Christianity. Hungary had the second largest Jewish population in Europe, after Poland, and the majority were staunchly patriotic. Yad Vashem historian Robert Rozett notes that Jews were the most educated segment of Hungarian society. Most were middle-class merchants or small-business owners, but many were also prominent intellectuals and artists.[21]

On the other hand, Israeli historian Jelinek Yeshayahu argues that Jews paid a high price for emancipation—one step in absolute assimilation and Magyarization. "As a token of gratitude for being accepted by the Magyar nation, both Orthodox and liberal Jewry took up the official language and ostentatiously demonstrated its patriotism and loyalty to the fatherland. The Jews from Hungary sustained this loyalty for a long time, even in the New World."[22]

Although there were incidents of anti-Jewish riots and demonstrations during the "Golden Era," rapid intervention by the government reinforced Jewish support for the state. Even after the First World War, Jews in Budapest lived relatively well. For many Jews in Budapest, their relatively conflict-free lives before WWII led to a kind of complacency. In her testimony for the United States Holocaust Memorial Museum, survivor Eva Brust described growing up in a wealthy, secular Jewish household in the capital in the 1930s.

> *Life before the war was very, very nice . . . We had religious education in the public school system. Besides the languages, arts,*

*geography, history, and math, everybody went to their own religious*
*classes during that particular period so as Jewish children went*
*to a class where a rabbi taught Jewish history, Hebrew, whatever.*
*Catholics went to Catholic class and Protestants went to Protestant*
*class and everybody mingled and got along very well, and I was never*
*aware of Jewish or not Jewish or anything else pertaining to religion*
*until much later.*[23]

How could this tolerance have quickly given way to the unparalleled slaughter of Hungarian Jews at the end of WWII? Randolph Braham calls the paradox one of the most perplexing questions in the history of the Holocaust.

*When the Jewish communities of German-occupied Europe were*
*being systematically destroyed during the first four and a half years of*
*World War II, the Jewish community of Hungary, though subjected to*
*harsh legal and economic measures and to a series of violent actions,*
*continued to be relatively well off. But when catastrophe struck with*
*the German invasion of the country on March 19, 1944, it was this*
*community that was subjected to the most ruthless and concentrated*
*destruction process of the war. This took place on the very eve of*
*Allied victory, when the grisly details of the final solution—the Nazi*
*drive for the liquidation of European Jewry—were already known*
*to the leaders of the world, including those of Hungarian and world*
*Jewry. The barbarity and speed with which the Hungarian Jews were*
*destroyed has been characterized by Winston Churchill as "probably*
*the greatest and most horrible crime ever committed in the history of*
*the world."*[24]

Braham argues that Hungarian Jews' history of extreme fidelity to an antiquated feudal regime for years prevented the development of a national Jewish consciousness that might have protected them after the First World War. The late timing of a Nazi crackdown in Hungary during WWII further promoted Jewish complacency. Yellow-star decrees, for example, were issued in several other German-occupied European countries beginning in 1939, but they were not mandated in Hungary until 1944.[25] Even after proof of Nazi atrocities began to emerge in the form of reports from Polish and Slovak refugees who had escaped from death camps, the majority of Jews believed that this could not possibly happen in "civilized Hungary where the destiny of the Jews and Magyars had been intertwined for over a thousand years."[26]

Sadly, the nationalism of Hungarian Jews and their sense of invulnerability was completely unwarranted. Not only were Hungarian Jews massacred, but their extermination could not have been carried out without the consent of the newly established right-wing government and the cooperation of powerful interest groups in the country.[27] Mid-level landowners and Christian business owners and bourgeoisie who hoped to eliminate competition from Jews in agriculture and commerce allied with civil servants and officers, dreaming that aggressive Nazi policies would help recover the lands lost after WWI under the Treaty of Trianon. The country and its politics were so obsessed with the idea of a complete (or at least partial) revision of the Trianon Treaty's national borders that all other issues or considerations became insignificant. Nazi Germany was the leading revisionist power on the European continent, seeking to revise the Treaty of Trianon. When Germany explored its economic and political influence on Eastern Europe, Hungarian leaders did not hesitate long to accept the help of the Third Reich. In November 1940, Hungary signed the Tripartite Pact with Germany, Italy, and Japan, committing Hungary to armed conflict.[28] Antisemitism was further exacerbated by successful attempts to brand Jewish bankers, industrialists, and businessmen as the cause of the economic crisis suffered during the Depression between 1929 and 1941.[29]

Tara Zahra summarizes how major Western powers failed to protect central European Jews from slaughter because of opposition to lifting immigration quotas in their own countries.[30] Facilitating the immigration of eastern European refugees to Africa and South America was viewed as an alternative. In addition, after the Great Depression, the US implemented a "public charge" policy to restrict the admission of Jewish refugees. It wasn't until 1938 that President Roosevelt permitted some modifications to refugee quotas but without increasing the limits. That same year, he convened an international refugee conference in France, promising attendees that their countries would not be asked to raise immigration quotas. After the conference, an Intergovernmental Committee on Refugees was created to find a haven for refugees. One especially egregious policy came out of negotiations with the Nazis to use confiscated Jewish assets to pay for resettlement—a policy that led to fines for emigration in eastern Europe that left Jews without funds to pay the fees charged by receiving countries.

In 1942, Treasury Secretary Henry Morgenthau tried to get President Roosevelt to develop a plan to save millions of European Jews who were being threatened with extinction by Hitler, but he was stymied by a series of intentional delays and obstruction by officials in the US State Department and by opposition from the British government. An important *Politico* essay by Andrew Meier describes how officials in the US State Department went so far as to deliberately try to stop the news of the mass murder of Jews in Poland and Romania from reaching anyone in the United States in order to prevent President Roosevelt from implementing a plan to accept large numbers of refugees.[31] Documentarian Ken Burns put it succinctly:

> *We're not responsible for the Holocaust. We did as much as any nation to try to relieve it both on the battlefield and in the number of people we accepted, but we failed ultimately because we did not yell loudly enough about it. We did not yell early enough about it, and we did not save as many people as we could have saved. We could even have filled the meager quotas and saved five times as many people as we did, but the State Department was always changing the requirements, raising the bar, moving the goalposts, and making it too hard for even Otto Frank to get his visa. I think maybe if he had gotten his visa maybe Anne Frank would still be alive.* [32]

Pope Pius XII was also complicit in a coverup of Nazi atrocities. A recent book by David Kertzer sheds light on the role of the Pope ignoring reports of the slaughter of Jews from his vast network of bishops and priests across occupied Europe. Pius refused to confirm reports of Nazi mass murders to President Roosevelt and he never spoke out against the Nazi persecution of Jews, even after the Jews of Rome were rounded up by the Nazis on October 16, 1943, for deportation to Auschwitz. Pius's sole concern was for the release of baptized Jews and those in mixed marriages.[33]

In Hungary, conditions deteriorated rapidly after the German invasion in March 1944, at which point every Hungarian agency cooperated in the deportation of Jews. Even government midwives were sent to railroad stations to search Jewish women for hidden jewelry.[34] The extent to which ordinary Hungarians turned in their neighbors to the Nazis is one of the most disturbing aspects of the Holocaust in Hungary. They were responsible for the transformation of Budapest—and particularly Pest—into what Cole has called "Holocaust City," with dizzying speed. In May 1944, there was no closed ghetto in the city, but by the end of June, ordinary citizens helped the Arrow Cross restrict Jews to 1,948 yellow-star houses where they were confined for twenty-one hours a day, with only three hours in the afternoon for medical treatment, cleaning, and shopping. The restrictions also included segregated bathhouses, hotels, restaurants, bars, and cinemas within the ghetto.

As deportations of Jews from Hungary to Auschwitz were reported in the international press, pressure mounted on Regent Horthy.[35] After the Allied landing of troops in Normandy in June 1944 and the massive Soviet offensive against the German Army, Horthy began to replace some of the extreme right members of his government. If you were a Jew, you were defined by your religion, regardless of whether you had been baptized as a Christian, went to a Christian church, or were a believer. At the end of June, some 7,400 Hungarian Jews were housed in "protected" yellow-star houses on the basis of promised exit permits from the Swedish Red Cross and the Swiss. To accommodate them, 3,000 Jews were evicted from homes on Pozsonyi Avenue and replaced with "protected Jews" who had been offered diplomatic passes for emigration.

In July, after finally being petitioned by Pope Pius XII, President Franklin Roosevelt, and King Gustav V of Sweden, Horthy halted the deportations. He then reached an agreement with Hitler to permit a limited number of Jews to emigrate from Hungary to Sweden and Palestine as long as the general deportations resumed. Jews in the Budapest ghetto continued to live in designated houses and many believed that the worst was over. By August, some of the restrictions against movement within and outside of the Budapest ghetto were eased, and more privileges were accorded to "Christian Jews," including converts and those in mixed marriages.

In October, Regent Horthy again tried to disengage from the Axis, but he capitulated when the Gestapo kidnapped his son. Horthy was deposed and jailed and replaced by ardent Nazi sympathizer Ferenc Szálasi. Restrictions confining Jews to yellow-star houses in the ghetto were hardened, and Adolf Eichmann returned to Budapest demanding fifty thousand able-bodied Jews to build fortifications against the approaching Red Army. Gangs and police forced their way into the yellow-star houses in the middle of the night and forced the conscription of all males between sixteen and sixty and women eighteen to forty. Among them was Ferko's nephew Denes Noti, who was marched with thousands of other young men to perform labor for the Third Reich, beginning in early November.

Jews remaining in Hungary and in yellow-star houses in Budapest were divided into six categories. Ferko's sister Borbála and his mother, Rózsa, were in the category of Jews who held foreign protective passes and were given permission to emigrate. Those not permitted to depart immediately were placed into an international ghetto. Cole writes that "by the winter of 1944, the homogenous category 'Jew' no longer existed—if it ever had— and multiple categories of 'Jews' were subjected to multiple territorial solutions."[36] By November 12, 1944, fifteen to seventeen thousand "protected" Jews were moved into the international ghetto and spread among 122 houses assigned to Swedish, Swiss, or a few other legations. The majority were on Pozsonyi Avenue, although some were located in other parts of the city. A sign on the gates of the Swedish houses said, "these premises and inhabitants possess extraterritoriality," meaning something akin to diplomatic status.[37]

## What Did Ferko Know?

I woke up the other night dreaming about December 1944. The dream wasn't about the murder of my great-aunt; it was about Ferko trying to learn the fate of his family members. I can't imagine what this must have been like, and I'm haunted by the question of what he knew of events in Hungary while he was employed by the US government and when he learned of his family members' deaths in 1944 and 1945.

My grandfather's work in the Coordinator of Information office and then the OSS spanned four years. He began working with the COI Oral Intelligence Unit in December 1941, six months after Hungary joined the Third Reich in declaring war against the Soviet Union. His early career there coincided with severe increases in antisemitic actions by the Hungarian government. Four months earlier, Prime Minister László Bárdossy instituted a Nuremberg-type racial law to deport thousands of Jews to a German-occupied city in western Ukraine, where they were slaughtered.[38] By January 1942, a Hungarian major general informed the Germans that Hungary was interested in transferring twelve thousand "alien" Jews to Russia. Events such as these are likely to have been known to the COI and to Ferko as he interviewed refugees escaping the region and arriving in New York, and communicated with his family members in Budapest.

As early as October 1941, an internal diplomatic memo revealed that twenty thousand Jews were being deported from Germany to the ghetto of Lodz in Poland,[39] and by the spring of 1942, the broad outlines of the Holocaust in Europe were beginning to leak to the public. Vatican sources and informants in Switzerland and Poland reported on Nazi plans for systematically exterminating Jews, although the details were incomplete and not wholly accurate. A member of the Polish underground met personally with President Roosevelt and British Prime Minister Eden, and the US government confirmed these reports in November.[40] The information was publicized soon thereafter. Nevertheless, some individuals in the US government considered the report exaggerated and others worried that coverage of atrocities against the Jews would undermine support for the war. Skeptical journalists prevented early news of massacres of Jews from being fully publicized.

German tactics to suppress information about deportations and murders throughout the Third Reich also had some success. In 1942, Jews sent to transit stations on their way to concentration camps from Berlin and elsewhere were warned that they would be deported or shot if they revealed the horrendous conditions that they had witnessed—public body searches, children separated from their mothers and packed into rooms with little air and no heat, people jumping to their deaths.[41]

In June 1942, when the COI became the OSS, Ferko was transferred to the OSS Strategic Intelligence Branch in New York, where he should have had even greater access to intelligence about events in Nazi-occupied countries, including Hungary. That September, Adolf Eichmann suggested that Hungarian Jews be exterminated rather than deported to camps, and in October, the Third Reich presented this as a formal request that was rejected by the Hungarian government of Prime Minister Miklós Kállay. In the last five months of 1942, the US government received information from OSS officials on German plans to deport and exterminate Polish Jews. However, the Department of State viewed the reports as unconfirmed allegations that required more proof, even though credible reports of Polish gas chambers had been published and were available to the public by that time.[42]

Why was so little done to save European Jews after the truth of the massacres leaked out? University of Chicago historian Tara Zahra says one reason is that persecution of the Jews was welcomed by many:

> *Well before the Nazis occupied eastern Europe, many Polish, Czech, Romanian, and Hungarian officials and citizens had been hoping (and planning) for the evacuation of Jews from their territory. It is therefore hardly surprising that there was so little organized protest when Hitler fulfilled these fantasies.*[43]

In the US, government officials argued that retaliatory action would impede the broader war effort, and even some Jews worried that aggressive responses to the atrocities might produce antisemitic backlash. As late as November 1942, censors in the US Office of War Information prevented theologian Paul Tillich from broadcasting a warning to the German people about participating in the persecution of Jews. Finally, in December the Allies issued a joint declaration condemning the Nazi's plans to exterminate the Jews.

Ferko would likely have learned of Nazi atrocities from OSS documents well before the Germans invaded Hungary. I found the following

OSS official dispatch in the National Archives, dated March 10, 1943, that described the slaughter of Jews in Germany:

### Germany: Extermination of Jews

*From a Berlin source which our agent considers reliable, we have the following report on changes in the Nazi Jewish policy:*

*The new Nazi policy is to kill Jews on the spot rather than to deport them to Poland for extermination there. High officers of the SS reportedly have decided that Berlin shall be liberated of all Jews by mid-March. Accordingly, 15,000 Berlin Jews were arrested between January 26 and March 2. All closed trucks were requisitioned; several hundred children died; several hundred adults were shot. Extension of these methods to other parts of Germany in the near future is expected.*[44]

Hungarian Prime Minister Horthy met with Hitler in April 1943. By the end of that month, Hungarian Jewish labor servicemen were massacred in Ukraine, and in July, the Germans and Hungarians signed an agreement to transfer Jewish laborers to work in Serbian copper mines.

At the end of January 1944, President Roosevelt created the War Refugee Board. Representatives of the Hungarian opposition parties appealed to the Kállay government to change its course, but the pattern had been established years before. In the years between 1938 and the German occupation on March 19, 1944, the Hungarian government issued nearly three hundred anti-Jewish laws and decrees reversing the rights accorded to Jews at the end of the nineteenth century.

Two days after the German occupation, an eight-member Jewish Council was established. The council appealed to Hungarian Jewry for obedience and calm after the government of Regent Horthy issued a series of antisemitic decrees, including a requirement for Jews to wear the Star of David. By April the Sztójay government had turned fifty thousand Jewish labor servicemen over to the Germans and initiated plans for Jewish ghettos in Northern Transylvania. On April 28, 1944, the first trainload of Hungarian deportees was sent to Auschwitz, and in May, plans were made for the "total deportation" of Hungarian Jews. Over the

next three months, approximately 440,000 Hungarian Jews were deported—almost all of them to gas chambers at the Auschwitz concentration
camp (320,000). Thousands were also forced into labor and sent to the
Austrian border. The only concentration of Jews remaining in Hungary
were those residing in Budapest.[45]

As chief of the Balkans Field Station of X-2, Ferko was in charge
of gathering and analyzing top-secret intelligence data from Yugoslavia,
Bulgaria, Albania, and Hungary. Much of this information came from
the interrogation of refugees from Nazi-controlled territories. It seems
indisputable that Ferko knew about the massacres of Jews in the region,
the conditions in Budapest that led to the confinement of his mother and
sister in a yellow-star house, and Borbála's murder in December 1944.

In addition, Ferko and his older brothers were in touch with their
family members who remained in Budapest. Through them, they would
have received reports of atrocities from Hungarian soldiers who returned
home after serving in the east or who were themselves survivors of Jewish
labor battalions. In addition to the human toll, the transformation of
railroads into networks of cattle cars that shipped Jewish men, women,
and children to imprisonment and death must have been another shock
to Ferko, given his family's close connection to the Austro-Hungarian
railroad system where his father worked as a station master. For much of
Ferko's childhood, the Kálnays lived close to important stations, and the
boys attended a school for the children of employees.

Even without access to official and personal sources of information
on events in Hungary, by 1944 my grandfather would have been informed by Western news broadcasts and published newspaper reports
that provided explicit accounts of the conditions leading up to the massacre of Jews in Hungary.[46] I used ProQuest and "TimesMachine" to
search historical archives of the *New York Times* in that year. From the
1944 *New York Times* articles alone, Ferko would have learned of the dire
danger faced by his relatives in Budapest, as shown by the list of titles
of articles listed below. Ferko's declassified government files helped me
develop a chronology of his work in the OSS during WWII, but they
reveal none of the accompanying emotions. What must he have felt as he

read about thousands of Hungarian Jews being confined in ghettos and prison camps and deported to gas chambers in Poland, and learned of the tepid response of the US and British governments?

**Selected Titles of Articles from *The New York Times* on Events in Hungary in 1944**

| | |
|---|---|
| May 4 | Hungary Liquidates Jewish Businesses; 16,000 or 30,000 Confiscated with Aid of Gestapo |
| May 10 | Jews in Hungary Fear Annihilation—Gas Chamber Baths on Nazi Model Reported Prepared by Puppet Regime |
| May 17 | Hungary Herds All Jews—Spokesman Says 800,000 Are in Ghettos or Prison Camps |
| May 17 | Russia's Aid Sought for Jews in Hungary—Committee Here Cables to Stalin Urging Him to Intercede |
| May 20 | Savage Blows Hit Jews in Hungary: 80,000 Reported Sent to Murder Camps in Poland—Non-Jews Protest in Vain |
| June 4 | Senators Appeal on Hungary's Jews—Foreign Relations Committee Pleads with People to Stop 'Cold Blooded Murder' |
| June 18 | Hungary Policy Assailed: Group Meeting Here Denounces the Extermination of Jews |
| June 22 | Hungary Warned by Congressmen—House Foreign Affairs Body Demands Halt to 'Inhumane Conduct' |
| June 27 | Hull Backs Move to Warn Hungary: House Protest on Abuse of Jews Called For, He Says, Stressing Allied Policy |
| July 2 | 350,000 More Jews Believed Doomed: 400,000 Sent to Poland from Hungary Up to June 17 |
| July 6 | Hungary Deports Jews, Eden Says—He Confirms Massacres—Says 'Country Ignores Protests by Allies and Pope' |
| July 10 | Massacre of Jews in Hungary Scored: Special Services of Protest Held by 2,000 in Bronx and Manhattan |
| August 18 | U.S. and Britain Aid Jews of Hungary—Accept Budapest Proposals to Offer 'Temporary' Haven to Persecuted People |
| August 23 | Concessions to Jews Reported by Hungary |
| December 4 | Hungary Threatens More Jews |
| December 29 | Jews' Death March in Hungary Bared: 100,000 Driven from Budapest, 75,000 Reached Austria, A Witness Reports |

What is less clear is whether Ferko would have had direct personal information about the murder of his sister by the Hungarian Arrow Cross in December 1944 or his nephew's death in a labor camp in February 1945. I posed this question to Zvi Bernhardt, then deputy director of Reference and Information Services at Yad Vashem.* He replied, "The short answer to your question is no, a US intelligence officer in Europe would probably not have known the information on death of family members in the postwar years. Contrary to popular belief, the Nazis and the regimes that collaborated with them did not make lists of all the people they murdered." When I asked him when the names of victims became known, he gave a more detailed response:

> In general, information about the murders in Europe—and this is even more true about murders toward the end of the war that were done openly in the middle of a city—were quite quickly known in diplomatic circles, and frequently published within a finite period in newspapers. However, the exact details were frequently confused or misleading. An interested diplomatic service—or even an avid reader of newspapers interested in Hungarian Jewry—probably knew quite quickly that "Jews were murdered in Budapest." He or she might or might not have known for many months who the perpetrators were, or the number of Jews murdered.
>
> Right after they were liberated—which happened differently in different places—many of the survivors searched for information about their loved ones. Most of the information at first was finding someone who had been with them during the war. In most cases, lists of survivors from various sources were compiled quite quickly and attempts were made by various organizations to send them to interested individuals and organizations. Lists of those murdered were less common.

Peter Black of the Center for Holocaust Studies responded similarly to my question, writing that "there is no question that the OSS knew

---

* Sadly, Svi Bernhardt died on April 30, 2020, after a distinguished career.

in general what was happening in Soviet-encircled Budapest from their contacts in the neutral legations (including Wallenberg, who was an agent of the War Refugee Board). Whether they knew of specific killings prior to the fall of Budapest in February 1945 seems doubtful." From this response it appears likely that, at the very least, Ferko knew that his mother and two sisters (Borbála and Ilona) had received protective passes from Wallenberg. It is difficult to know if he had a hand in securing the passes. I asked Peter Black about this possibility, and he replied that such influence or pressure to issue protective passes would not likely have been documented since it would have occurred outside formal channels.[47]

The Soviet Army liberated Budapest on February 13, 1945—little more than two months after Borbála's murder. Ferko would surely have learned of the fate of his family members, then from friends or remaining relatives in Hungary. However, because he never spoke of his family in Budapest, we have no way of knowing when that may have been or whether he was in touch with them. From Ferko's nephew Esteban, I learned that Ferko's brothers Andrés and Jorge were in contact with their mother and Borbála in the years leading up to the war. Ferko traveled to Budapest many times over the course of his life, but I don't have information on the dates of trips or whom he may have visited.

What seems indisputable is that Ferko must have received pleas from family members and friends trapped in Hungary or elsewhere in Europe as the Nazis began rounding up, deporting, and exterminating Jews. Even if not all of his friends and relatives knew that he was working for the OSS, the fact that he had been living in the US for twenty-six years would have been enough to convince people that he could secure a lifeline for them. In her memoir, *Paper Love*, Sarah Wildman investigated the life of her deceased grandfather, who fled Nazi-occupied Vienna in 1938. She came upon a stash of letters that included pleas from relatives begging for his help and demanding to know why he hadn't rescued them or responded to their entreaties.[48] Fully half of her father's Austrian medical school classmates beseeched him for visa money or passage to the US or Palestine and affidavits of financial support. She quotes a passage from a letter from her grandmother's niece:

*Dear Aunt,*

*I would again try to write you and my sister and my brother [and] perhaps you would, after 2 1/2 years, have some emotions for me and give me an answer. It is . . . a story from heaven how you left me behind, ill. You probably know very well—you don't think about asking us if we are still alive. I am ashamed when other people are asking if I receive letters from you to say I haven't heard anything from you. And I don't get any sign of life.*[49]

When Ferko received desperate cables and letters like these, as he must have, how did he respond? Did he try to use his influence to intervene by helping people get protection from Wallenberg or international agencies? Did his inability to save loved ones leave him with a deep sense of guilt or anguish? Was his anguish so deep that he suppressed all mention of the tragedies? Although I have shown that Ferko had news of the slaughter of Jews in Budapest in 1944, and most likely learned of the fate of his sister and nephew by 1945 or earlier, in the remaining four decades of his life, he never once spoke of their murders or the plight of other people close to him. Only in his last years did he even acknowledge our family's Jewish ancestry.

What is also remarkable is that Ferko's love for Hungary and Budapest remained undiminished after the war. Perhaps grief and guilt made him sublimate thoughts of the fates of those left behind. His whitewashed memories of Budapest are like Sarah Wildman's grandfather's descriptions of Vienna—a city he escaped in 1938— as a place of beauty and culture, world-renowned art and music. Wildman recalls that:

*He never spoke of persecution, not to his children, and certainly not to his grandchildren. . . . He never talked about the virulent xenophobic wave that drowned his Vienna when Hitler was received like a Messiah; he did not speak of leaders of the Jewish community scrubbing the street on their hands and knees, of windows smashed or painted over with the word Jude, a word that would come to feel like a curse rather than a description, or an identity. . . . he did not speak of what it felt like to walk those streets the moment that*

*somehow everyone, overnight, had arm bands and flags that identified*
*them with their Nazi Party. He did not speak of that error that the*
*marching hordes brought with them, the bands of men with their*
*arms raised who rode through the streets on trucks, nor the shouting,*
*ecstatic Viennese girls thrilling to the presence of German Nazi officers.*

*Nor did he speak of the looting that began overnight,*
*immediately—the stealing from Jews that ranged from resting the*
*works of great art held by high families to the pillaging and destruction*
*of humble shops. He neglected to mention that when he first returned*
*to Vienna in 1950, it was not so much simply to visit, but to look for*
*survivors . . . Instead, what we heard, what we were schooled in, was*
*the importance, the near perfection, of Vienna Symphony and art and*
*parks, of Goethe, and Zweig and Schilling and Schnitzler and Freud.*
*For my grandfather . . . in the early years of the twentieth century*
*Vienna was Europe . . . It was the city of his friendships, his essence,*
*his very being. Only rarely were there hints of what lay beneath.*[50]

## Generations of Silence

What accounts for the silence of my grandfather and his family regarding the deaths of their close family members? I have come to learn that
such silence is common among Jews around the world and among
other victims of large-scale trauma. French historian Stéphane Gerson
cites research documenting this reaction among African Americans after
emancipation. Many felt such shame and pain over the racial and sexual
violence they had experienced that they didn't pass on their own stories.[51]

After the Second World War, denial of the atrocities of the Holocaust
and the erasure of Jewish identity was characteristic not only of the per-
petrators but also of victims. Once I learned this, I came across story after
story of hidden Jewish ancestry. Susan Rubin Suleiman is a Hungarian
émigré and a professor of comparative literature at Harvard who has
written about memory and the Holocaust. She distinguishes between
"working through" a tragedy through analysis and self-reflection and
merely "turning the page" out of a desire to wipe the events from memory. Hungary is a special case since close to 100,000 Jews remained in the

country after the war, but "the majority lived in some form of silence, if not downright amnesia about their identity and history."[52]

In 1990, *New York Times* reporter Judith Miller interviewed a Hungarian woman who learned from a class film that she was Jewish and that the numbers on her mother's arm were concentration camp tattoos. She didn't dare discuss this with her mother and only later found Shoah records documenting that eighteen of her family's relatives died in the Holocaust. She reasoned that her family's strategy for protecting her was not to let her know that she was a Jew. Similarly, Ariana Neuman delved into her family history and learned that her father was arrested in Czechoslovakia in 1941 and sent to Auschwitz. Of thirty-four members of his family before the war, twenty-five were slaughtered by the Nazis. Yet, years later, after immigrating to Venezuela and building a life there, he never spoke of his experiences or even acknowledged that the family was Jewish.[53]

In her poignant memoir about her grandparents who committed suicide together when they were in their seventies, Johanna Adorjan recalls that they would reply, "We don't talk about that" when asked about their time in Hungary during the Holocaust or her grandfather's experiences in two concentration camps.[54] Joachim Savelsberg describes a similar phenomenon among survivors of the Turkish slaughter of Armenians during the First World War—grandparents who survived the genocide but who never spoke of it to their grandchildren because they wanted to protect them. Novelist Julie Orringer's grandfather served in a forced labor battalion in Hungary. He rarely spoke of the experience until Julie began to ask questions for a novel she was writing.[55] From these stories it is easy to conclude that we construct our identities on the basis of highly selective memories that reveal more about present than past events.[56]

Like Ferko, Aaron Levine was an Allied spy who interrogated German prisoners of war. Also like Ferko, he never revealed those experiences to his children. His daughter Deborah Levine learned of his exploits fifty years later when he finally shared with her a box of over a hundred letters he had written to his wife during the war.[57] Levine's father helped liberate a Nazi death camp but never spoke of it to his children.

Joseph Skibell wrote his novel *A Blessing on the Moon* to break the silence of his grandfather, who never spoke of or mentioned the names of the eighteen members of his family who were murdered in the Holocaust.[58] Skibell attributes the silence to unbearable grief. Biographer Michael Frank described another motive in his moving portrayal of Auschwitz survivor Stella Levi—reluctance to be defined as a victim or to fill the role of narrator after the voices of her parents, aunts, uncles, neighbors, and friends were silenced.[59]

When anthropologist Carol Kidron conducted in-depth ethnographic interviews with the children of Holocaust survivors, she noted a profound silence within the families, sometimes as a strategy to avoid the pain of reliving something unspeakable, and other times as a defense mechanism to protect oneself or relatives from an actual threat. In *The Elephant in the Room,* Evistar Zerubavel describes silence as complicity between survivors who never speak of their experiences and their descendants who fear learning the truth. Such conspiracies can be passed from generation to generation, increasing in intensity with the passage of time and the number of people participating in the concealment. Even more insidious is the fact that the silence itself is rarely discussed among the conspirators, and that individuals who break it are considered disloyal.

In *Paper Love*, Sarah Wildman quotes a physician whose father survived Auschwitz but who never spoke of the experience. The son compared his father's state of mind to a pressure cooker that would explode if opened while boiling. At night, he woke sweating and shouting, but refused to speak of the content of his dreams.[60]

French author Adam Biro describes a refusal on the part of his Hungarian grandparents to acknowledge any tragedy, from the death of a pet cat to the murder of family members in the Holocaust.[61] Their motive was to dissimulate the truth to protect the children. There was no talk of death, illness, accidents, or crime, and especially no mention of the tragedy that had engulfed Hungary and the whole of Europe. In Biro's description of the silence, "all the shushed, protected children, bloody and broken, were held in its grip."

Julia Vajda and Eva Kovacs report that many Hungarian Jews went into "hibernation" after the Second World War, suppressing all mention of what they had endured and shedding everything, including names that reflected their religious identity.[62] In Hungary, the denial of Judaism was compounded by a communist government that stopped prosecuting war criminals soon after assuming power. Throughout central Europe, communist regimes described the war as an "anti-Fascist struggle," and the persecution of Jews was almost never mentioned.

Another Hungarian whose parents never told him he was Jewish is journalist John Temple.[63] Like me, John discovered as an adult that he was Jewish and had a relative who died in the Shoah. Temple's mother confided that she hadn't known that her husband was Jewish until years after they left Hungary and immigrated to Canada. Temple's father hid the fact from his own wife and then from his son. The revelations motivated Temple to seek out relatives in the US, the UK, Australia, and Hungary to learn more about his family history. Of twenty-nine cousins who attended a family reunion that he organized, many had not known about their ancestry, and only one had been raised Jewish from birth. In his words, "The past. Forgotten. Or at least a key part of it. That's the way they wanted it."

Jews like the Kálnays were ardent nationalists who considered themselves fully assimilated into Catholic society. It was they who were most traumatized by the brutality of their treatment in Budapest, the collaboration of the Hungarian authorities, and the apathy and the seeming indifference, or even callous satisfaction, of their Christian neighbors. For many, their treatment caused denial and profound identity crises. In particular, many converts could not absorb the fact that the government still considered them Jewish and thought they had been imprisoned by mistake.[64]

Another possible reason for Ferko's silence about his Jewish ancestry may have been remorse over the fate of his family members. He may have been racked with guilt over his inability to save them or perhaps by fear that his work for the American government may have jeopardized their safety. After the war, there was collective guilt among Hungarians, and the remedy for the pain caused by the guilt was forgetting. The trauma of the Holocaust became a national secret, and open discussion was taboo. "Real" emotions could only be shared within the Jewish community. This dual communication system was passed on to the next generation, and many Hungarian Jews concealed their family background from their children. Today, although only one percent of the population in the country are recognized as Jews, the ancestry site *My Heritage* reports that Hungarians have the second highest percentage of Ashkenazi Jewish heritage of any country in the world (after Israelis). Eight percent of five thousand Hungarians tested had over 25% Ashkenazi genes in 2019.

Suppressed Jewish ancestry has been revealed by several famous Americans whose parents immigrated to the US from other parts of Europe. The parents of diplomat and author Richard Holbrooke apparently hid their German Jewish heritage so he could grow up "as an American." And US Secretary of State Madeleine Albright famously asserted she was fifty-nine years old when she first learned that she was Jewish and that three of her Czech grandparents were killed in the Holocaust. Similarly, Aarons and Berger discuss a number of contemporary third-generation writers—Jonathan Safran Foer, Nicole Krauss, Julie Orringer, Daniel Mendelsohn, Johanna Adorjan—and others whose research into the lives of their ancestors entailed first discovering and exploring their own Jewish roots.[65]

In the UK, acclaimed playwright Tom Stoppard learned in his fifties that both of his Czech parents were Jews and that a majority of his relatives had been murdered in the Holocaust.[66] His "endless willingness not to disturb my mother by questioning her" describes my own reluctance to push back at my mother's refusal to discuss our suppressed heritage.

Of course, it wasn't only Jews who kept silent about events during the war. Burkhard Bilger spent ten years researching his German grandfather's hidden role as a Nazi official. Such silence is understandable given the stigma of party membership, but there are also many cases of US veterans who were awarded for heroism but who kept silent about their experiences. In 2023, a *New York Times Magazine* article described one such soldier who began having nightmares about combat only when he turned one hundred. For most of his life, he hid his two Purple Hearts and never spoke of his exploits because it seemed unbecoming to "seek attention." In response to the article, several readers wrote letters to the editor describing their own veteran relatives' refusals to talk about their experiences despite receiving Medals of Honor or experiencing severe injuries.[67]

In the case of the Kálnay family, our hidden history didn't start with World War II; it began much earlier with the negation of Rózsa's hospitalization and even her existence. The family propagated a fiction that she died in 1900 when Ferko was a year old. After Rózsa's institutionalization, Ferko's father, József, replaced her with a stern Catholic woman, Erzsébet Szentgáli. My own mother recalls meeting Erzsébet as a child when she was in Hungary with her parents. She referred to her as "Ferko's mistress." Furthermore, as I mentioned earlier, József may never have divorced Rózsa. On the other hand, the Kálnay children began to refer to Erzsébet as their mother on official documents. In the 1940s, Ferko listed her rather than Rózsa as his mother in the biographical section of an OSS personnel form. Shame over Rózsa's psychiatric illness and fear of discrimination as Jews in Hungary may have motivated this cruel lie. The religions of family members were recorded on public documents and were well known, but, as adults, Ferko and his siblings hid their Jewish ancestry. Their adopted identification as Christians continued through generations and led to a hundred years of subterfuge about our family's Jewish origins.

### CRACKS IN THE WALL OF SECRECY

The murders of Borbála and Denes were insufficient to force the facts of our family history into the open. Instead, their deaths became part of a continued coverup. It was only after relatives in the US and Argentina had died or were near death that the truth of our Jewish ancestry began to emerge. The following examples of end-of-life or post-death confessions come from a complex web of Kálnay parents, children, aunts, uncles, and cousins.

On the American side of the family, the first hints came not from Ferko but from his ex-wife, my grandmother Elsie. After she and Ferko divorced, Elsie lived in Brewster, New York, and our family was divided into an East Coast contingent (Elsie, my mother, and my immediate family) and West Coast (Ferko and my Aunt Peti and her family). Like Ferko, Elsie's family was Jewish. But although I grew up with Elsie and knew her intimately, I had no idea. Finally, at the end of her life—and unbeknownst to me— she confided in Peti, who, in turn, told my cousin Wendy who reconstructed the conversation as follows:

> *My mother called me in 1979 when I was in grad school. Elsie was ill and at the end of her life when she finally confided to my mother that our family was Jewish. I was surprised but not shocked. I don't recall the details of our conversation, but I do remember how upset my stepfather was at the revelation—so much so that, for a brief period, my mother thought that he might divorce her because she was a Jew. That concern didn't last long, but my stepfather was adamant that we never talk about our ancestry or let his professional associates in California find out; he was very worried about his standing in the community. We forget how much antisemitism there was in that generation.*

Another incident that may be related to the coverup occurred when my mother was in her late seventies. During an Argentine cousin's trip to Minnesota, my sister Tess pulled out a photo album to ask what Eugenia remembered about several members of the Kálnay family. The conversation ended abruptly when my mother became extremely agitated and had an uncharacteristic angry outburst. It's possible that her reaction was related to as-yet-undiagnosed dementia—the condition that took her life a few years later. However, her anger may also have been triggered by deep-seated fears of revealing our family history.

Ferko died in California in 1992 at the age of ninety-three. At the end of his life, Wendy tended to him. Just before he died, Wendy finally got acknowledgment of his true background. That evening, Wendy and her partner picked Ferko up from his assisted living facility and brought him to their home. After dinner, Wendy asked him to show them on a map where his family lived in Hungary. Ferko became agitated and whispered in a hushed voice, "I need to tell you something. I was born in Croatia, not in Budapest. My parents were Jewish, and our original family name was Klein, not Kálnay." He added anxiously, "It was so long ago; it doesn't matter."

Ferko had a son, Peter Kalnay, from his second marriage to Gloria Mladineo. Peter lived in Davis, California, and saw his father from time to time. After learning of our family's Jewish ancestry, he plied his father with questions, but to no avail.

Many more years passed before I could research our family history. By then I had retired from my job as a university professor and had time to devote to the quest. In May 2018, I went to Marbella, Spain, to meet my mother's cousin Esteban Francisco Kálnay, the son of Andrés, one of Ferko's architect brothers. Esteban was raised in Argentina, where he studied architecture like his father. He left Argentina and immigrated to Germany when he was twenty-eight years old and later moved to Spain.

Esteban is an expert on Kálnay family history and a source of much information on our ancestors. He was extremely open and generous when I visited him, and I learned that my great-grandfather, József, while not openly Jewish, observed Shabbat and that his wife Rózsa had a Sephardic maiden name, Margulit (sometimes spelled Margalit)—which means "pearl" in Hebrew. However, not long after Rózsa was institutionalized in 1900, he and the children began to pass for Christian. Esteban believes that when his father, Andrés, and his uncle Jorge immigrated to Argentina in 1920, they decided not to reveal their Jewish ancestry, and sent their children to Catholic schools. He didn't learn this until after the death of his father in 1982, when Esteban was twenty-two and his mother sat him down and revealed the truth of the family ancestry. She added that most Kálnays of their generation had agreed to keep it hidden.

For German-speaking architects like Andrés and Jorge Kálnay, associations with powerful German-Argentinian businessmen may have been a motive to suppress their Jewish identity. During the First World War, Argentina remained neutral, and the sizable German population there attracted investors and manufacturing plants such as Mannesmann, Krupp, Thyssen, Klockner, Bayer, Merck, and Schering. When Andrés and Jorge arrived in 1920, there were so many Germans living in the country that Germany considered it a transatlantic colony with separate police, intelligence and collection agencies, post office, and schools. After WWI, as many as 130,000 additional German immigrants arrived, and there was a rapid growth in German schools, churches, sport and musical clubs, welfare and mutual assistance funds, a hospital, a job-placement bureau, and regional associations. With the rise of National Socialism in

Germany, there was pressure on many of these organizations to support the party.[68]

Andrés's most important building in Buenos Aires was the popular Cervecería Munich (beer hall), built in 1927. In 1931, he redesigned the interior of the German Evangelical Church of Esmeralda in Buenos Aires.[69] Two years later, the church was embroiled in controversy over its association with the German Nazi Party. Andrés also designed the headquarters of the newspaper *Deutsche La Plata Zeitung*, which later supported the Third Reich during the war.

Even before World War II, being openly Jewish would have been a liability since the Argentine Nazi Party was strong and growing. Although being Jewish in Argentina was far less dangerous than in Hungary, Buenos Aires was not a peaceful sanctuary. In 1937, thousands of Argentinians marched at a German Youth Festival and celebrated the Third Reich. By 1938, the German-speaking population of the country was estimated at 237,000, not including German Jews. Also in 1938, a "Day of Unity" rally attracted twenty thousand Nazis to Luna Park Stadium (designed by Jorge Kálnay in 1931) to celebrate the annexation of Austria into the Third Reich.[70] The rally provoked anti-German backlash in the country, and relations between Germany and Argentina soured in the following year.

Nonetheless, Argentina remained neutral during World War II. Afterward, President Juan Perón halted Jewish immigration to Argentina, introduced Catholic religious instruction in public schools, and welcomed a number of fugitive Nazis. There was another wave of antisemitism after Perón was overthrown in 1955 and again during the country's military dictatorship between 1976 and 1983.[71]

Whatever the motives, the Kalnay family suppression of our Jewish ancestry persisted for many years. In his study of the Armenian genocide, Savelsberg found that, over time, such silence becomes self-reinforcing and intensifies with increases in the number of people participating and the length of time transpired.

*Moving from two- to three-person, let alone wider, conspiracies of silence involves a significant shift from a strictly interpersonal kind of*

*social pressure to the collective kind we call group pressure, whereby*
*breaking the silence actually violates not only some individuals'*
*personal sense of comfort, but a collectively sacred social taboo,*
*thereby evoking a heightened sense of fear.[72]*

This appears to be what happened in our family as more and more people colluded in erasing our family's Jewish ancestry, particularly among the Argentine Kalnays.

A large majority of Argentines are Catholic, and the country's constitution grants the religion preferential legal status. Although Argentina has the largest Jewish community in Latin America, the country has veered from periods of welcoming Jews and other immigrants during the First World War, to periods of overt discrimination and the sheltering of Nazi war criminals after WWII. In 1919, the year before Andrés and Jorge settled in Argentina, there was a general strike in Buenos Aires, and many Jews were beaten and murdered after being accused of Bolshevism, as they were in Hungary and the United States. The attacks on the Jewish quarter in Buenos Aires occurred with the acquiescence of the army and the police. Many firms fired all of their Russian and Jewish employees.[73] Despite this, there were over 150,000 Jews in Argentina in 1920, and they were integrated into most sectors of society. During the subsequent decade, Jews prospered economically and had relatively good relations with government authorities.[74] The climate was one that permitted Andrés and Jorge to develop a thriving architectural business. Their embrace of Catholicism likely enhanced this success.

Ironically, however, even in Argentina, the supposedly deeply-held secret of our Jewish ancestry appears to have been widely known, though never mentioned openly. I learned that from a conversation with another of my mother's cousins—a daughter of Jorge Kálnay. Eugenia is a renowned meteorologist at NASA and the University of Maryland. Her mother, Susanne Zwicki, was a devout Swiss Catholic who is remembered as a divisive figure in the family.

I asked Eugenia if she knew that our family was Jewish when she was growing up. She replied that she had no idea. Like Esteban, she didn't find out until after her father died in 1957.

*I learned that my father—to whom I was very close—was Jewish
only after he died. My mother said that she didn't know either,
but that after many years of marriage she looked at his Hungarian
passport and, although she couldn't read it, she saw the word
"Izraelite" stamped on it. When my father came home, she asked "Are
you Jewish?" And my father replied: "Yes. Do you want to divorce
me?" My mother also told me that when he was dying of cancer at
age sixty-three, my father wondered if it was punishment for the
family's renunciation of Judaism. For some reason my mother seems to
have told these things only to me, of her eight children.*

As it turns out, Suzanne didn't divorce Jorge after discovering his
passport, but in a bizarre coincidence, I learned much later that she was
an antisemite. In 2020, I made a lunch date with a new Brooklyn friend
who happened to mention that her brother is an architect who lives in
Buenos Aires. I replied that he was likely to know of my great-uncles,
Jorge and Andrés Kálnay, since they were prominent architects there
years ago. Ellen spoke to her brother and called me to say, "not only does
he know of them, but his Argentine partner, Susi, was the girlfriend of
Marco Aurelio, one of Jorge's sons." I was speechless, and immediately
emailed Susi and arranged a phone call.

In her first email to me, Susi said Marco Aurelio's mother was a "Swiss
Nazi" relocated to Argentina, who refused to invite Susi to their home
because Susi's father was Jewish! I later spoke to her on the phone, and
she said by "Nazi," she meant an antisemite, not a party member.

Sadly, a legacy of shame over my family's Jewish ancestry continues
to this day. Many—and perhaps most—Kálnay family members in New
York and Europe and Argentina know the truth but never speak of it
openly, fearing that others would be disturbed. As Jorge Kálnay said when
his wife found his passport with the stamp, "Israelite," "Do you want to
divorce me?" That same wife rejected her son's girlfriend because she had
a Jewish father. Others refuse to discuss our Jewish ancestry because of
their conviction that it would be too upsetting to ardently Catholic relatives in Argentina.

Ironically it is most often the suppression of the truth rather than the
secret itself that produces the most trauma. Dani Shapiro is the author

of a book about family secrets and the host of a podcast on that topic. She has interviewed hundreds of individuals who expressed a deep fear of revealing their secrets. From those interviews, Shapiro concluded that the fear that people would "die of shame" was not only unlikely but that it was never true. In her experience, with the fullness of time, it can be painful to reveal a secret, but it is always liberating.[75]

In my view, open discussion of our Jewish ancestry is something I owe to my great-grandmother Rózsa and to our other Jewish ancestors. Such honesty is especially important today in the face of rampant antisemitism and the whitewashing of history in Hungary and in some prominent factions in the US.

### Remarriage, and Love Affairs

Ferko remarried in 1943, when he was in his mid-forties and at the height of his work with the Office of Strategic Services. He and his second wife, Gloria Mladineo, may have met while he was undergoing top-secret training in Maryland. Gloria was a twenty-six-year-old Croatian American, only a few years older than Ferko's daughters.* During the war, she was a member of the Women's Army Corps (WAC) with the Second Signal Battalion in Washington, DC, an agency specializing in deciphering enemy radio transmissions. Women in the Second Battalion worked as cryptographic code clerks and operators of teletype machines, switchboards, and radios, intercepting coded enemy messages and forwarding them to the Signal Intelligence Service for decryption.

Gloria was tall and intelligent. She was proud of her work but was mortified by the slanderous backlash against women in the military, which led to a national campaign branding WACs as promiscuous or lesbians. Gloria was authoritative in manner and speech, though she had wells of insecurity that were not apparent on the surface. She was deeply in love with Ferko and wounded by his love affairs with other women. Their first marriage lasted five years, though they never lived together for a sustained period. This was partly because Ferko didn't get along with Gloria's mother, who lived with her in Van Nuys, California. My

---

* A personnel form dated November 30, 1943, lists Gloria as his wife. I don't have the precise date of marriage.

cousin Wendy recalls that Gloria's mother and Ferko argued all the time in Croatian.

In 1946, Gloria and Ferko had a son: Peter Kalnay. They divorced in 1948 but stayed in touch and then remarried in 1965 while Ferko was in Mexico. Their second marriage lasted eight years.

Of Ferko's many extramarital liaisons, perhaps the longest was with Sylvia Press, whom he recruited in 1942 to work with him in the New York office of the Strategic Intelligence Branch of the OSS. Sylvia and Ferko worked closely on all of his assignments throughout the war.

*Gloria Mladineo in WAC uniform. (From the author's personal collection)*

Sylvia began as an editorial assistant and stenographer but worked her way up to become an intelligence analyst whose work included interrogating German internees in Italy and translating interviews. In the 1950s, she wrote *In the Care of Devils*, a novel that was a thinly veiled autobiography according to critics and to Ferko himself. I describe the details of how Ferko began working at the OSS and the political events in the novel in a separate chapter, but here I present her descriptions of "Felix Wittner," her supervisor—presumably Ferko, although Felix was Viennese rather than Hungarian. He was a likable and charming host whom everyone adored, as well as a linguist and a "promoter" who had broad contacts that allowed him to recruit individuals to the OSS. "Above all he was a brilliant man with practical imagination and audacity that emanated so surprisingly from that graying, elfin figure that often seemed more sprite than flesh-and-blood man."

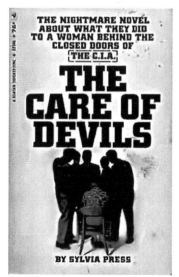

THE NIGHTMARE NOVEL ABOUT WHAT THEY DID TO A WOMAN BEHIND THE CLOSED DOORS OF [THE C.I.A.]

**THE CARE OF DEVILS**

BY SYLVIA PRESS

*Photo of book cover by author.*

In the novel, the female protagonist denies any romantic involvement with Wittner, but in real life there were formal allegations of an affair between Ferko and Sylvia Press. In a 1945 top-secret—and blatantly sexist—report, the former chief of the American Military Unit in Bucharest wrote about meeting Sylvia Press in 1943.

*Sylvia Press.*
*(From the author's personal collection)*

> *She worked closely with Francis Kalnay, doing just what was never very clear, although it was said that she and Kalnay had maintained quarters in the Roger Smith Hotel some six months to recruit personnel but never recruited any . . . When Francis Kalnay visited Bucharest, he spent less than an hour in our office. I let him and Miss Press have my car and they toured the country for a day or two. After that I know she wrote to him often. . . . She is a frustrated woman who is not getting any younger and probably took quite a jolt when Kalnay married another woman. She is typical of thousands of that unmarried age group of women who work for the government.*[76]

Ferko's marriage to Gloria in 1943 doesn't appear to have soured his relationship with Sylvia Press. The two continued to work together at every post he assumed until they left Europe together in November 1945 and sailed to New York on the ship *Randolph*. A photograph of Sylvia after the war was inscribed, "To Ferko, my companion in war, my friend in peace. Sylvia."

Two wives and countless girlfriends are likely to take a financial toll. However, the full picture is elusive because Ferko was private about his finances to the point of being furtive. We know that he evaded his obligations to his ex-wives and children and that, although he didn't live extravagantly, he always seemed to have enough money to live well and to be generous with friends and the children of his employees in Mexico. Wendy's father, who filed taxes for Ferko during the years he lived outside the US, felt he was working with incomplete information about properties bought, developed, and sold in Valle de Bravo.

The character purported to be Ferko in Sylvia Press's book tried to hide the sale of a beach bungalow from his first wife because he was worried that she might claim the property while he was overseas with the OSS. Sylvia signed the papers for him and, when asked why she had done that, her character in the novel responded:

> *It was the midst of a war. He was leaving on a secret mission for our government. He was straightening out his personal affairs and had to make all sorts of final arrangements quietly as we all did when we were shipped out so as not to break security. He was my boss and I trusted him. When he asked me to do him a personal favor he did try to explain it to me, but I can't help if I'm stupid about those things. I mean real estate. It looked as though I was going to remain in for the duration. It was a small thing. What did he ask? He didn't want . . . anyone to know he was leaving the country. There was a question of some checks that would have to be deposited. I think it also had something to do with his wife. I think he was afraid she might get hold of the property while he was gone and before the sale was completed . . . there was no love lost between them.*

Apparently, Ferko never lost his charm, even in old age. Long after his OSS career, when he was seventy-four years old, he scandalized family members by dating a woman in her thirties in Carmel, California. They were designing and producing elaborate clothes of the era, with funky buttons, brocades, embroidery, and flowing tunics.

# IV

# END OF THE WAR AND
# LEAVING THE OSS

## PREPARATIONS FOR A PEACETIME INTELLIGENCE AGENCY

In the last months of the war in Europe, Ferko's work with the OSS Secret Intelligence Branch operations moved beyond planning operations in foreign capitals to training American and "volunteer" Axis POW recruits to penetrate Nazi Germany. These individuals were given special clothing, documents, and equipment to operate within the Third Reich without detection. In cases where American recruits were captured or executed, Ferko was often left with the task of writing bereavement letters to the family. On May 26, 1945, he wrote to the uncle of recruit John Perich: "John volunteered for a special mission requiring great courage and highly specialized knowledge. A few weeks ago, I learned that my dear friend John was killed with many others by the bestial Nazis in the western part of Germany. He died, according to my information, on the 24th day of February 1945."

In the spring of 1945, the Third Reich collapsed as the Soviet Red Army closed in on Hitler's forces from the east, and western Allied Forces fought their way toward Berlin from Italy. The Führer committed suicide on April 30, 1945, and Germany surrendered unconditionally on VE Day: May 8. In Italy, Liberation Day is celebrated a few weeks earlier in memory of a nationwide strike and uprising against the Nazi occupation on April 25, 1945. I don't have records of the public celebrations that Ferko witnessed from his vantage point in southern Italy, but from web photographs, it appears to have been similar to the VE Day celebration that OSS spy Wayne Nelson witnessed in France:

> *The town was hysterical. It developed that the Germans had left in force at 4 or 5 a.m. that morning. They were invited to the mayor's house for fine wine and champagne that had been hidden during the occupation. Mike and I were kissed by all the girls, had photos taken, and given photographs. We signed more autographs than Frankie Sinatra. I received the mayor's speech and replied with one of my own.[1]*

The end of hostilities in Europe led to many strategic changes for the OSS, and Ferko was closely involved in the planning, although the precise nature of his work is shrouded in mystery. Below is a map of OSS missions and bases in Europe and the Near East in 1945.[2]

*Source: CIA. Public domain document. Note: The Central Intelligence Agency has not approved or endorsed the contents of this publication.[3]*

A week after VE Day, a figure with the code name "Puritan" wrote to James R. Murphy, the head of X-2, saying "Jester" had recommended Ferko leave Italy and be reassigned to England.* "Puritan" was Norman Holmes Pearson, head of European X-2 operations (the same officer who had lauded Ferko and nominated him for a Certificate of Merit.) In the memo, Pearson argued that Kalnay was needed to interrogate returning OSS agents. Italy was a prime location for such work because of its attraction for Axis defectors, who could easily masquerade as refugees at a time when apprehending and prosecuting war criminals was a high priority for the Allied powers. One OSS scholar found a document stating that Ferko had made an agreement with Angleton a year earlier that he would resign once the situation had stabilized in Italy.[4]

Several weeks later, Ferko was given a promotion and a higher-grade appointment. His specific assignment was with "special funds," a division that had responsibility for financing operations of the Secret Intelligence and Special Operations Branches. Nevertheless, at the end of May, he was relieved of his duties in the Mediterranean Theater of Operations in Caserta and ordered to Washington. Ferko, Sylvia Press, and several other Special Funds employees left for DC on June 13, 1945. Exactly a month later, Ferko reported to Fort Totten, Long Island, for transportation back to his permanent station in Caserta, Italy. The KAY Project was in full gear and expanding to the Middle East. Robert Huse of the Special Operations Branch of the OSS sent a memo to higher-up William Mudge, detailing a long list of personnel "hand-picked by Mr. Kalnay" who were being considered for the KAY Project, including one hundred Greeks and a handful of eastern Europeans. He closed the letter by asking, "Am I correct that it is our present policy to recruit as many men as possible for the KAY Project?"

World War II ended on September 2, 1945, with the surrender of Japan. In October, the OSS was dissolved and a new group called the Strategic Services Unit (SSU) was created from the Secret Intelligence and Counter-espionage Branches to create a permanent peacetime intelligence agency. On December 10, 1945, Ferko resigned from his position as a special funds employee and chief of X-2 Balkans Field Station. He

---

* I have not been able to verify the identity of "Jester."

sailed to New York on the ship *Randolph* for yet another assignment. He appears to have transferred to the SSU to continue undercover work.

Before leaving, Ferko wrote a memo requesting reimbursement for having paid for his housing in Bari "for reasons of security." The request was denied. It's possible that Ferko's motive for the housing change was actually to live in cushier quarters. In many parts of Italy, OSS personnel requisitioned villas to be used as homes, offices, and interrogation centers. Some included cellars of fine brandy and other liquor. In Caserta, the OSS communications office shared a 1,200-room royal palace of the Bourbon Kings with the headquarters of the MEDTO Supreme Command of the Allied Forces.[5] In Cairo, the OSS living accommodations included beautiful accommodations with a tennis court and Sudanese servants. In Florence, an OSS operative stayed in an apartment in a palazzo.[6]

Ferko had spent time in Bucharest with Major Robert Bishop, an officer in the X-2 Division of the OSS who wrote about the sumptuous meals there. "Romanian tables groaned under the load of plenty: an iced dish with fresh caviar from the delta of the Danube; sliced salami, smoked sturgeon, little meat rolls, all taken with sips of tuica, a mild prune brandy." The work was also financially lucrative for some. A special funds officer in Algiers from September 1943 to July 1944 reports that "there was hardly a mission that went to France, Italy, or the Balkans, which did not take a supply of gold coins in addition to bank notes of the country they were dropped in."[7]

## SECRECY WITHIN THE OSS

The precise nature of Ferko's SSU assignment remains a mystery. Since its inception, secrecy was so strict within the OSS that potential recruits never received word from the agency that they were under consideration while being scouted and even trained. In his book about OSS officers working behind enemy lines in the Balkans, Eric Lichtblau noted that they weren't even supposed to know the identities of other agents at the base, and agents' letters were censored so that none of their family or friends knew where they were going or what they were doing.

After the war, this culture of secrecy became rampant throughout the federal government. Within a decade, overclassification of documents had grown exponentially, and by 1961, the National Archives had over 100,000 cubic feet of classified records. Many others were destroyed or never declassified. For decades, the classification of OSS materials precluded an objective analysis of many of its actions or even the rationale behind Truman's decision to close the agency.

In her book *Classical Spies*, about her father's work as an archeologist with the OSS, Susan Hueck Allen describes how documents were combed over by the CIA after World War II. The most sensitive materials were removed and only those considered harmless were declassified and surrendered to the National Archives. To wit, the papers of Col. Buxton—Ferko's superior in the early days of the OSS—remain classified to this day.

I obtained my grandfather's personnel records in response to a FOIA request to the CIA (successor to the OSS). However, other sensitive documents I sought were not included. I also sent a FOIA to the FBI to ask if Ferko was ever under investigation. The response, which neither confirmed nor denied an investigation, was phrased in typical government "non-speak:"

> . . . the mere acknowledgment of the existence or nonexistence of such records is itself a classified fact protected by FOIA exemption (b)(1) and/or would reveal intelligence sources, methods or activities protected by exemption (b)(3) [50 USC & 3024(i)(1)]. This is a standard response and should not be read to indicate that any such records do or do not exist.[8]

If the overclassification of documents has been a barrier to general search for OSS materials, it is an even greater impediment to accessing the records of X-2, an elite within an elite that hid its activities even from other OSS personnel. Elements essential to the analysis of X-2 are still missing from the public archives today, despite the declassification of scores of thousands of other documents. This culture of secrecy clearly contributed to my grandfather's silence about his activities during the war.

A confidential notice in Ferko's file before his 1945 departure to OSS Europe read:

*CONFIDENTIAL — SECURITY*

*The main thing to remember about security is that you should never let anyone outside of your part of the organization know anything about the operations, personnel, or other activities of X-2 branch.*

*It is not wrong to tell people that you work for OSS, although it is best to avoid this. However do not sound mysterious about it. If you do state that you work for OSS, just say that you do a routine job, such as clerk, stenographer, supervisor, etc., leaving the impression that your work is of no particular interest to avoid further questioning.*

*If you are going overseas the best policy is just not to tell anyone of this, except possibly your immediate family. If you do tell your family, caution them not to mention it to anyone else.*

*When you go to the POE [Port of Embarcation], do not advertise it. If you have friends or relatives in the city at which the POE is located, tell them you are there on a shopping tour, a vacation, or give them some other excuse. <u>Never</u> tell them you are waiting for a boat. The bottom of the ocean is a long way down and you are dealing with hundreds of other lives in addition to your own, <u>so be careful</u>.*[9]

When Ferko first began his assignment at the US Army's European Theater of Operations in London in December 1943, he was given a code name and asked to sign the OSS Oath of Office, swearing: "I will not disclose or reveal either by word or by conduct any information which I may obtain by reason of my employment by the Office of Strategic Services, and I will forever keep secret any information so obtained by me." He was also required to swear that he had read and understood the "Espionage Act" and bound himself to abide by it. The consequences of violating the Espionage Act were imprisonment or death.

These government admonitions appear to have been effective. I belong to an "io" email group in which individuals share or seek information about their relatives who were former OSS members. In posting after posting, people reveal that their fathers or grandfathers refused to talk about their experiences in the organization.

## ABRUPT RESIGNATION FROM GOVERNMENT WORK

In March 1946, Ferko abruptly left the SSU. Why did he leave when he seemed to have a promising future ahead, planning for the transition of OSS operations? Was it the result of his politics, his ethnicity, or his shortcomings? In the following pages, I reflect on three possible explanations.

### Theory 1: Anti-Communist Sentiments

Ferko may have been a victim of the growing anti-communist fervor in the US and the related animosity of FBI Director J. Edgar Hoover toward Donovan and the OSS. From his first years in New York, my grandfather had several friends who were sympathizers and active members of the Communist Party. This is unsurprising, given his close ties to European émigrés and artists. After the First World War, eastern European residents comprised a majority of members. At the height of membership in 1939, there were only about 66,000 members of the Communist Party of the USA, but Jews and artists were heavily represented. Others were active in organizations created by the party, such as the American League Against War and Fascism.

As mentioned earlier, many of Ferko's closest friends and associates in the 1920s and 1930s were members of the Communist Party or sympathizers. In spite of this, Ferko himself was not a communist, and he was likely wary of association with the party from his earliest days in the United States. In 1918, the year before his arrival, Congress authorized the deportation of immigrants who advocated revolution, and in January 1920, the US Justice Department carried out a sweep known as "the Palmer Raids" and arrested some ten thousand alleged Bolsheviks.[10]

In her book about her affair with Dreiser, Yvette Szekely referred to Ferko and Julian DeMiskey when she wrote, "My mother, like her intellectual friends, was among the radical elite who, although propounding revolution, didn't really believe [in] the International Soviet."

Ferko did, however, define himself as a socialist. His best-selling book, *Chucaro*, can be read as an allegory of exploitation of pure-minded workers by the wealthy. As a journalist in New York, he was a regular contributor to the socialist news weekly *Magyar Szó* that was "dedicated to the ideals of socialism and to the task of organizing workers in trade."[11] Ferko is acknowledged in a book about the publication that lauds such prominent communists as John Reed, C.P. Snow, and Paul Robeson as well as a number of Hungarian labor organizers in the US.

On the other hand, Wendy reports that Ferko was never very political and that he was unable to sit through an hour of political analysis. Furthermore, he was determined to keep his political leanings as secret as his Jewish identity. It's not difficult to understand how the combination of antisemitism in Europe during both World Wars, within the OSS, and during the scourge of McCarthyism made Ferko nervous and fearful. When he was elderly, Wendy recalls him saying to her conspiratorially, "You and I may be socialists, but we must never tell anyone."

The fight against Nazi Germany in WWII naturally entailed close alignment with communists, since the Soviet Union was an ally of the US, and several communist nationalists throughout Europe were instrumental in opposing the Axis Powers. However, these alliances didn't eliminate fear of communism within US government circles or the OSS. When the war ended, the recruitment of anti-Nazi, pro-Tito partisans in Yugoslavia, which had been lauded at the highest government levels when Ferko was in Europe, began to be vilified as subversive and "pro-communist." According to Wendy, Ferko scoffed at these attitudes, saying, "they thought we were all Tito Yugoslavs, but not all Yugoslavs supported Tito." However, Wendy studied under Manfred Halpern, a German Jewish professor who asserted that anti-Soviet left politics in the OSS were both widespread and widely known. Historian Michael Holzman says that "socialist" may be a euphemism and that OSS personnel included many small "c" communists, some Communist Party members, and even some Comintern agents.[12] Director Donovan may have intentionally hired some communists to enlist their help working against Fascist regimes in occupied Europe.[13]

In his book on the OSS, Richard Harris Smith wrote that Pittsburgh investment banker Joseph Scribner, assistant chief to the Special Operations Branch in Washington, suspected what he called "Kalnay's Yugoslavs" of being communists and questioned Ferko's own political motives. R. Davis Halliwell, chief of OSS Special Operations, was generally a fan of Ferko's, but Smith writes that he shared Scribner's concerns about the "communistic tendencies" of several Yugoslav Merchant Marine crewmen recruited by Ferko after they were stranded in New York.

Smith also referenced Sylvia Press, the OSS officer who had worked closely with Ferko in X-2 and was later interrogated by OSS officials and forced to resign without a pension. Smith notes that "one charge brought against her was that she worked in the OSS with Francis Kalnay, the Hungarian writer whose recruitment of pro-Tito Yugoslavs had so upset OSS Headquarters—a full decade before." Press herself was criticized for being pro-Soviet, and this may have influenced others' views of Ferko since she was known to be both his assistant and his lover. In a section of Major Bishop's report on X-2 activities in Bucharest, he wrote:

> Her views are of some interest. Most of us were shocked by Russian actions and treatment of the Romanian people. She thought them justified. When the Soviets deported all Romanians of German ethnic origin for slave labor, she thought it quite proper. I attributed this to the fact that she was Jewish and bitterly anti-German.

It is true that many OSS field personnel strongly identified with the resistance forces to which they were assigned, and some were clearly communist sympathizers. Some were so ardently pro-Partisan that the OSS brass branded them biased, a charge that may have had some basis. A scandal erupted when large parts of a classified OSS document were printed in the pro-communist journal, *Amerasia*. As anti-communist sentiments grew in Washington, so did suspicions of OSS officers. At the same time, J. Edgar Hoover tallied leftists and communists employed by the OSS as ammunition to bring down Director Donovan. At one point, Donovan had said, "I'd put Stalin on the payroll if I thought it would defeat Hitler."

Perhaps the OSS director intentionally removed Ferko at the end of the war when Donovan's own views of the Yugoslav Partisans changed. At that time, a number of OSS personnel were reassigned or removed in what was seen in the field as a purge. One example was someone Ferko would have known well—Major Francis Arnoldy, the head of the Yugoslav section of the OSS in Bari in 1944. A Slovene American who worked for US Military Intelligence succeeded in getting Arnoldy removed because he was regarded as pro-Partisan.

At the end of the war, Roosevelt had his chief White House military aide conduct a confidential investigation into the OSS. Donovan's plans for a postwar organization that reported directly to the president were leaked from the report and enraged the Joint Chiefs of Staff. Roosevelt asked Donovan to submit a revised proposal, but the president died before that was accomplished. Harry Truman succeeded him on April 12, 1945. Unlike Roosevelt, Truman was not convinced that the country needed a central intelligence agency, particularly with a politically prominent Republican like Donovan as its chief.[14]

Truman abolished the OSS because he thought there was no need for the intelligence agency during peacetime. Shortly thereafter he realized this was incorrect and he authorized the creation of the Central Intelligence Agency (CIA), the National Security Council (NSC), and the Air Force Office of Special Investigations (AFOSI).[15]

Within a few months, Truman issued an executive order abolishing the OSS and terminating Donovan, effective October 1, 1945. He then scaled down the OSS espionage operation and placed them under the War Department in a Strategic Services Unit. On the date of Donovan's termination, the X-2 Balkans office was relocated from Rome to Venice, and two months later—on December 10, 1945—Ferko submitted his resignation as chief of X-2 Balkans and moved to New York for his short-lived assignment with the Strategic Services Unit.

## Theory 2: Internal Politics and Antisemitism

Ferko may also have been the victim of internal politics and rivalries within the OSS. Despite his many fans, he had some critics within the organization and some advisory agencies. In April 1945, Major Robert

Bishop, an X-2 officer, brought Ferko and Sylvia Press to help expand OSS operations in Bucharest. In Bishop's report, he stated Frank Wisner, head of OSS operations in southeast Europe, had taken a strong dislike to Ferko, and told Bishop to get him out of Bucharest. There was no explanation except for the bizarre statement that "he thought that Kalnay was a spook who gave him the creeps."*

Attitudes like this may have their origins in antisemitism. Although many eastern European Jews were recruited to the OSS because of their language skills and connections in key countries, prejudice was rife in the government. Indeed, as the publication *The Jewish Forward* disclosed, the US government conducted widespread domestic spying during World War II that targeted Jews, Jewish organizations, and Zionist activity. A specific example of antisemitism can be seen in a report on Tibor Keszthelyi, a war hero who became chief of the OSS Hungarian desk. In the report, Keszthelyi is described as follows: "racial origin . . . Hebrew, although physical as well as mental characteristics are non-Hebrew." Another is found in a memo to Ellery Huntington that Ferko wrote in July 1943 proposing candidates for the Balkan area. One was Dr. Moses Hadas, a professor of Greek and Latin at Columbia University who had worked on the Survey of Foreign Experts. In the memo, Ferko complained that although Lt. Smolianinoff had never met the professor "he does not believe Hadas would be a good agent because (1) he is not tough physically, and (2) he is a Jew. 'Case closed.'"

Another antagonist who may have led to Ferko's problems in the OSS was Ulius Amoss, a Greek American businessman who served as OSS executive officer in Cairo, where he aspired to assume control of operations in the Balkans. In the summer of 1943, when Amoss was relieved of his post, Ferko assumed responsibility for OSS operations in the Middle East. Several years later, when Senator Joseph McCarthy promoted the theory that the CIA (successor to the OSS) was rife with "communist agents," Amoss was one of his inside sources.

Antagonism from Amoss or others described above may have curtailed approval of Ferko's appointment as a major in the Army. That proposal, made by Ellery Huntington, languished until Ferko himself withdrew the application.

---

* According to Merriam-Webster's online dictionary, a spook was a term for a spy. *Merriam-Webster*, s.v. "spook (*n.*)," accessed August 16, 2023, https://www.merriam-webster.com/dictionary/spook

**MEMORANDUM**

To:         Ellery Huntington
From:       Francis Kalnay
Date:       July 8, 1943

Six months ago (on Jan 12, 1943) I was asked by the OSS to fill out and return "at once" an application for a commission in the United States Army. I had no further work until, upon your instructions, the necessary papers were sent to me on April 13th and promptly completed and returned. On May 1st I appeared before the OSS Board and subsequently I was told by various individuals that it was just a matter of a few days before I would be commissioned, probably with the rank of a major.

Since it appears to me that there has been undue delay or hesitancy in this matter, and since I am about to leave for the Base, I wish to withdraw my application for a commission. As you may know, I have no personal ambition in these matters, and I shall perform my duties to the best of my ability under any circumstance.

I know that you have done your best in this matter, and I greatly appreciate your efforts.

The date of the letter is curious since it coincides with a key moment in the KAY Project. Also on July 8, Ferko wrote to Commander Halliwell, the chief of Special Operations, informing him that three consecutive groups of recruits for the project were trained, provisioned, and ready to be sent on their missions behind enemy lines. On the other hand, at the end of 1943, a negative appraisal of some of Ferko's recruits came from Lt. Col. Paul West, chief operations officer, OSS-ME. In a memo to J.M. Scribner, assistant chief of the Special Operations Branch in Washington, West argued that five of the Yugoslavs Ferko had recruited as agents were unclear about their mission and unprepared for hazardous duties.[*]

More serious criticism came from James J. Angleton, who was head of the OSS Secret Counterintelligence "Unit Z" in Italy that handled ULTRA intelligence. In April 1945, Angleton wrote a top-secret

---

[*] See Appendix D for full memorandum.

memorandum questioning the usefulness of Ferko's reports on the
Balkans:

> *Future operations on Balkanites in Italy must follow the well-*
> *established pattern which in our experience has been to interrogate*
> *and break a person of considerable stature, who in turn, throws out*
> *undeveloped leads which are followed up; all such information being*
> *continually incorporated into a schematical, or diagrammatical*
> *presentation and analysis of the intelligence network uncovered.*
>
> *Otherwise it is quite impossible to control or act on penetration*
> *agents reports. Our present difficulty is mainly that of evaluating the*
> *various reports which have been produced by yourself, No. 5 SCI*
> *Unit and the SIM/CS (Italian CE), and SCI Unit Z, Trieste. I feel*
> *that the time must come to carefully examine and control the Balkan*
> *information obtained in Italy during the past four months, and*
> *therefore we would appreciate your comments.* *

When the OSS disbanded in 1945, Angleton stayed in Italy to run
operations for the successor organizations to the OSS. If he had concerns about Ferko's work, it would have had serious consequences. David
Robarge of the Center for Security Studies at Georgetown University and
chief historian of the CIA told me that he suspects that "Angleton might
have been concerned that the reporting on the Balkans potentially was
corrupted with communist or partisan misinformation."

### Theory 3: Perhaps the Nazi Ratlines Provide a Key

Things are often not what they seem in the formal records of a spy
agency. I described above the dismissal of Ulius Amoss from the OSS
in the summer of 1943. Ostensibly, he was fired for ordering targeted
assassinations in North Africa and Europe. However, much later, declassified documents revealed that Amoss was kept on payroll for clandestine
work. Perhaps the same was true for Ferko. In his personnel records, he
lists intelligence work in Argentina as one of his areas of operation in the
OSS, but I found no record of that work in his declassified files.

---

* See Appendix E for full memorandum.

By 1939, Latin America was probably Germany's most important theater of operations. The Third Reich maintained close contact with its German citizens in the region through commerce, diplomacy, social organizations, and German intelligence operations.[16] The largest concentration was in Argentina. Because hundreds of thousands of German immigrants were living there after the war, President Juan Perón secretly ordered diplomats and intelligence officers to create escape routes for SS officers and Nazi Party members. He also recruited Nazis with military and scientific expertise. As a result, some five thousand Nazi officers and collaborators used these "ratlines" to flee Europe and seek sanctuary in Argentina.

Perhaps Ferko worked with the Allies to track German businesses in Argentina in the early 1940s or to identify Nazis there after the war. Identification and prosecution of Nazi war criminals was a priority for some Allied leaders. As a fluent Spanish speaker with work and family ties in Buenos Aires, Ferko would have been a good candidate for such work. On the other hand, although I know that Ferko traveled to Argentina after 1945, his visits there must have been short in duration since he moved from New York to California immediately after resigning. Furthermore, information on the ratlines and financial assistance to Nazis in Argentina has been shrouded in secrecy to this day. A 2019 report from the Simon Wiesenthal Center revealed that even eighty years after WWII, there are still unanswered questions about how Swiss banks provided financial assistance to Nazis in Argentina.[17] While the release of reams of formerly top-secret documents has shed light on some of the mysteries surrounding my grandfather's other work in the OSS, questions about whether he was involved in the OSS Secret Intelligence Branch work infiltrating Nazi organizations in South America may never be answered. Sadly, there is no one left to ask now that nearly ninety percent of the sixteen million Americans who served in the war have died.

After the war, the US issued thousands of immigration visas to Nazi collaborators at a time when concentration camp survivors faced larger barriers. Furthermore, many war criminals were recruited as spies, informants, and scientists to work in the US, Europe, Latin America, and the Middle East. It is conceivable that Ferko severed ties with the OSS/CIA intentionally because of disgust over these policies.

**Theory 4: Financial Improprieties**

A more mundane reason for Ferko's abrupt resignation from the OSS may have been that he was under suspicion for having moved money among several bank accounts. Before her death, his daughter Peti voiced this suspicion, saying she didn't know if the funds were hidden from OSS executives or from wives and mistresses (Ferko had at least two girlfriends at that time, in addition to his wife Gloria). In his book on the OSS and Yugoslavia, Blaz Torkar describes a series of financial errors identified in payments of a Yugoslav OSS agent. Torkar did not directly implicate Ferko in the improprieties, but they would have occurred on his watch as chief of X-2 Balkans.[18]

## SENATOR JOE MCCARTHY INVESTIGATIONS & FERKO'S FLIGHT TO MEXICO

Immediately after his resignation from the OSS in December 1945, Ferko changed his home address from Riverside Drive in New York City to Los Angeles. He was still married to Gloria at that time, and their son, Peter Kalnay, was born in California in August 1946, but within two years they had divorced.* By the end of the decade, Ferko lived in Ojai, California, north of San Francisco, where he had bought a small farm and vineyard. He harvested grapes to sell to local winemakers and built and sold stone ovens.

Then, in 1954, Ferko abruptly packed up and fled to Mexico, where he lived for two decades. Why? Escape from ex-wives and mistresses may have provided some motivation to leave the US, but the more powerful motivator was likely to have been his fear of growing anti-communist fervor in the US.

In 1947, a former colleague was suddenly targeted by the FBI. The man was a press attaché in Rome and a progressive Catholic who once described himself as a socialist. He was accused of being a homosexual and a communist—common allegations used to discredit Jews and left-leaning émigrés. The following year, US Communist Party member Elizabeth

---

* Ferko and Gloria stayed in touch and remarried in 1965, only to divorce again in 1973.

Bentley caused a national furor when she testified before Congress that Soviet spies were implanted in the OSS.

Ironically, Ferko's much-heralded success in recruiting communist Yugoslav Partisans to collaborate with the OSS was a strategy used against him after the war. He confided in Wendy that the OSS had been under suspicion by the House Un-American Activities Committee (HUAC) for employing many anti-Fascist Tito Yugoslavs and eastern European Jews, even though that occurred at a time when the Soviet Union was a US ally.

Another European immigrant who was targeted by right-wing members of Congress was Louis Adamic, someone whose life closely paralleled that of Ferko. Adamic founded the Common Council for American Unity—a successor organization to the FLIS where Ferko began his quasi-government work. Both men spent many years working to promote the integration of new immigrants in the United States. Ferko wrote *The New Americans* with Francis Collins, and Adamic wrote *A Nation of Nations*. On the other hand, the two books are very different. The Kalnay-Collins book is an encyclopedia of resources for new immigrants, while Adamic's book is a discussion of the contributions of immigrants to American society. Both men supported Tito's Partisans during the Second World War. As a result, after the war, Adamic was targeted by Senator McCarran, an ardent anti-communist who sought to expose leftist sympathizers in the US. His interrogation must have greatly disturbed my grandfather.

In 1948, when HUAC hearings began, Adamic and Alger Hiss were portrayed as two of the most prominent "communist spies." During the hearings Adamic was charged with passing on secret information to a pro-Tito Moscow agent.[19] It was also falsely alleged that he had done so while working for the OSS. The parallels with Ferko's career are startling and Adamic's hearings were widely publicized. How must Ferko have felt as he watched Adamic's image change from that of a lauded, successful immigrant to a foreigner trying to subvert the American way of life?

Unlike Ferko, Adamic was a very public figure who published widely-read anti-Fascist books and articles, although the Truman Administration and the HUAC hearings effectively silenced him and tarnished his reputation. He lost invitations for speeches, public appearances, and avenues for the publication of his articles and books. In 1949, Adamic began to receive death threats from Croatian Fascists and Soviet agents who had entered the United States, and two years later, on September 4, 1951, he was found dead of a gunshot wound. Although the death was ruled a suicide, historian John Enyeart reviews the evidence and concludes that it was most likely a political assassination.[20] The Truman Administration and HUAC hearings effectively silenced him and tarnished his reputation.

In 1947, President Truman created a federal loyalty program to appease conservative Republicans and Democrats who asserted that, during the New Deal, communists had infiltrated the federal government. Between 1947 and 1956, FBI agents interviewed more than five million federal employees, and 25,000 were under intense scrutiny. Of these, 2,700 were fired and 12,000 quit.[21]

In an earlier chapter, I mentioned OSS officers Ulius Amoss's and Frank Wisner's antipathy toward Ferko. After the war, Amoss worked for Wisner and served as a key informant to Senator Joseph McCarthy. It may have been these two who fed negative information to the CIA Director of Security on Sylvia Press and Ferko.

### Implications in His Lover's Memoir

Ferko had already been traumatized by the bombings and carnage he witnessed in the war, and the HUAC investigations were the last straw. Although he was no longer working for the government and therefore wasn't directly approached by HUAC, many of his colleagues came under suspicion. Most alarming to Ferko was the interrogation, dismissal, and denial of pension to his lover and assistant, Sylvia Press, in 1954. Sylvia had stayed on with the CIA after the war, but she paid dearly for her earlier relationship with Ferko; in the words of Professor of US National Security Christopher Moran, her dismissal was directly related to their collaboration:

> *The fact that she had known Francis Kalnay, a Hungarian-born professor who had angered OSS headquarters by recruiting Yugoslavs allied to the communist revolutionary and statesman, Josip Tito, was also used against her. She appealed directly to CIA Director Allen*

*Dulles, but to no avail [and she was] thrown as a bone to McCarthy,*
*who was threatening to launch a full-scale investigation of the*
*Agency. Clearly, the last thing the CIA wanted was the demagogue*
*senator digging into its files.*

Ironically, the criticism of Ferko during the Sylvia Press interview failed to mention that his support of Tito and the Yugoslav Partisans, both during WWII and after the Tito-Stalin split, aligned with official US policy. Furthermore, some of the allegations against Ferko for his "communistic tendencies" began while he was still employed by the OSS supporting the foreign policy objectives of the US government. In this too he was similar to Adamic, who commented in 1946 that one section of the Department of Justice was trying to paint him as a communist foreign agent while another section sent him on tours to persuade people to buy war bonds.[22]

Press's book, *In the Care of Devils,* was such a thinly disguised memoir of her years in the OSS and CIA that the agency apparently spent over $50,000 buying up copies to keep it from circulating. Some friends told her that CIA officials intentionally borrowed library copies and never returned them and that there was an unwritten directive for anyone who found a copy to seize it and turn it over to security.

During Press's CIA interrogation, she was asked numerous questions about Ferko's seaside bungalow. In her book, she quotes the agency's head of security as suggesting the house was an out-of-the-way location for clandestine meetings and that her help in the paperwork for the sale of the property was "a pattern that the communists often use . . . they keep transferring ownership to create confusion." She was also told that some of the individuals recruited by "Felix" (Ferko's character) in 1943 were Cominform agents. The interrogation planted seeds of doubt in her mind.

*Was it possible? Had Felix—the charming, Felix the perennial*
*Viennese, Felix whom everyone adored for his quaint humor, his*
*amusing helplessness in the face of the practical—had he involved her*
*in some far-fetched, long-term mess that was only now, after all these*
*years (after Felix himself was long since gone!) coming home to roost?*

*Unthinkable. Yet, suppose it was true? There was a catlike quality*
*about Felix's ability to extricate himself when things threatened to*
*become unpleasant or onerous.*

According to national security expert Christopher Moran, the interrogation and dismissal of Sylvia Press intimidated CIA employees for
years to come. He attributes this to the agency's penchant for secrecy. As
a result, CIA Director Dulles was able to control information that was
released to the public.

There may also have been negative reports about Ferko from other
sources in the OSS. The organization was famously rife with elites from
wealthy families, such as the Vanderbilts, Morgans, Whitneys, and
Mellons, who were ideologically opposed to OSS cooperation with communist insurgents during the war. Ferko's numerous trips back to Hungary
and other parts of Europe after the war may have raised suspicions.

### REFUGE IN MEXICO

Soon after Sylvia Press's dismissal, Ferko left the US and moved to the
small city of Valle de Bravo, two hours southwest of Mexico City. He was
not the only political exile in Mexico in the 1950s. Many American film-
makers, writers, poets, literary agents, and artists immigrated to Mexico
City and Cuernavaca after the end of the war. Some had been blacklisted
and prevented from publishing or exhibiting their work after President
Truman issued an executive order identifying many leftist institutions
as "subversive" and calling many prominent individuals before HUAC
to answer questions about "communist infiltration." Some fled to avoid
being subpoenaed to testify.

Several American expatriates in Mexico were teachers, doctors,
journalists, business professionals, college professors, and government
employees who had been fired from their jobs because of their anti-
Fascist, leftist views. Others fled to Mexico seeking a more welcoming
intellectual and artistic climate. One was the award-winning screenwriter
Dalton Trumbo; another was the screenwriter and producer Ray Spencer,
who moved to Valle de Bravo before Ferko and was a frequent guest at
the Kalnay residence there over the years.

Mexico was also attractive because it was affordable, and because in the early 1950s, Americans didn't need passports to travel or resettle there. They generally received tourist visas upon entering the country and then could apply for permanent resident status to be able to work. That usually took a year, during which the applicants had to travel back into the US every six months. This was particularly stressful for naturalized US citizens like Ferko because they could lose their citizenship if arrested by the Immigration and Naturalization Service.

Many Americans returned to the US after the censure of Joseph McCarthy in 1954 and in the late 1950s and early 1960s, but Ferko had just begun to create an idyllic life in Valle de Bravo on a picturesque plot where he cured meats, baked bread, and grew grapes, coffee beans, fruits, and vegetables. He also found other ways to earn money: building smoke ovens, designing houses, teaching English, and giving cooking lessons and demonstrations. And of course, there was the added attraction of exile to a country where he spoke the language and was not far from family in California.

Diana Anhalt interviewed sixty American families who sought refuge in Mexico in the late 1940s and throughout the 1950s. She found most were leftist artists and intellectuals, some of whom were members of the US Communist Party; others were fleeing criminal charges or vindictive spouses. They were attracted to Mexico because of the low cost of living, the country's reputation for harboring political refugees, and the fact that passport requirements were waived for American citizens. Although many settled in Mexico City, others went to rural areas in the provinces where the cost of living was lower, and where they felt better hidden from the FBI, which surveilled suspected US citizens in Mexico and passed on reports to the CIA. In some cases, Americans residing in Mexico were served subpoenas to appear before the Senate's McCarran Committee. In other instances, pressure from the US government on Mexico led to "unofficial extraditions" of US Communist Party members back to the US during the 1950s. Those extraditions convinced many American expats to apply for Mexican residency, as Ferko did in 1959.

For a few years, Ferko taught English at the high school in Valle de Bravo. As was true in each of his other endeavors, his students loved him. One of them was Fernando Hernández Rebollar, a Mexican high school student, whom Ferko helped to spend six months in the US on an exchange program. Hernández considered Ferko a kind of godfather. As an adult, Fernando worked on a book titled *Francis Kalnay: A Hungarian American Who Left His Imprint on Valle and Other Places*, which he presented at a festival in Valle de Bravo in November 2017. I was invited as a guest of honor but had to cancel because of the Mexico City earthquake of that year. After the seminar, Fernando served slices of sweet pumpernickel made from Ferko's recipe published in the Safford book. Sadly, despite repeated attempts, I have been unable to stay in touch with Fernando or to read his thesis about Ferko. In his original email to me, Fernando wrote:

> *Allow me to introduce myself: my name is Fernando Hernández, I am a historian, born and raised in Valle de Bravo, Mexico (a beautiful small town near Mexico City, where your grandfather lived and developed some of his creative "passions" for about eighteen years). It happens that your grandfather was kind of a godfather to me—in the best sense—when I was a teenager: indeed, I was his (English) teaching "assistant" during high school, 1957–1959, and he arranged for me to go to the United States in 1960 (where I spent six months with wonderful people and greatly improved my English skills). I have therefore many reasons to be grateful to him and therefore embarked on a project related to Francis as a kind of tribute to him.[23]*

What do we know of Ferko's love life in Mexico? Rather than cultivating new girlfriends in Mexico, Ferko maintained a relationship with his ex-wife Gloria, who would visit him during vacations from the US high school where she was a vice principal. Their son, Peter, spent several summers there as well. In 1965, Ferko and Gloria remarried, but they divorced a second time in 1973, the year before he left Mexico and returned to California.

In all Ferko spent two decades in Mexico. During that time, he reinvented himself and embarked upon several new careers with enormous success—as a gourmand whose cooking and hospitality earned him considerable recognition, as an award-winning children's book author, and as an architect who changed the face of a Mexican town. He had three workers in Mexico—Inez, Rafael, and Inez's daughter. Inez and her daughter kept the house and did the shopping and cooking when Ferko did not. Rafael did maintenance and worked in the garden. Ferko taught Inez cooking and Rafael beekeeping, pruning, and much else. When he decided to return to the US, he was concerned about their welfare and left them some funds.

## Golden Years as a Gourmand

In Mexico, Ferko continued and expanded his interests in cooking and entertaining. His home became a B&B for visiting Americans and the site of exquisite meals. One such visitor was Virginia Safford, the *Minneapolis Star Tribune* food columnist. Safford was so impressed with Ferko's cooking that she included a description in a book she wrote about the best meals she had ever eaten. The meal sounds fabulous—with homegrown roasted coffee beans, home-cured meats, local honey, fresh greens, wild berries from the garden, and fresh baked bread. Perhaps it was this experience that led Safford to retire in Mexico the following year. She was not the first American woman to be charmed by Ferko.

**Chapter from *Friends and Their Food* by Virginia Safford, Dillon Press, New York, 1969:**

**Menu**

"Antipasto Kalnay"
Smoked turkey cured with honey from his own hives
Radishes
Oven-baked rye bread made with stone-ground flour and baked in an
    oven designed by Kalnay
Hungarian cabbage rolls
Mexican squash soup
Garden-fresh salad greens
Hungarian rum cake with wild strawberry jam and coffee

Most all of us have come across an unforgettable character. It can be a man or woman, rich or poor, but one who, for a variety of reasons, stands out in our memory. It was in a little, out-of-the-way Mexican village called Valle de Bravo, 45 miles from Toluca on a twisting mountain high-way that I first met Francisco Kalnay. Because of a letter of introduction I was invited to stay in his house for a few days. In fact he occasionally takes paying guests. I found the village of Valle de Bravo fast becoming a new resort with a delightful hotel called El Refugio, with well-to-do Mexicans seeking a quiet weekend retreat.

The 1968 Olympics put Valle de Bravo in the news with the featuring here of the equestrian events. In a way it is something of a miracle that Kalnay ever found this village, but it is also something of a miracle for the village to have found him.

Before coming to Mexico Kalnay had been an actor, author, journal-ist, and farmer, as well as a beekeeper and coffee grower. He could also be called a miller as he grinds all the flour that goes into the making of the various delicious breads he serves to his guests.

His book for children, *Chucaro: Wild Pony of the Pampas*, won first prize among 400 entries in the annual New York Herald contest for children's books some years ago. After World War II he settled on a California grape vineyard. He decided after five years it was too much for him and began to look elsewhere. "The place I was determined to find," he told me as we sat lingering over supper in his kitchen, "had to have five things: first, a perfect climate year-round, lush tropical vegetation, an abundance of water, the right altitude and a picturesque background." Somehow he found Valle de Bravo, a town that appeared to have every-thing he wanted.

The village is small, but he found an old building with an abandoned orchard in which he planted 60 coffee trees that seemed to be compat-ible with climate and altitude. Soon he found he was growing excellent oranges, avocados, chirimoyas, and other strange, exotic fruits.

Once he had fixed up the old house Francisco never stopped building. When I was there it had become a complex of five buildings. Incidentally, he knows so much about construction that he's regarded as the"chimney doctor" around the village. One day when there was a swarm of bees around his place he established a hive that for years has served him well with honey.

"How do you get all the things done that you must do in one day?" I asked him, aware of the fact he also teaches a daily class in English to 100 high school students and adults in the little town. "My day always be-gins no later than 6:00 AM," he told me, "and never do I think of going to bed before midnight." He has three trained staff to help around the house and garden. A young Mexican boy was doing most of the baking when I was there. I will never forget the tantalizing aroma of freshly baked bread when I first entered his kitchen.

One of the things that makes "Francisco" such a food personality is his accomplishment in smoking meats. He showed me an underground smokehouse and explained that into it, from time to time, go luscious bits of sausage, hams, bacon, and nice, fat geese and turkeys. He uses a honey cure from honey that his bees produced, and when he speaks of his coffee it is with warm affection. "The coffee tree is kind to everyone," he says. "It is beautiful and it is healthy, and never does it rest—the picking goes on everyday, and from December to April the branches shoot forth new blossoms."

I saw a load of various beans drying in the sun on his terrace, and the smell of the freshly brewed coffee was almost as tantalizing as the bread. Everything we ate at the simple wooden table in his little kitchen, with the cooking going on in full view, was delicious. We started out with what might be called country antipasto. In the middle of a table were crisp radishes and small green onions garnishing a platter of sliced, smoked turkey breast to be eaten on buttered rye bread. Then came the soup. Mexican soups are wonderful, though one seldom knows what goes into them. But the main course I want to tell you about are the authentic Hungarian stuffed cabbage rolls.

One could simulate the rum cake he served me by dousing slices of frozen pound cake with rum and then spreading them with jam from wild strawberries and a dab of whipped cream. But first you would need to find wild berries. Unquestionably, baking bread is Francisco's specialty. Because he grinds his own flour, one can be sure that nature's vitamins have not been removed. His pumpernickel is a marvel of good eating.

*Ferko's bread oven. (From the author's personal collection)*

## Author

While in Mexico, Ferko wrote several articles on cooking for the American magazine *House Beautiful*, including "Give Yourselves the New Thrill of Smoke Cookery" (1953), "Enter the Wonderful World of Marinades" (1959), and "What! Flowers in Cooking?" (1960).

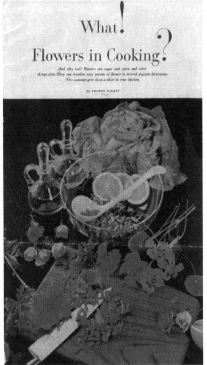

*Francis Kalnay. "What! Flowers in Cooking?"*
House Beautiful Magazine, *April 1960,*
*pp. 161–94. Fair use.*

And of course, it was in Mexico that Ferko wrote his award-winning book, *Chucaro: Wild Pony of the Pampa,* with illustrations by his friend and fellow New York artists' camp owner Julian DeMiskey. In 1958 Harcourt, World & Brace published this coming-of-age story of a boy on the Pampas in Argentina. The following year it was selected as a Newbery Honor book and *The New York Herald Tribune*'s Spring Festival Award. It is a story about Argentinian cowboys, or gauchos, that can also be read as a metaphor for socialist class struggles and the exploitation of the working class by the rich and powerful. The protagonist is a twelve-year-old boy, Pedrito, whose father is an aging drunkard. Pedrito becomes the protégé of Juan, a gaucho who teaches him to tame a beautiful wild pony. When the spoiled son of the wealthy ranch owner wants the pony for himself, Pedrito and Juan challenge the boy to succeed at catching Chucaro or else leave the pony with Pedrito. The ranch owner's son fails

Chucaro *book cover photo by*
*author. Fair use.*

and Juan is fired, but in the end, he and Pedrito leave the ranch and ride off to another part of Argentina.

Ironically, I found the original copy-edited manuscript of *Chucaro* and correspondence with his editor at Harcourt, Brace & World when I was teaching at the University of Minnesota, a place I doubt Ferko ever visited. The documents are held by the Kerlan Collection of children's literature at the U of M Libraries.

The Richest Boy in the World.
*Photo of book cover by author.*
*Fair use.*

Also in 1959, Ferko published *The Richest Boy in the World*—a book described in Chapter 1 of this book relating to his childhood years in a boarding school in Croatia.

Before the publication of *Chucaro*, Ferko also wrote a little-known children's play, *The Song of the Wooden Doll*, which was copyrighted in 1952. No copy of this play remains. Another missing publication is a book of poems called *I Am the Cat*, published with Curtis E. Avery and Harry Behn.[24] His next children's book, *It Happened in Chichipica*, was published in 1971, over a decade after *Chucaro*. Chichipica is the name of a small Mexican village where the young protagonist, Chucho, lives with his uncle and works in a local bakery. Chucho's chances for a scholarship are almost lost when he is falsely accused of theft and threatened with reform school.

It Happened in Chichipica.
*Photo of book cover by author.*
*Fair use.*

Ferko imbued everything he did with a storyteller's sensibility. In his later years, he identified with being a writer, although his last children's book was published in 1971, twelve years after *The Richest Boy in the World*. Perhaps he berated himself for filling his life with other projects and procrastinating. Writing his last book, in particular, was a long and painful process. He may also have suffered from the pressure of living up to his success with *Chucaro*. He referred to himself as "a writer who did not write."

I asked Wendy to re-read Ferko's books and analyze them from her perspectives as both a granddaughter who was close to him and as a renowned political scientist. She responded with the following letter.

July 1, 2022

Dear Kathy,

I have just finished re-reading Ferko's three English-language books for children, *Chucaro, The Richest Boy in the World*, and *It Happened in Chichipica*. We had thought that I might be able to draw out the moral-political parables of each, and perhaps connect these to something of Ferko's life—his beginnings as a romantic poet and member of the Hungarian Navy in World War I, his immigration to America and early work as a journalist, actor, and small farmer, his service as an intelligence officer in World War II, his wanderings and habitats in Argentina, New York, California, Europe, and Mexico, and his life-long pacifism after the wars.

I couldn't quite do the assignment, however, because I found so much more in these books. Above all, re-reading them brought back to life Ferko's extraordinary imagination, his radical sensibilities, his worldview. So this letter to you is mostly about that.

I did find traces of Ferko's life in the books. They are dotted with his own experiences as a nearly starving student in a Hungarian boys school, as a poet whose mind wandered to the play of language while engaged in dull tasks like supervising those boys, as an improvisational English teacher in a Mexican village, as an expert handler of horses and appreciator of all animals, as a cook and gourmand. They feature his knowledge of farming, his love of languages and language play, his appreciation of village life in Mexico and shepherd life in Argentina, his delight in whimsy and mischief, and more.

It is also the case that each book does carry a moral lesson—*Chucaro* about the wrongful entitlements of power, *The Richest Boy in the World* about the soul-corrupting effects of riches, especially ill-gotten wealth, and *Chichipica* about the senselessness of old enmities among neighbors. However, the politics in these books go beyond parables or morality tales. In all three, there is a sustained and often subtle critique of hierarchy, especially class, and a profound respect for the knowledge, hearts, and lives of those at the lower end of hierarchies. Peasants, gauchos, villagers, artisans, children, but also animals and even landscapes—each has integrity, dignity, and stores of deep and important knowledge. Ferko imbues them all with more capacity to sustain life, express love and joy, and knit together communities than those at the top—directors, politicians, inspectors, visiting royalty. Those at the bottom are always at risk of violation and abuse by exploiters and rulers, or by those who do not really know the ways of the world and simply dominate it or take what they want from it. But even in this, the stories feature dignity as well as power drawn from living closer to the bone and living well. Officialdom is mocked along with power, whether through a curtain rod of sausages falling on a cruel school director's head while he surveyed the starving boys below or through the ostentatious failure of a rich and spoiled child to claim a beautiful pony belonging to a poor gaucho's son, or through mockery of officious language and procedures.

These political themes run through every story. Yet they are not developed crudely or didactically. Rather they emerge almost organically from the stories, which are told from the perspective of the earth-bound and earthly, whether animals or humans, rivers or storms.

Yet even this appreciation of the lowly and connected does not exhaust the unique voice and worldview contained in these books. Above all, what re-rereading them brought back to me was Ferko's extraordinary imagination and unconventionally radical sensibilities. He is an exceptional writer, to be sure, especially for someone writing in a second language. But above all, he was an author who saw the very nature of the physical, sensible, and human world differently from most, and struggled to convey that vision through his writing.

What is that vision? All three books feature not merely the proximity but the intermingling of human and animal natures and habits. Ferko dedicates paragraphs to the subjective pleasures of a pony being scratched, and chapters to the stubborn determination of a burro who repeatedly leaves his own yard for that of a despised neighbor, indifferent to cajoling and beatings alike. He populates his stories with humans eating and sleeping in animal ways and with animals who are emotional, canny, and mischievous. He does not erase the distinction between humans and animals; indeed, expert human handlers of animals are minor heroes in the books, and he also regards humans as uniquely prone to false airs, strange conceits, officialdom, and abuses of power. Still, Ferko sees the animal in the human and he sees mind and spirit—not merely instinct—in the animal. He also reveals the comedy and sometimes the tragedy of humans trying to escape their animality, ignore the spirit of non-humans, or treat animals like machines or slaves.

Perhaps more important than these crossings and intimacies between animals and humans, Ferko animates everything in his writing: trees, insects, food, landscapes, wind, forests, panchos, lassos, tortillas, bandanas, lakes, facial hair. Everything has a life force, a personality, along with requirements for well-being. It would be a mistake to call this anthropomorphism, because it is not that Ferko humanizes everything. Rather, he decenters human agency as he proliferates agency everywhere else in the universe. Today this viewpoint and philosophy is named "vitalism"—a school of philosophy that regards the so-called material world as alive and interdependent rather than inert and isomorphic. It is a view that has become hugely important to ecological thinking and eco-critiques of instrumentalist and anthropocentric relations to the "environment." Vitalism recognizes aliveness itself as full of agency and vulnerability, as dependent and interdependent, and above all as being conditioned.

Ferko's vitalist imaginary is fecund and extraordinary, and it is what makes his descriptive passages so riveting. Nothing is ever merely there; everything is alive, everything has personality and dynamism. Thus, accounts of a cold wind whipping around a building, of a peasant woman's face, of the sharpening of a machete, or of a donkey standing in a garden, are all action scenes. Here, for example is his account of The Lake in the opening pages of *Chichipica*:

> At night that nameless lake was hard at work, washing the foot of the mountain. But before dawn the wind vanished without a sound, and one by one the weary waves stretched flat until the whole lake fell asleep.

Here is his description of a baker who hired the story's young protagonist:

> The baker himself, Chucho discovered, was like his bolillos: coarse and crisp outside, but inside his heart he was nice and soft.

And the depiction of the gaucho in *Chucaro*:

> One thing he missed pitifully—a beard. The little black mustache, which curved and pointed toward his nostrils, seemed so insignificant and lonely. Only when he smiled, the little mustache began to feel fine, jumping up and down on his wide, red lips. So whenever you saw the mustache jump, you could rest assured that all of them were in a high mood—Juan, the mustache, and Pedrito.

The vitalism in Ferko's writing also relates to his critiques of power. It is almost always those at the top of human hierarchies who fail to understand the complex composition, interdependencies, and animation of the world, the sustenance provided by the earth, the ways of fauna and flora, of village life, or of children. Those at the bottom are more likely to grasp and honor these things. It is not that former is civilized and estranged from "nature" while the latter is brutish and close to nature. Rather, his writing implies that the more distant one is from how life is supported and made, the less likely one is to have regard for or even notice those practices.

A passage from *Chichipica* captures this. A townsperson interrogates Pepe about why he is trying to revive a ranchito that his parents had owned but which has been ruined from over-use by tenants:

> "Don't be a fool, Pepe, throwing good money after bad! Your land is worth nothing. Sell it!"

> "Strange. You want me to sell something that is worthless? Wouldn't that be dishonest? Besides, who the devil would buy it? In any case, the earth is no longer mine."

> "How come? Didn't you get the land from your parents? Don't you have the deed?"

> "What is there in a deed? A sheet of old paper with small words planted in long rows. Can you harvest it? Can you eat it?"

> "Are you joking? The deed is a precious document to prove that that piece of earth belongs to you."

> "Don't fool yourself, amigo, The earth belongs to youngsters who take our place when we are gone. You and I are only caretakers—caretakers who really don't care. You sound exactly like so many others I have known . . . ready to murder for a chunk of land, and once they have it, they waste or abandon it!"

One might expect such a passage in a contemporary children's story but it is astonishing to find it in one penned in the 1960s. Ferko's appreciation of what we now call sustainability and ecological interdependence is everywhere in his work. He even understood composting (and used the word!) as a means of regenerating soil depleted by poor farming techniques.

Ferko's mobilization of every sense—smell, taste, touch, sight, and sound—also contributes to the imaginative and vitalist way he paints the world. He dwells on how fresh green grass tastes to a burro, how the sun feels on a dog snoozing by its master's feet, how morning air on the pampas opens one's lungs and lifts ones spirit, how insects on the ground move, how a horse experiences a brushing. Detail in Ferko's book is almost always bound to the senses and with this too, he disrupts an instrumental, exploitative, or alienated relation to the earth and to others with his radical vision of our interconnected and material nature.

Ferko's writing also affirms the beauty and sustenance of human work. Indeed, he makes all good work into fulfilling and artistic craft, what today we might call "artisanal," for him was simply what intelligent provision for needs should be. From tortilla-making to weaving a poncho or saddling a horse, sustaining life is depicted as intelligent artistry, not merely toil.

Pleasure, work, and creation of a livable habitat are intermingled and do not compete with one another. Toward the end of *Chucaro*, he describes the gaucho and his charge, Pedrito, leaving their village for a new home:

> Juan rode in front, and Pedrito followed close behind on Chucaro [the pony]. Bundles and bags hung from their saddles on either side. They had so little and still so much—clothes, a guitar, a few keepsakes, and some tools. . . . Mrs. Pizetti had insisted on sending some roast chicken and bread. . . .

Music, tools, food, and a few objects carrying memories of loved ones and places—these are what Ferko believed sustained life. Beyond sustenance, he also cherished imagination, stories, art, kindness, and alertness to the humor and whimsy of a universe in which everything is alive and has personality. Together these things animated Ferko's writing and were also what he foregrounded in it. That he had a remarkable way with words was a gift that I remembered. That he used this gift to draw the world as he thought it should be is what took me by surprise as I re-read his children's stories this past week.

## Architect

Although he never studied architecture or engineering, the time spent with his architect brothers in Argentina served Ferko well. When he first moved to Valle de Bravo, he bought and renovated a guest house named "Quinta Llama," adding terraces and planting fruit trees, flowers, shrubs, and huge pots of geraniums.

Ferko earned additional money from teaching high school English, taking in paying guests, and other activities. He invested it in designing and building homes—first one, then another and another under the auspices of a company he called "Mi Ranchito." In all, he designed twenty-five charming homes in Valle that inaugurated residential tourism there during the 1950s and 1960s and helped convert a sleepy village into a destination for foreign tourists and wealthy Mexicans.

The real estate developer Pablo Riveroll visited Valle de Bravo during summers in his youth. In 2007, he published an article in the Mexican journal *Revista de Arte y Cultura* in which he described Ferko's long-standing influence on Valle de Bravo and its transformation into a

"Pueblo Mágico" known for Kalnay's European-influenced architectural style—chalets with terraces, traditional kitchens, and large stone ovens. All the houses had stunning views and were situated in old sections of town over narrow, pedestrian streets.

*Interior of one of the homes designed by Ferko in Valle de Bravo listed in Spanish as "The Most Beautiful House in Valle."*

*Exterior of one of the homes designed by Ferko in Valle de Bravo.*
*(From the author's personal collection)*

Ferko's houses had a popular, distinctive style that other architects began to copy. Riveroll suggests his displacement by these competitors influenced my grandfather's decision to move back to the US in 1974.

# V

# IMPACT

### RETURN TO THE US AND FINAL YEARS

Because he was isolated in Valle de Bravo, it took Ferko a long time to realize the extent to which the political anti-communist climate in the US had thawed. Finally, after twenty-one years of exile, he returned. In 1974, at age seventy-five, he moved to Carmel, California, where he lived in an apartment complex called Hacienda Carmel. While there, he scouted land to build another house and found what he wanted on a cliff overlooking the Carmel Valley and the Pacific.

What we will never know is how Ferko, who had been away from the US for a quarter century and did not drive, faced the daunting task of purchasing land, getting permits, hiring sub-contractors, and building a house exactly to his specifications on a hilltop perch, not to mention acquiring furniture and other household accoutrements. During construction, did someone pick him up every morning and drive him to the site and to tile stores, lumber yards, and fixture stores? Wendy recalls a pair of brothers who were devoted to Ferko and may have served as day laborers who helped him in Carmel. In addition, as Wendy's father used to say, "Ferko was a world-class hitchhiker," meaning that he expected everyone to like him and help him, and they always did. He was also happy to offer a small bribe, even when it wasn't appropriate.

Ferko had always been drawn to places of extraordinary beauty—the rolling hills of his farm property in Putnam County, the pine-covered ridges surrounding the lake in Valle de Bravo, and the incomparable ocean views from his house in Carmel. People told Ferko it would be impossible to build on the cliff because the driveway was almost vertical. However, he constructed a small house there and walked up and down every day to get his newspapers and mail. Like his homes in Valle de Bravo, the Carmel house had a charming Mediterranean patio filled with potted plants and a smokehouse where he prepared fish and meats that others brought to him from the sea or nearby forests. I visited him there once with my husband, and we spent a leisurely afternoon enjoying the view and a wonderful home-cooked Hungarian lunch.

Ferko was later convinced by his doctor to sell the house because heart problems made the long, vertical walk up the hill ill advised. However, he missed the place so much that he ignored the doctor's orders and rented it back not long after moving out.

In Carmel Ferko built and sold smokehouses and outdoor ovens, and gave cooking classes as he had done in Valle de Bravo. Below is a photograph of a bread plate that he invented and marketed through the "Grateful Bread Company," a pun on the "Grateful Dead" rock band that was still popular in that era.

As always, Ferko loved to cook and entertain, and one can imagine how enchanted neighbors and visitors were with his delectable

*Greatful Bread Pan. (From the author's personal collection)*

meals—particularly the mature ladies who flocked to his cooking classes. Ivor Westley was a B&B guest in Mexico who later visited Ferko in Carmel. He remembers that "The Hungarian" dedicated his final years to giving cooking classes to a group of older women who were captivated by the charms of this European who was an insatiable traveler and a storyteller with vivid memories of many foreign lands.[1] However, Ferko's own romantic interests tended toward much younger women. In his mid-seventies, he lived with a girlfriend about half his age.

As mentioned earlier, in California, Ferko was closely involved with the local Gurdjieff Society. Members of the group doted on him and helped with errands and shopping since he had given up driving many years earlier before the war. Most of the Gurdjieff crowd worshipped him because he was older, and he had known some prominent figures in the movement. Wendy recalls that family members viewed the society as a cult, but Ferko resisted this and tried to talk to them about Gurdjieff's philosophy:

> He sometimes brought members around when I visited or when he visited my mother in Modesto. They were very Moony-like. Lots of smiling white women in their twenties and young couples. When he died, some showed up at the small memorial service we had for him. Some family members were worried about them taking Ferko's money and property, and were relieved to discover they weren't mentioned in his will.

At the end of his life, Ferko was forced to leave his mountaintop chalet and move to a senior apartment complex adjacent to a shopping center in Carmel Valley. He lived there for a couple of years and had continued support from members of his Gurdjieff community. But, as he aged, his faculties declined—he would leave pots burning on the stove and routinely lose things. Although he received food from "Meals on Wheels," when Wendy visited from Santa Cruz she found almost a dozen unopened meals stacked in a corner of the kitchen. That led her to hire assistants for him, although none lasted long. One attendant even stole an old car Ferko had bought for them to run errands and ended up in jail. When it was time for Ferko to move to an assisted living facility, he chose

*Ferko in his eighties. (From the personal collection)*

one in Santa Cruz close to Wendy. It was a place near the wharf called "Sunshine Villa" with a third-floor room that had a beautiful ocean view. However, the staff soon insisted he move down to the first floor, near the dining room, because his memory was fading rapidly and he could not always remember how to get back up to his room. Sunshine Villa had no memory care unit then, but fortunately, the staff were charmed by Ferko and protected him from being evicted. Occasionally, Gurdjieff community members visited him at the facility, but this became less frequent over time, as he had difficulty recognizing them.

Like many elderly individuals with dementia, Ferko became a bit paranoid at the end. Occasionally he would say people stole from him or accused him of wrongdoing. Wendy says that he expressed regret over his estrangement from his brothers, and imagined that his brothers had visited him in Santa Cruz, although Jorge had died in 1957 and Andrés in 1982. Still, Ferko had lucid moments when he could hold up his end of a simple conversation. He retained his charm and warmth and won over almost everyone he dealt with. Wendy remembers picking him up from assisted living and bringing him to her house for dinner and hearing the same bad puns and jokes he had told his whole life. "You only live twice—now and then," he would say with such mirth that it made her laugh every time.

Ferko made Wendy promise never to take him to a hospital because he was sure he would die there. She was forced to break the promise only once when he got pneumonia, and she spent several nights sleeping in his hospital room until he was discharged. Then, one morning, Ferko dressed with the help of an assistant and said he was feeling tired and wanted to rest on his couch for a few minutes before going to breakfast. When the attendant checked on him later in the day, he was still sitting on the couch with his beret on, head tipped back, not breathing.

In a sad stroke of irony, Ferko's death on December 2, 1992, occurred precisely on the forty-eighth anniversary of his sister's murder at the Arrow Cross headquarters in Budapest.

### HISTORICAL LEGACY: WHO WAS FRANCIS KALNAY: CONFLICTING VIEWS

Now that I have completed several years of research, I return to the initial questions that motivated my quest: How did Ferko achieve his rapid ascension within the OSS, why had he abruptly resigned and then fled to Mexico, and how did this impact his life and our family?

Suppose you were tasked with identifying crucial information that could be used to help the Allies plan a strategy for winning the war in Europe. Where might you begin in an era with no internet or high-speed communications beyond operator-to-operator radio signals?

\* \* \*

It is December 1941. Germany and the Axis Powers have declared war on the United States, and you are recruited to gather information that will assist the Allies in planning combat in Fascist-controlled Europe. There is no internet to search for information about opposition groups that might be infiltrated; no database of war materiel or blueprints of the location of industries being used for the manufacture of weapons; no instantaneous reports about the status of railway and shipping lines for the transport of troops. What would you do? Where would you begin?

Identification of foreign-born informants with information on their home countries would be a logical start—in other words, a Survey of Foreign Experts.

Review of OSS records helped me gain a clear picture of Ferko's ascension. His knowledge of languages, extensive contacts in the immigrant community, and keen interest in "Americanization" made him an ideal candidate to help the government identify potential informants knowledgeable about life within Nazi-occupied Europe. Under his direction, the survey expanded into a comprehensive index of new immigrants in the US and their potential as sources. He supervised a cadre of interviewers who contacted these individuals and maintained files on their backgrounds. As the survey database grew, so too did Ferko's success in recruiting informants and potential spies. Eventually the survey expanded to other continents and provided information on such diverse topics as communication systems in Czechoslovakia; roads in Fukien, China; anti-Nazi personalities in Denmark; and the production of explosives and chemicals within enemy-occupied Europe.

The offices Ferko created within the OSS had a direct role in each of two essential components of effective espionage: to identify the enemy's assets and structure of their organization, and to controvert the enemy's mission either directly or by recruiting their agents to your cause. For the Survey of Foreign Experts, potential sources were identified from passenger lists of individuals arriving in New York from Axis-occupied countries. Survey personnel vetted these lists, interviewed targeted passengers, and then recruited those deemed likely to have knowledge about manufacturing, mining, transportation, infrastructure, and political organizations and opposition groups in each of these countries. By 1943, the survey had indexed thousands of individuals residing in the United States, recent arrivals from neutral or enemy-occupied countries. Some were native-born Americans, others were refugees from war-torn Europe. Many had strategic knowledge of conditions and personalities, business contacts, relatives, or friends in enemy-occupied countries. The result of the work was a database that catalogued the human and tangible assets of the Fascist governments in Europe and beyond.

Ferko served as an invisible linchpin in the war in Europe. As Ellery Huntington wrote in a recommendation for his commission as a major in May 1943, "Mr. K is doing currently one of the most intelligent organizational jobs in connection with his mission which I have ever seen done in the annals of OSS."

Three weeks after VE Day, General Dwight D. Eisenhower, Supreme Commander of the Allied Expeditionary Force, remarked:

> *In no previous war, and in no other theater during this war,*
> *have Resistance forces been so closely harnessed to the main*
> *military effort. . . . I consider that the disruption of enemy rail*
> *communications, the harassing of German road moves and the*
> *continual and increasing strain placed on the German war economy*
> *and internal security services throughout occupied Europe by the*
> *organized forces of Resistance, played a very considerable part in our*
> *complete and final victory.*

What Eisenhower described was, of course, the heart of Ferko's work. When he left Strategic Intelligence and moved to Strategic Operations to head the eponymous KAY Project, he oversaw the recruitment of individuals who became counteragents working behind enemy lines. The extensive record system he had helped to assemble became the basis for preparing X-2 agents for their own counter-espionage work. As head of the X-2 Balkans substation, he helped gather top-secret intelligence from intercepted Axis radio transmissions that were decrypted, provided to British and American commanders, and used by X-2 agents to identify and sabotage enemy military units, transportation, and supply systems. During the two years of existence of the X-2 division of the OSS, it gathered data that no other agency did, employed methods unlike any other, and operated where no others could. It is not an exaggeration to say that without this work the war might have been lost.

It is surprising to me that "Francis Kalnay" remains unnamed in so many histories of the OSS and the Allied presence in central Europe and the Balkans during WWII. This is the result of an extraordinarily high level of secrecy regarding X-2 that prevails to this day. John Chambers, a professor of history who was commissioned to write a history of OSS training procedures during WWII, notes that little is known about the X-2 branch because of this policy.[2] Fortunately, however, although much of Ferko's work is still shrouded in "top-secret" designations and destroyed documents, there are several declassified reports and memos that provide evidence of some of his remarkable contributions to the war effort. We know, for example, that he personally recruited, trained, and supervised resistance fighters who operated in the heart of Axis territory and carried out sabotage and propaganda efforts in Yugoslavia, Serbia, Northern Italy, Bulgaria, and Hungary. Norman Holmes Pearson, head of European X-2 operations, credited Ferko with helping infiltrate the German Intelligence Service and neutralize many enemy espionage activities. In his nomination of Ferko for a Certificate of Merit, he wrote, "On numerous occasions, Mr. Kalnay's careful piecing together of fragmentary evidence revealed facts about Abwehr and [Reich security] functioning in central and western Europe, which the activities of agents and controlled enemy agents in those regions had failed to uncover." That is a remarkable statement—that my grandfather's meticulous work revealed facts about Nazi work that the activities of other agents had not.

Of all the countries on the European continent from which the OSS mounted secret operations against the Germans, none was more important than Italy, particularly after Mussolini's surrender to the Allies on September 8, 1943. After that, southern Italy became a strategic location for targeting Germans and forcing them back up the Italian peninsula. By extension, the Balkans were vital to both the Allies and the Axis powers because of their proximity to Italy across the Adriatic. After the fall of Mussolini and Hitler's defeats on the Soviet front, Churchill and Roosevelt saw an opportunity to attract Bulgaria, Romania, and Hungary away from Nazi control and to use the Balkans as a launching ground for incursions into Germany. OSS Director Donovan had additional reasons for interest in the Balkans. He was strongly anti-Soviet and feared that Soviet armies might advance through southeastern Europe without Allied deterrence. Furthermore, the partisan groups already waging guerrilla war against the Germans made the region an excellent site for OSS spies and saboteurs—actions that could be undertaken without escalating turf wars with the British SOE.

In his declassified personnel records is a sheet on which Ferko summarized his work in Italy: While armies fought the most visible battles of the war, Ferko was instrumental in supporting the covert war behind enemy lines, recruiting and training individuals who decoded Nazi communications, carried out acts of sabotage, and organized resistance fighters. His work spanned three of the major OSS departments created by Director Donovan: X-2 Counter-espionage, Secret Intelligence, and Special Operations for which he headed the eponymous KAY Project to recruit counteragents behind enemy lines.[3]

Given his remarkable accomplishments, why does Ferko not figure more prominently in the literature on the OSS and World War II? Today, he is far better known for his children's books than for his service to the United States. Perhaps it is due to the covert and top secret nature of his work. The release of reams of formerly top-secret documents has shed light on some mysteries surrounding his activities in the OSS, but many questions remain. As O'Donnell wrote in his book about OSS spies:

*While the most visible part of World War II was fought by armies, navies, and the air forces, a largely invisible and covert war was also raging around the globe. Saboteurs were demolishing railroad tunnels; spies were stealing secrets and "operatives"—uniform soldiers trying to fight behind enemy lines—or parachuting into occupied countries to organize and lead resistance fighters.[4]*

An important, unanswered question is why Ferko abruptly resigned from the federal government at the end of the war and then, eight years later, abandoned family and friends to move to Mexico for twenty years. There are two possible answers to this question, and a combination of them seems likely. First, the beginning of the McCarthy era terrified Ferko and other Americans who had worked with anti-Fascist Yugoslavs. Although the Soviet Union was an Allied power in WWII, after the war fear of communism cast suspicion on individuals like Ferko, who had worked closely with the Tito Partisans. The persecution of several of his friends and colleagues led him to believe that he too might be subject to interrogation or worse. The key to Ferko's primary motive for fleeing to Mexico may have been his realization that Germany's surrender in May 1945 would not mean a cessation of warfare. He was deeply distressed to find that the Allies were merely changing their focus from fighting the Nazis to planning responses to threats from the Soviet Union. If this was, indeed, Ferko's final epiphany, it was motivated by his deep abhorrence of war and his leftist sympathies.

In addition to political motives, there was the matter of Ferko's questionable financial decisions that may have put him under scrutiny in the OSS. Moving to Mexico held the allure of distancing him from those problems and the demands of his ex-wives and children.

## A FAMILY DIVIDE

It is ironic that I should be the one to chronicle my grandfather's life, because, unlike my West Coast cousins, I barely knew Ferko, and because I was influenced by my mother, Elizabeth, who never fully forgave her father for abandoning the family and leaving them in perilous situations. Unfortunately, my grandparents' divorce led to competing "camps" within the family.

Ferko and Elsie's divorce was bitter, and Peti and her children were drawn closer to Ferko, while my mother's sympathies were with Elsie, a resilient but emotionally fragile woman who overcame abandonment, poverty, and limited formal schooling out of sheer determination and love for her daughters. On the other hand, to Ferko—and to some extent to Peti and her children—Elsie was seen as an angry and controlling ex-wife, while Ferko was viewed as a loving and creative soul.

The families were divided by more than geography and parental allegiance. Peti was known as the romantic daughter, and Elizabeth as the practical one—roles that they embraced. When they lived on the farm with Dan Steinbeck, Peti felt unfairly criticized for being a free spirit while my mother was praised for her strong work ethic. On the farm there was no time for writing, creativity, or the arts, all of which appealed to Peti. While my mother studied home economics and prepared to be a teacher, Peti pursued a master's degree in psychology at Berkeley. The divisions persisted.

After her divorce from Ferko in 1934, Elsie remained on the dairy farm in Brewster with Dan while the girls went to college at Cornell. After they graduated, the East Coast-West Coast division began. Elizabeth remained in New York, while Peti settled in California where Ferko lived before and after his sojourn to Mexico. In his later years in Carmel, Peti's daughter, Wendy, oversaw his care and helped him move to assisted living. Peter, Ferko's son from his second marriage, lived in Davis, and later in Washington state, and saw his father sporadically.

Peti and her family had a very close and warm relationship with Ferko, although he often frustrated them by harboring secrets about our Jewish ancestry, his financial affairs, or what properties he owned. Wendy comments that no one really understood Ferko's finances. Her father used to say that in the forty years he had known him, Ferko had no visible means of income. He did make some money in real estate, including in Valle de Bravo, where he bought land and built and sold several houses to other expats. Before that, he earned something from the various farms he lived on. And there were modest book royalties ranging from less than ten dollars to a few hundred dollars per year in the 1990s, but that doesn't explain how Ferko could live and employ three full-time servants (a cook, a housekeeper, and a gardener/maintenance man) during his twenty years in Mexico and then live comfortably in the Carmel Valley in his later years. He had a knack for building homes on sites with magnificent views that others said were unbuildable. He did this in Valle and again in Carmel. As a result he bought the land cheaply and then reaped a good sum when he eventually sold the properties. He also had Social Security and a modest pension.

Ferko attempted to keep his love affairs secret. When he was in his eighties, he tried unsuccessfully to keep the family from finding out that he had a girlfriend in her twenties. Peti hated his philandering. She understood the pain of abandonment and was upset watching Ferko desert his second wife, Gloria, more than once.

Peti was also afraid that her father was being taken advantage of. On the other hand, she loved him as a charming, refined man who was very different from the people around her in the culturally flat Central Valley of California. Ferko gave her a window out of that world.

My mother reacted very differently. Her resentment of her father was intense. On the other hand, her childhood experiences shaped her into the capable, resilient woman we all admired. Unlike her sister, my mother had little interest in psychology or introspection. Instead, she maintained a steadfast, pragmatic focus on what steps she could take to "fix" any problem faced by her or her family, and a determination to handle challenges on her own. This was likely the result of having to assume responsibility for an emotionally fragile mother and a younger sister while she herself was very young. Peti loved Elsie too, although there was some friction between them. She knew that her mother had had a hard life, and was saddened by her insecurity and status consciousness.

In addition to their allegiance to different parents, another source of division between Peti and Elizabeth was a perceived class divide. Wendy recalls that her mother felt insecure and inadequate in relation to my parents and felt judged by my father.

> *There was a significant class and culture gap between the two families, not just a continental abyss. My father was an engineer at a chemical plant in the Central Valley; yours was a senior partner at one of New York City's most prestigious accounting firms. We went camping for most summer vacations; your family went to Europe. My father drank cheap bourbon; yours had a wine cellar. My parents were a little bit bohemian (Ferko's influence)—yours decidedly were not.*
>
> *Elsie accentuated this difference and made it matter more. When she visited us, she talked about your family constantly and admiringly. She was not only grateful to your parents for taking care of her, but enormously impressed by and proud of their cultured life. She was similarly proud of you and Tess and talked about you constantly to Greg and me.*

Despite their separation, my mother revealed her deep love for her sister when Peti developed breast cancer. She was distraught at Peti's decision to forego traditional medical treatments and to seek herbal and nutritional treatments in Mexico. That decision was more the result of Peti's commitment to Adele Davis and the natural food movement than to a direct influence of her father. On the other hand, Ferko too disdained formal medical interventions and boasted that he had never been to a hospital.

After Peti's death in 1983 at age fifty-seven, my mother was concerned about Wendy and Greg and wanted to be a maternal figure to them although we were separated by three thousand miles. For her part, at the end of her life, Peti felt deep remorse that she and her sister hadn't been closer and guilty that she hadn't helped my mother tend to Elsie as she aged.

In her pragmatism and rejection of sentimentality, my mother was unlike Ferko, but like him, she was generous, compassionate, frugal, and free of class consciousness. Wendy concurred with this assessment, saying:

> My experience of your mother was that she was utterly unpretentious
> and without class airs, and averse to pretension in that domain. Her
> down-to-earthiness seemed such a deep part of her identity. Mine
> was apart from class preoccupations in a different way. She chose
> her friends according to whether they were genuine, interesting, and
> caring.

Both daughters absorbed from Ferko the idea that class was neither the measure of the person nor should it determine the range of one's pleasures and activities. It's impossible to define Ferko's social class. Wendy commented:

> More than anyone else I've ever known, Ferko was almost outside of
> or apart from class. In the Marxist sense he was also one of the least
> alienated people I have ever met. Work was not annoying to him
> or something to be gotten through so that he could get to pleasure.
> He chose work that brought gratification and strove to make all
> work pleasurable, from baking bread to building houses to cleaning
> a smokehouse. Ferko was cultured but not refined, appreciative of
> books and arts but not deeply educated in any of them, ready to do
> hard work like framing a house or pouring a cement patio but also a
> writer—I don't know anyone else like this anymore. I think it draws
> not only from a different time, but from Europeanness. Cooking,
> designing homes, adding a new nook to an existing balcony, keeping
> bees, making a smokehouse—all of these things gave him great

*satisfaction and he approached them artistically and with gusto. He loved working with his hands and using his muscles, but he also loved using his imagination and playing with language. He did not see one as better than the other.*

Ferko approached work as art, or as self-realization. In his fiction and even food writing, his world was lyrical, imagistic, impressionistic. For him there was no line between work and pleasure, work and stimulation, or work and sociality. His relationship to work contrasted somewhat with his daughters' adherence to the Protestant ethic in which work justifies one's existence, and according to which a person should never sit idle while others worked for you. My mother was literally unable to stay seated while someone else was preparing a meal or cleaning or doing any other chores. Both she and Peti employed occasional cleaning women but worked alongside them. On the other hand, my mother derived great satisfaction from her hours of cooking, gardening, and working alongside my father to clear land or repair the house.

In some ways Ferko was a man of an earlier era. He did not drive a car or understand complex technologies. On the other hand, he was extremely versatile and capable in the everyday world. He taught himself many things—beekeeping, how to smoke meats and care for a vineyard, and how to design and construct beautiful houses with intricate mosaic benches, trellised patios, and dining nooks. He designed a bread plate that yielded crusty bread and then worked with a ceramicist to refine it. What is especially remarkable is that a man who never went beyond high school not only learned new skills but excelled at them. After he taught himself to cook, he became the subject of a chapter on outstanding meals in a book written by a food critic; although he had no formal training in architecture beyond what he learned observing his brothers, he designed buildings that changed the face of a Mexican town; he wrote children's books in his second language and earned one of the highest awards in the profession. And, most remarkably, he was a foreign-born refugee who rose to a high rank in the American spy agency.

Ferko was adamantly secular, a characteristic passed on to his children and grandchildren, none of whom attended religious services or subscribed to a particular religion. Although he was self-taught—or perhaps because of that—he greatly valued higher education and encouraged his children and grandchildren to study. I can see his influence on my mother's adaptability and in her belief in education and self-improvement, as well as her willingness to pick up and change course in response to adversity. She first met my father, Donald Fennelly, through her college roommate at Cornell who asked her friends to write letters to her older brother in the war. When my mother and Donald finally met, she proved her gumption on a day when the sump pump broke in his parents' house. Without a word, she hiked up her skirt and helped bail out the basement.

When the war ended, Donald and Elizabeth married. Unlike her father who could never sustain a long, nurturing relationship, my mother's relationship with my father was one of mutual love and respect in a marriage that lasted for almost fifty years. At the beginning of their life together, she taught home economics and he worked as an accountant. They moved around the country more than a dozen times, as my father accepted positions within his company in different cities—something that would have been untenable for other wives but that my mother took in stride. Early in their life together, when they had very little money, they devised a contingency plan based on Elizabeth's knowledge of cooking, baking, and farm work and Donald's carpentry and construction skills. The plan was to rent themselves out as a couple who could live with a wealthy family, handling cooking, housekeeping, and maintenance. Since she found a job teaching high school and he found work teaching business classes at Columbia University, his alma mater, they never activated the couple-for-hire plan. Later, my father became a partner in the Big Ten accounting firm of Arthur Young (later Ernst & Young), and my parents moved from working to middle- and then upper-middle-class. Together they went to the symphony, opera, and museums in Manhattan, and my mother gave cooking classes out of her beautifully appointed home kitchen. Yet my parents never lost interest in physical labor or doing their own home maintenance. When they lived in a wealthy suburb in New Jersey, my mother would climb a ladder to help my father paint the house—much to the chagrin of the neighbors.

Like her father, my mother loved working the land and raising and preserving fruits and vegetables. After my parents retired, they bought a small farm in western New Jersey that they converted first into a vineyard and later a Christmas tree farm where they grew most of the produce the family consumed. When we visited, I often found my mother driving a tractor, pruning grape vines, tending to her fruit trees, or harvesting herbs and vegetables. Her hardscrabble upbringing and resilience had left their mark.

*Elizabeth Kalnay Fennelly on tractor and painting a house.*

My mother demonstrated her resilience in the way she managed after my father's death in 1994. Theirs was a long and unusually close partnership, and she was extremely distraught during his long illness, barely sleeping as she cared for him and handled their affairs. Yet, after his death, she packed up and moved once again in order to be close to me and my sister in Minneapolis. Once there, she made friends, took a literature class, worked as a docent at the Minneapolis Institute of Art, sat on the board of her cooperative, was active in the League of Women Voters and the Friends of the Minnesota Orchestra, and taught English to immigrants and refugees. And, of course, she continued to prepare delectable meals for her children, grandchildren, and friends. My daughter Leila wrote this tribute to my mother in 2020:

> *On the tenth anniversary of her death, I will be cooking something from Betsy's Kitchen, the family collection of my Argentinian-born, New York-raised, Hungarian grandmother's recipes. I am so grateful to have been her first grandchild and to have had her as such a present force in my life for three decades. I use the household and streetwise lessons she passed on nearly every day. She was the most capable person I have ever met and raised her children and grandchildren to appreciate the value of all that is locally made, homemade, and well made.*

My mother was also a lifelong feminist who supported women's rights. In 2022, after the Supreme Court struck down *Roe v. Wade*, Leila wrote:

> *I have been thinking of my grandmother so often in these past few weeks, for many reasons both personal and political. In addition to the culinary legacy she passed down to two generations (and counting)—she was also a staunch supporter of reproductive rights and bodily autonomy. I'm glad she's not here to see the rollback we're facing right now. And I treasure her example as a fierce defender of what is right. Channeling her indefatigable spirit as things get much worse before they get better.*

Both Elizabeth and Peti and their children have attributed to Ferko and Elsie their love of food and cooking, something Ferko most likely learned from his siblings in Budapest and Buenos Aires. He was a wonderful host and employer. He always had someone working for him—building a smokehouse or a Mediterranean patio filled with pots of geraniums and herbs—and he was decent and warm to them. When people visited him in beautiful Carmel, California, it was difficult not to be disarmed by this worldly man who entertained guests in his mountaintop house as he had done in Mexico, preparing delicious meals of home-cured meat, fresh-baked bread, and garden vegetables. This description could well be of my mother, Elizabeth, instead of her father, although she and Donald did their entertaining on East Coast suburban patios or at their rustic retirement farm. Like Ferko, she befriended anyone who worked for her and cooked them delicious lunches that they ate together each workday.

The photograph below is from a rare visit by Ferko to my parents' home in rural New Jersey in the 1980s. Wendy recalls it as a tense afternoon because of my mother's quiet hostility toward her father.

*Picnic with Ferko at Elizabeth's home in New Jersey.*

For me, the search for my grandfather became a self-exploration and reflection of how his life may have influenced who I became. I share his sense of adventure, love of languages, and appreciation of beautiful natural settings and art from around the world. After Ferko died, I inherited several things that reflected his travels and eye for local art. They include dozens of Moroccan and Mexican pillows and a few exquisite drawings and paintings, including three distinctive lithographs by Ben Sullivan, an intricate, graphite sketch of two elderly Chinese men smoking opium, and a lyrical watercolor of a street scene in Morocco by Lauly.

There is also some overlap in our professional backgrounds. Although I was certainly not a spy, the substance of Ferko's early OSS assignments is remarkably like my own specialization in survey research. He spent years developing questionnaires and interviewing newly arrived immigrants—something that mirrors my work as an academic studying US immigration, albeit with a different purpose.

Migration, of course, is a theme that represents so much of my Hungarian family's history and the plight of Jews throughout the world, leading up to and after WWII. From my research on Latinx migration to the United States, I recognized a number of parallels with the vilification of Jews and the use of forced migration and deportation to alleviate "the Jewish problem" long before the Second World War. I have also been struck by the tragic irony of fear of the immigration of large numbers of Jewish refugees that prevented both the American and British governments from fully acknowledging Nazi atrocities during WWII.

My initial motive for writing this biography was to find answers to many puzzling questions. As I dug deeper, the quest became the motive—"the journey is the destination," as they say. I nominated myself as Ferko's designated biographer because his story deserves to be told and there is no one else who will write it.

During the search, I learned about relatives I never knew existed, historical events of the previous century, and their impacts on Kalnay family members, near and far. I found that the research made me hyper-aware of current and historical antisemitism. One minor event that brought the two together was the discovery that the two volumes of Randolph Braham's *The Politics of Genocide: The Holocaust in Hungary* that I had borrowed from the Russell Sage College Library via inter-library loan were stuffed with copies of antisemitic flyers designed to look like Confederate States of America currency. On one side was a Star of David with passages from the New Testament, as well as quotes from a Jew who had "seen the light" and converted to Christianity. I wrote to the reference librarian at the college and urged them to check the shelves on Jewish History for similar propaganda. They found more, and a Google search revealed similar occurrences at other college libraries in New England. Although the propaganda would come as no surprise to most Jews, it was unsettling to come across the flyers while reading detailed accounts of antisemitism in Hungary before and during World War II.

It is easy to react with incredulity over Hungarian Jews' denial that they would be next in line during the expansion of the Third Reich, but is that so different from my own complacency as I observe encroaching American Fascism from my vantage point in an ultra-liberal town in "left-wing" New York City? Examples of overt Fascism and antisemitism at high levels of government in the United States abound, such as then-President Trump's statement that "You had very fine people on both sides" after a white supremacist march in Charlottesville, Virginia, in 2017 at which Neo-Nazis chanted, "Jews will not replace us."[5] The similarities to antisemitism in Hungary are dramatic. As I write this, highly-placed Republican leaders in the US are coddling up to Viktor Orbán and his right-wing Fidesz Party. Like many American conservatives, Orbán often talks about threats to "Christian democracy" and Christian ethnic heritage that he believes he is uniquely positioned to thwart, and his plans to "keep our . . . Christian heritage for ourselves, our ethnic heritage." In 2022, the American Conservative Political Action Committee held its annual conference in Budapest, and in recent years Orbán has hosted a number of prominent conservatives. In 2021, former Attorney General Jeff Sessions praised the Hungarian government for their attempts to "return to our Christian roots based on reason and law, which have made Western civilization great."[6]

In the course of my study of Ferko's life, some of my original questions were answered—particularly those that could be addressed with information from declassified OSS/CIA files, or that were answered by a broad network of individuals and scholars who had written about the era that I was studying or the Kalnays themselves.

When Ferko "confessed" his Jewish ancestry to Wendy at the end of his life, he intimated that the family surname had been changed from

Klein to Kálnay to hide the fact and to allow his brothers to enroll in a school for railroad employees. This turned out to be a red herring as I learned after obtaining copies of Andrés and Jorge's secondary school enrollment forms that had "Izr" under their names—short for "Izraelite." Further investigation led me to the realization that religion was openly known and recorded on most public documents in the Habsburg Empire. I became fascinated with the field of onomastics and contacted Tamás Farkas, a specialist in the study of name changes, who directed me to a database that proved that Ferko's father changed the family surname in 1878 when he was nineteen years old—long before he had children himself. Rather than hiding the family's ancestry, the motive for the change would have been to demonstrate fidelity to Hungary, as many Jews were pressured to do.

Questions about Ferko's life that remain unanswered or subject to conjecture have to do with the personal motives of my grandfather and other family members. The omissions taught me as much as the findings—in particular that we can never really know our family histories beyond an assemblage of stories and personal interpretations. In my case, this was especially true because neither Ferko nor any of his siblings are alive, and I was only able to interview two second-generation relatives who saw him occasionally as children. Both of these (Esteban, son of Ferko's brother, Andrés, and Eugenia, daughter of Ferko's brother, Jorge) contributed mostly second-hand stories recalled from conversations with their parents.

Who was my grandfather? While his declassified files helped me develop a chronology of his life before and during WWII, it is a dry narrative that describes his work and successes in the OSS but nothing of his interior life. Those parts of the mosaic are left to conjecture.

How, for example, can we reconcile the high praise heaped on Ferko by his superiors and his evident skill at designing and carrying out complex, high-level government assignments with his personal life as a romantic who followed a Russian mystic and left a long trail of lovers? Perhaps nothing illustrates my grandfather's romanticism so clearly as his selection of the name of the Bengali poet, Tagore, as part of my mother's very long name: Böske Herminia Francisca Tagore Kalnay. Yet, despite this romantic nature—or perhaps because of it—Ferko prioritized his free lifestyle over close relationships with his own children.

Ferko's lifelong espousal of pacificism is another mystery. In California he was active with the pacifist group World Beyond Wars. This was remarkable given his ancestry and his direct involvement in war and its horrors. Very few Jews of eastern European ancestry were pacifists. One notable exception was the poet Allen Ginsberg, who was Buddhist.[7] Ferko's abhorrence of violence likely derived from his interest in Gurdjieff, who did not call himself a pacifist but who taught that "a conscious man refuses war" and spoke of "one world." Like Ferko, Gurdjieff grew up during the global power struggles among the Russian, British, and Ottoman empires and the onset of the first World War. He believed that preventing war was his mission in life.[8]

Gurdjieff's follower J.D. Ouspensky, a contemporary of Ferko's, rejected all negative emotion.[9] Ferko was an ardent proponent of their views on peace and harmony. He despised violence of any kind and was drawn to a utopian vision of a conflict-free world. If he engaged with someone who was in any way conflictual, he would say, "that person is very rough, and we need to avoid them." He wanted only smooth waters. This made it difficult to have certain conversations with him, but it was also part of his charm.

Ferko's son is adamant that his father would have been aghast to read praise of his government service.

> *Ferko would not want his wartime involvements to be retold as martial exploits that he had ever been proud of. He would abhor having them presented in any way that might be admired or ever emulated by his progeny. . . . Ferko's disillusionment with war knew no bounds. He rejected the idea that it could ever henceforth serve humanity, even in extreme cases. Nor was he in the slightest willing to concede to the idea warfare might have to be tolerated or condoned any longer as a necessary or ineradicable evil. Ferko taught that war was an atavistic, obsolescent, absurd form of mass insanity, the continuation of which would certainly spell the definitive dead end for humankind, or "finita la commedia," as Ferko liked to say.[10]*

One key to my grandfather's personality was his worship of Ernest Hemingway, a contemporary who shared Ferko's leftist views and abhorrence of war and who achieved enormous acclaim as an author. Like Ferko, Hemingway was a voluntary expatriate. My grandfather was deeply shaken by Hemingway's death by suicide in 1961. I wonder if Ferko knew Hemingway's son Jack from the young man's time in the OSS. Or, he may have known of Hemingway's trauma when his son was wounded and then held as a German prisoner of war in late 1944 after being captured in Nazi-occupied France.[11]

## TRAUMA AND SELECTIVE MEMORY

To me the most disturbing aspect of Ferko's coverup was his refusal to acknowledge the existence of his mother or the murder of his sister, even to close family members. Tragically, Rózsa was erased three times: once when she was institutionalized, a second when she died of heart failure at the height of the siege of Budapest in 1944, and finally throughout her life when several of her children failed to acknowledge her as their mother. In this Ferko colluded with several of his siblings and his father.

I find Rózsa's story deeply personal but also remote, although as a new grandmother it has taken on more meaning. I am extremely close to my young granddaughters and am aware that they will only remember me if others reinforce the memories after I die. The idea that my mother neither knew her paternal grandmother nor spoke her name is unbearably sad. Furthermore, Rózsa's obliteration by her own family members represents a kind of victory for the Hungarian Nazis whose goals were to destroy not only individuals themselves but also evidence of their existence.

In his memoir *The Lost,* Daniel Mendelsohn traces the lives of his great-uncle, great-aunt, and their four daughters who were victims of the Holocaust and then, like my great-aunt and her son, were erased from his family's history. He writes that "their omission is an interruption, a severing and discontinuity in the family saga, a disconnection that breaks the ethical, familial, and characterological bonds of lineal descent, as the larger history of the Holocaust does to Jewish cultural descent."

Mendelsohn suggests that "[t]he people who killed them wanted to erase them. That was the agenda. Not just to kill them. But that nothing would be left. No memories. No stories . . . That's the tragedy of these people."[12]

My family members' initial motives for obliterating Rózsa involved fear of mental illness. In 1900, as today, schizophrenia was a source of shame and fear for many families. In her book *Shanda,* the Yiddish word for "secrets," Letty Cottin Pogrebin comments that young people raised in our era of ubiquitous social media cannot begin to fathom the importance of privacy to earlier generations or the sense of shame that accompanied the divulgence of any family matters, let alone ugly secrets.[13]

The stigma of mental illness may have been the first motive to erase Rózsa Margulit Kálnay from family history, but it also proved a convenient time for the family to assume a Christian identity when József took Erzsébet Szentgáli as his mistress. The subsequent coverup of the murder of Ferko's sister, Borbála Kálnay Noti, and her son, Denes Noti, represents something darker—a not uncommon protective response to violence, and discrimination against Jews during the Holocaust. Equally disturbing is the perpetuation of the myths by subsequent generations who fostered the fiction of our family's Catholic heritage. Some of this response may be due to fear. In an article about Jewish assimilation in modern-day Hungary, András Kovacs argues that many Jews consider themselves to be Jewish only when faced with antisemitism. In cases where Jewish identity is seen as a stigma, it evokes fear of any kind of social or political conflict.[14] During the Fascist period in Hungary, there were many other reasons to be fearful of being identified as a Jew. One was the extraordinary collusion of ordinary Hungarian citizens with the Nazis. As Susan Faludi notes in her book about her Hungarian father, "in the first eight days of the Nazi occupation of Budapest, citizens filed 30,000 denunciations against Jews and Jewish property, compared with 350 in the first years of occupied Holland."[15] I read this terrifying sentence several times: thirty thousand denunciations in eight days; anyone who had lived through that kind of treachery would have been traumatized for life.

What I will never know is how much my mother and her sister knew about Kalnay family history. Clearly they knew of our Jewish ancestry. When I received the results of my DNA test, what struck me was the size of the result: 98.4% Ashkenazi heritage on my mother's side. That's not from a distant ancestor hidden in our family tree. It means that *all* of my mother's aunts, uncles, cousins, parents, and grandparents were Jews.

Late in life, Peti briefly acknowledged our Jewish ancestry, but neither she nor my mother ever mentioned the murder of their aunt by Arrow Cross guards in Budapest or the death of their cousin Denes in a forced labor camp. What makes this especially puzzling is that my mother was someone who never dissembled or even exaggerated, and for whom unequivocal honesty was a defining characteristic. How could she have participated in such an enormous coverup?

To a certain extent I can identify with the sublimation of horrific memories. I have always been able to compartmentalize difficult experiences—although mine have been minor and cannot be compared to the trauma of losing loved ones to war and violence. Still, I wonder if my ability to quickly move on without dwelling on painful events is behavior learned from my mother's stoicism.

What has shocked me even more than my mother's silence about Ferko's family was her denial of her maternal ancestry. It's not surprising that I knew little about Ferko's life before embarking on this book. I never knew him well, and he lived thousands of miles from my home on the East Coast when I was growing up. However, writing about my grandfather has made me realize how little I knew about two people who were constants in my life throughout my childhood—my mother and my grandmother. I was astonished to learn that my mother and all her relatives were Jewish. Astonished because both my mother and her mother were fiercely anti-clerical. In my lifetime, neither of them set foot in a church or synagogue, other than as tourists, or spoke to me or my siblings in a personal way about religion. In contrast, my father was raised as a Presbyterian by his devout German-ancestry mother. He considered himself to be agnostic, while my mother declared that she was an atheist.

Much literature about World War II describes the Holocaust as the central defining feature of Jewish lives. In my family the opposite has also been true, with *denial* of Jewish ancestry as a central defining feature in the form of ardent secularism, like that of my mother and grandmother, or devotion to Catholicism on the part of some of our Argentine relatives. This has been explained to me as an attempt to honor earlier promises of secrecy, but the implication is, of course, that there is shame in being Jewish. Although it may be tempting to maintain secrecy to avoid upsetting others, that silence reinforces shame and antisemitism. It is long past time to reveal the truth of our ancestry.

My reckoning with my family's origins is abstract and somewhat academic, but the realization that my mother and maternal grandmother were complicit in a coverup of our roots is more visceral. I didn't grow up with Holocaust survivors who taught me about their struggles and how they overcame them. Instead, my mother and grandmother's survival was contingent upon their silence, forcing me to excavate the truth that drove it. Like many other members of the third generation, I became a "dogged sleuth, digging around in the ruins of memory."[16] It's a never-ending quest, as each question raises others to be investigated and unraveled. With the passage of time and the deaths of members of the *second* generation, this becomes increasingly difficult. And, in the case of relatives of Jews from Hungary and other parts of central Europe, towns and neighborhoods and even countries have "changed hands" multiple times and vanished as well.

The frequency of selective memory among victims of severe trauma and their children has taught me that there are many motives for coverups—guilt, conscious or subconscious beliefs that denial can help to erase an event, the desire to protect others from knowledge of unspeakable horrors, and political forces that attempt to whitewash the history of genocide. In short, family narratives are always unreliable and particularly so in the face of severe physical or psychological injury. Repression is, of course, a mechanism for survival.

In their book on memories of the Holocaust, Aarons and Berger discuss the tension facing the generation of Holocaust survivors "between the need to bear witness to the past and the anticipated taboo against doing so." They point to examples from literature and film that demonstrate that "the meaningful things were always left unspoken, leaving the question of how one reclaims a memory that is not one's own." The psychologist Dan Bar-On describes this as the distinction between "historical truths" about what happened and "narrative truths" or how people tell what happens.[17]

A Yivo Institute for Jewish Research exhibit at the United Nations in New York describes the varied reactions of survivors of the Holocaust:

> *The expression of grief was not straightforward, however. Survivors*
> *experienced complex emotions that included feelings of powerlessness,*
> *bafflement about survival, and fearing the experience of joy, as*
> *a betrayal of those who did not survive. For some mourning was*
> *perceived as an act of treason against their loved ones, as it suggested*
> *an acceptance of their deaths.*[18]

Arnon Goldfinger, the director of the Israeli-German film *The Flat*, first discovered as an adult that his great-grandmother had been murdered in a Nazi concentration camp. When he confronted his mother, she said that she never knew how or where her grandmother had died, and that she was forbidden from asking questions. Goldfinger came to realize that his family lived only in the present. When he queried one of his mother's cousins, she responded: "Why do only the third-generation Germans ask these questions? I'm glad that you didn't know."[19]

Even when family members have factual knowledge of the historical truth, they may resist its divulgence. Like Goldfinger, I am a member of the third generation—a group that Aarons and Berger describe as fixated on details. When my generation tries to confront the past, we are characteristically received with resistance by parents who tried to protect their children from the knowledge of the realities of the Shoah and by grandparents who are resistant to the efforts to uncover that which was secreted in their own attempts to repress and compensate for both individual and collective grief.[20] "The third generation comes to [family] stories through a kind of traumatic interference, events filtered, more often than not, piece meal, through the events and blockades of the intervening decades."[21]

How strange that I am working hard to uncover details that my grandparents and my mother were determined to keep buried. And, how ironic that I, an atheist, should be the one to highlight our family's heritage and to follow the Jewish imperative defined in the Book of Joel: "Tell your children of it, and let your children tell their children, and their children another generation."[22] Through the process of writing this book I have come to appreciate the words of Marcus Garvey: "A people without the knowledge of their past history, origin, and culture is like a tree without roots."[23]

How much of our family history did my mother know beyond her Jewish ancestry? Did she discuss the past with her mother, Elsie? Did she ever reveal details to my father? Did she have nightmares about what would have happened to the family had she and Elsie and Peti not fled Hungary in 1933? I will never know the answer to these questions, but I am saddened by my own lack of curiosity about our history until it was too late to talk to my mother or grandmother about their experiences.

Before writing this book, if you had asked me what it meant to be half Hungarian, I would have given examples so superficial and positive that they might have been conjured by a director of tourism. I think of my grandmother Elsie's love of Hungarian music and how she would get up to dance the *Csardas* when we took her to Hungarian restaurants in New York to celebrate her birthday. I think of Ferko's soft Hungarian accent—cultivated and maintained after half a century in North and South America. I think of my mother's delectable stuffed cabbage leaves and homemade pastries. I remember her pleasure when a Yorkville shopkeeper said in Hungarian, "*kezet csókolok*" (I kiss your hand), as she left his shop laden with cans of paprika, caraway seeds, and smoked sausages. Years later, when she was dying and could no longer communicate with us, my nephew memorized the phrase and was rewarded with delighted giggles each time he said it aloud. I understand now that these colorful images mask the horrors my family members lived through in the 1930s and 1940s. In fact, not a day goes by that I don't think about their fates and my own Hungarian heritage.

When my mother was ill, her recollection of past events was much sharper than her recollection of the present. There were two memories of her family that haunted her and that she recounted over and over. One was Ferko's refusal to let her stay in his apartment in New York when she needed a place to live in her first year of college at New York

University. The second was her frustration with her sister when they moved to Hungary and Peti put her head down on her desk and refused to reply to the teacher's questions. "She wouldn't even try," my mother complained. I replied that Peti had been dragged to a new country and a new and unfamiliar school where the instruction was in Hungarian. "She was only five years old!" I protested but to no avail.

I realize now that my mother's response may reflect deep-seated resentment over the way she was thrust into an adult role looking after both her sister and her mother when she was still a child herself. And her stalwart refusal to discuss the darker aspects of the past is likely to have been a coping mechanism to deal with the trauma of her turbulent childhood. As Elizabeth Rosner wrote in *Survivor Cafe:*

> *Selective memory is a human characteristic, of course, our voluntary and involuntary preference for recalling the positive and erasing the negative. We may be driven by shame or resentment (or both, as they are interconnected), but regardless of the reason, we curate our stories both personal and collective. We airbrush the monstrous and highlight the angelic. We purify and we edit, even when we don't mean to, or know that we are doing so. We want to be better—to seem better—than we are.[24]*

The search to unravel the mysteries surrounding Francis Kalnay has taught me that all family histories are changed and edited from generation to generation. They are airbrushed to highlight successes and to erase fears and defeats, particularly after traumatic events. In such circumstances, we are all storytellers.

*Portrait of Francis Kalnay painted by Francis Cahill circa 1985. Printed with permission.*

# APPENDIX A:

## Kalnay Proposal for Balkan Division of X-2 METO at Istanbul

November 26, 1943

To: Lt. Col. Carroll Gray
From: Francis Kalnay
Subject: Some ideas and suggestions concerning the Balkan division of X-2 METO at Istanbul.

Latest reports indicate a desperate effort on the part of Balkan satellite nations to establish contact with Allied representatives. That's a "constant stream" of emissaries from the Balkans is arriving in Istanbul. It is, of course vital for Allied agents to smoke out these efforts. Furthermore, the deterioration of Nazi organizations and pro Nazi sympathies in every stratum in the Balkans; the shifting of vital German industries to save her regions in central Europe; the extreme need for protection from saboteurs of oil fields, refineries and communication lines in Romania and Hungary; the reluctance of satellite countries to supply additional divisions and industrial manpower to the Germans; the growing tension over territorial revisions and treatment of minorities between Hungary and Romania, Bulgaria and Romania, Hungary and Slovakia, Albania and Greece; the fratricidal battles between Serbs and Croats; the ever-increasing aid given to the Yugoslav, Albanian, and Greek guerrillas by the Allies; all these are forcing the Germans to multiply their agents in the Balkans and in Turkey, the neutral meeting ground.

Personnel: Because of the uncertainty of Turkey's next move, it seems advisable to process, as soon as possible, all individuals being considered for the following posts:

Chief of Balkan Division
Assistant
Two officers and six field operatives each for Bulgaria, Romania, and Hungary

There will be a need for at least two secretaries for this division. Cable, file clerk, and guards, it is assumed, would be covered by the over-all METO Istanbul office.

Physical set up and some security measures: cover, local regulations, housing, and other factors will determine location, size, and type of head-quarters. Under ideal conditions, the Balkan division would operate under one cover such as a bank, export import company, embassy, scientific institution, a particularly well-situated apartment house, etc. However from the standpoint of security, a breakdown into isolated units would be preferable since otherwise, should the enemy at any time penetrate into one unit, the entire organization might be endangered. Whatever the physical set up of the headquarters of this division may be, internally the isolation or separation should be fool-proof, to the extent that no documentary evidence of the existence of one section or area should be found in the files of another.

Division of work: the activities of the two officers in each of the geographic areas mentioned above could be divided as follows: one would be responsible for the handling of operatives in the enemy field (employment, dispatching into the field, maintenance of contact, collection of information, etc.) His colleague would concentrate on the enemy agents to be found among, or through his nationals on the immediate scene, and on the coordination of material concerning his area coming from other Middle East sources.

In addition one or both could be assigned, when necessary, to assist in protecting American government agencies located in Istanbul from enemy penetration. Again it would be their responsibility to prepare and keep up-to-date as complete a file as possible of all suspect individuals among their particular nationality groups, entering or leaving Istanbul; to analyze all political economic military and cultural ties between the country of their interest and Turkey; and to discover the identity, function and movement of Nazi agents through whatever medium presents itself.

Mobility of personnel: once there is any suspicion that his cover has been discovered, an officer should be transferred to a new post.

Field operatives: operatives would fall into two groups: one to be sent into enemy territory to accomplish a certain specific mission; the other to track down agents engaged in military, political or economic espionage, or sabotage in a given area. Probably the best type of agent to penetrate the field is the man who has legitimate business requiring his presence in one of the Balkan countries, with natural reasons to make occasional trips to Istanbul, such as representatives of a well-established industrial firm, engineers, government officials, officials of a transportation company, commercial travelers, scientists, press representatives, church dignitaries, etc.

Another potential source of operatives might be the dissident minority groups from each country. Some of these maintain underground contacts with parallel political organizations in neighboring countries (for example the Agrarian parties in Bulgaria maintain close relations with Machek's Croatian Peasant Party in Yugoslavia. This is also true of persecuted religious groups: Muslim, Catholic, Protestant, Jewish, etc.).

Field operatives should never be brought to Headquarters nor to field offices, except upon specific instructions from the chief of the division. While it might be expedient, occasionally for operatives to work in teams, for security reasons they will be employed individually by a single officer, and will maintain contact through him alone. In most cases the operatives will have no knowledge of each other.

Possible leads: the officer will find his leads through such sources as shipping companies, cultural relations organizations, industrial and commercial representatives, export and import companies, insurance companies, tourist bureaus, scientific organizations, motion picture companies, press and press photo bureaus, radio, religious organizations, schools, newspaper stands (particularly kiosks selling foreign periodicals), and booksellers. A considerable colony exists in Turkey of nationals of each of the Balkan countries and it may be there a few key people will be able to furnish the clues to such a "Who's Who." One of the tasks of the officer would be preparation of a dossier on suspect local residents of each nationality (the officer will find himself surrounded not only by Nazi espionage and counter-espionage organizations, including Ribbentrop's private political Espinoza bureau, but individual espionage units representing group interests from each of the Balkan countries).

Speculation on probable reshuffling of Nazi headquarters and Agents: the heavy bombing of the two major Nazi espionage centers, Hamburg and Berlin, gives rise to speculation as to where the Abwehr and other Nazi intelligence headquarters will be located. It seems likely that the new headquarters might be located somewhere around Vienna, where Balkan divisional headquarters have been established for some time. Should Turkey suddenly align herself with the Allies, it is likely that some of the well-known Nazi agents from Turkey will leave, while fresh agents will penetrate Turkey before the door is closed.

It is to be expected that this influx of new Nazi agents will have to be of the keenest type, possessing the best cover; therefore the most dangerous.

Cooperation with Allied intelligence agencies: It is to be assumed that, in addition to contact with British intelligence, X-2 will have liaison with other established allied intelligence units, such as the Free French, Polish etc. in Istanbul.

Flow of information from Washington: it is expected that METO X-2 headquarters in Washington will supply its Balkan division at Istanbul, through the usual channels, with available vital information which might be used in the field (R&A, SI, SO, MO, etc.).

It is suggested that an administrative assistant be situated to the office of the theater officer of X-2 METO, Washington who will collect, analyze, classify, and channel material bearing on X-2 Middle East activities. Particular attention should be paid to unearthing possible contacts in the Middle East or enemy-occupied countries who may be reached and used in the respective territories. As an illustration of a potential source within OSS for such contacts, there is the Survey of Foreign Experts in New York which has indexed thousands of individuals now residing in the United States, recent arrivals from neutral or enemy-occupied countries. Some are native-born Americans, others are refugees. Many of these have knowledge of conditions and personalities, business contacts, relatives or friends in those countries.

# APPENDIX B:

## Norman Holmes Pearson Nominates Ferko for Certificate of Merit

June 30, 1945

To: Commanding Officer, Office of Strategic Services, European Theater of Operations

1. It is recommended that Francis Kalnay, civilian, be awarded the Unit Commander's Certificate of Merit for his work with X-2 branch, Office of Strategic Services, European Theater of Operations.

2. Francis Kalnay, American civilian, was placed in charge of the Balkan desk in late spring of 1944, a time when American authorities were noticeably inexperienced in counterintelligence and related problems in the Balkan countries. Mr. Kalnay brought to his work a thorough knowledge of Hungarian, but his tasks soon passed beyond the purely linguistic ones as he brought to bear upon the field his very considerable knowledge of Balkan diplomatic and political intrigue. Through his efforts the desk established elaborate files of Balkan materials, and built up a reservoir of information so impressively useful that many enemy espionage activities were localized, and through being identified, neutralized, and important links between Balkan personalities and the German intelligence service in other countries were established. On numerous occasions Mr. Kalnay's careful piercing together of fragmentary evidence revealed facts about Abwehr and Reichssicherheitshauptamt functioning in central and Western Europe which the activities of agents and controlled enemy agents in those regions had failed to uncover. He was never at a loss for a helpful suggestion or a new insight into some aspect of the enemy's espionage system. With intense devotion to duty and a keen sense of urgency he kept himself thoroughly informed on complicated political, national, diplomatic, and military problems, and his work made X-2 inroads upon the German Intelligence Service easier and more deliberate. By his energy and intelligence he had formed the Balkan desk, in short, by the time of his relinquishing the post 1 January 1945, into an integral part of the X-2 organization.

# APPENDIX C:

## Selected *New York Times* Articles on Events in Hungary in 1944

Koestler, Arthur. "The Nightmare That Is a Reality." *The New York Times*. January 9,1944.Proquest.com.

> [Excerpt]: *At the present we have the mania of trying to tell you about the killing, by hot steam, mass electrocution and live burial of the total Jewish population of Europe. So far three million have died. It is the greatest mass killing in recorded history and it goes on daily, hourly, as regularly as the ticking of your watch.*

*The New York Times*. "Hungary Liquidates Jewish Businesses— 16,000 of 30,000 Confiscated With Aid of Gestapo." May 3, 1944. Proquest.com.

> *BERNE, Switzerland, May 3 — Invoking accusations of "leaders of the black market," "disseminators of defeatist propaganda" and "traitors who are on the point of selling the country's possibilities of resistance against the Bolshevist menace to the Anglo-Saxon powers," the Hungarian Government, assisted by the Gestapo, has virtually liquidated the affairs of more than 160,000 Jewish families since the German occupation, according to information received from Budapest tonight.*

Levy, Joseph M. "Jews in Hungary Fear Annihilation—Gas Chamber Baths on Nazi Model Reported Prepared by Puppet Regime." *The New York Times*. May 10, 1944.ProQuest.com.

> *ISTANBUL, Turkey, May 7. (Delayed) — Although it may sound unbelievable, it is a fact that Hungary, where Jewish citizens were comparatively well treated until March 19, is now preparing for the annihilation of Hungarian Jews by the most fiendish methods. Laughing at President Roosevelt's warning, Premier Doeme Sztojay's puppet Nazi government is completing plans and is about to start the extermination of about 1,000,000 human beings who believed they were safe because they had faith in Hungarian fairness.*

*The government in Budapest has decreed the creation in different parts of Hungary of "special baths" for Jews. These baths are in reality huge gas chambers arranged for mass murder, like those inaugurated in Poland in 1941.*

*Scores of thousands of Jews, including women with babies in arms, were murdered in these gas chamber baths. They were Jews from all over Europe, sent to Poland in cattle trains and forced into specially built chambers to which they were taken under the pretext of having baths prior to being sent to the Ukraine for colonization. Five and a half million Jews in Europe are reported to have been put to death in one form or another by the Germans since the war began.*

*Official diplomatic dispatches from Budapest declare that all Jews in Hungary are living in fear of imminent annihilation, from which there seems to be no escape. The dispatches written by a neutral diplomat who is known to be a great friend of the Hungarians, condemn in the strongest terms the present Hungarian government's treatment of hundreds of thousands of innocent loyal Hungarian citizens of Jewish faith. "Were I not here to witness it with my own eyes, I would never have believed that Magyars were capable of perpetrating such inhuman acts against honest, law abiding citizens, whose only sin is that they are members of the faith which is the mother of Christianity," the diplomat wrote. "Never in my career was I so eager to be relieved of my post as I am today. The cruelty of the government is beyond my comprehension, and I fail to understand how men calling themselves gentlemen and aristocrats can be so heartless and brutal to their fellow men.*

*"I am not justifying the Allied bombings of Budapest, but I cannot help but laugh when I hear members of the Hungarian government refer to the Allied air raids as barbaric and inhuman at a time when this government is daily committing the most abominable crimes against a million of their own countrymen."*

**The New York Times. "Hungary Herds All Jews—Spokesman Says 800,000 Are in Ghettos or Prison Camps." May 17, 1944. ProQuest.com.**

*The Nazi Transkontinent agency in a wireless dispatch reported yesterday by United States Government quotes Laszlo Baky, Under-Secretary of State in the puppet Hungarian Government, as saying that the program to herd Hungary's Jewish population of 800,000 into ghettos and concentration camps had been completed.*

*Meanwhile, the Hungarian MTI agency, in a wireless dispatch to the controlled Hungarian press also reported by the monitors, reported an article in the newspaper Esti Ujsag admitting that Budapest Jews had been forced to settle near war factories "which are threatened by enemy raids." The article was written by Francis Rajniss, a Hungarian Deputy and editor of the paper, and according to MIT reported him as declaring that the Allies "will be compelled to drop a rain of fire on their religious brethren."*

**The New York Times. "Russia's Aid Sought for Jews in Hungary—Committee Here Cables to Stalin Urging Him to Intercede." May 17, 1944. ProQuest. com.**

*In a cabled appeal to Marshal Joseph Stalin sent yesterday by the Emergency Committee to Save the Jewish People of Europe, Russia was asked to come to the rescue of the million Jews in Hungary whose lives are now endangered, and to reaffirm its intention to punish all "war criminals" convicted of persecution.*

*The appeal pointed out that there were now 50,000 Jewish refugees from the western Ukraine living in Hungary who might be exchanged for Hungarian prisoners of war held in Russia with guarantees that neither country would use them for combat service.*

*Among the signers of the appeal who met yesterday at the Hotel Biltmore, was Mrs. Ruth Bryan Owen Rohde, former United States Minister to Denmark, who declared that "when murder is announced in advance, those who don't attempt to prevent it are accessories before the fact."*

*A three-power warning from President Roosevelt, Prime Minister Churchill and Marshal Stalin would be effective in preventing Hungary from carrying out the German program of extermination according to Dr. Emil Lengyel, Hungarian author.*

*Gov. Henry F. Schricker of Indiana, Bishop James Cannon Jr., Sigrid Undset, Prof. Kirtley F. Mather of Harvard University, Bruno Walter, Serge Koussevitzky, Louis Adamic, Alfred Kreymborg and Dr. Guy Emery Shipler were among the forty signers of the cablegram.*

**Levy, Joseph M. "Savage Blows Hit Jews in Hungary: 80,000 Reported Sent to Murder Camps in Poland—Non-Jews Protest in Vain." Sent by cable to The New York Times. May 18, 1944. ProQuest.com.**

**The New York Times. "Speed Seen Needed for Jews' Rescue: 1,500,000 in Hungary and Rumania Can Be Saved Says Official in Palestine." May 20, 1944. ProQuest.com.**

*JERUSALEM. May 18 (Delayed) — Swift action by the Allies could save up to 1,500,000 Jews in Hungary and Romania, in the opinion of Isaac Gruenbaum, Chairman of the United Rescue Committee for European Jews.*

*If practical measures are not taken, however, it is felt that the same process of extermination as occurred in Poland will befall the Jews of these two countries. A memorandum on conditions there and suggestions for remedies were recently sent to the United States War Refugee Board, said Mr. Gruenbaum who, from 1918-35 was a Polish deputy.*

*Recent reports told of the arrival in Palestine of several hundred refugees from Eastern Europe and there are indications that more will arrive within the limit of 20,000 permits still available under the British White Paper.*

*85% of the money required to finance refugee aid here has been contributed by Jews in Palestine. Most of the remaining 15% came from South Africa and other countries.*

**Turkey Not Informed**

*In July 1943, Mr. Gruenbaum said, the British government made the statement that if escaping Jews reached Istanbul, Turkey, from Axis countries, they would receive Palestine visas under the White Paper quota. But no official communication to this effect reached the Turkish government and it consented to grant transit permits to only nine families a week, each from Romania, Bulgaria and Hungary.*

*Last March official assurances were given the Turkish government and transit difficulties were removed.*

*Obstacles also had to be overcome with regard to the exit from Romania. This was substantially achieved by the assistance of United States representatives after Ira A. Hirschmann completed his mission on behalf of the War Refugee Board. But the accelerated immigration that Mr. Hirschmann's assistance indicated never materialized, Mr. Gruenbaum said. One thousand Jews, many of whom were repatriated from Transdniestria, recently left Rumania.*

*Developments in Hungary have aroused grave anxiety. There have been signs that the tempo of the atrocities perpetrated there against Jews will be faster than in Poland.*

### More Money Asked

*Mr. Gruenbaum declared that Jewish communities outside Palestine apparently did not realize the acuteness of the Jews' plight in Hungary and Romania and had not contributed sufficient funds.*

*The three greatest obstacles to saving the Jews at the present time, he said, were the White Paper restrictions on mass admissions into Palestine and the barring of gates into other countries, the hindrances imposed by Axis countries against the departure of their Jewish victims and insufficient funds.*

**The New York Times. "Senators Appeal on Hungary's Jews—Foreign Relations Committee Pleads with People to Stop 'Cold Blooded Murder.'" June 4, 1944.ProQuest.com.**

*Characterizing the application of the anti-Jewish Nuremberg laws in Hungary as "cold blooded murder," the Senate Foreign Relations Committee yesterday called upon the Hungarian people to resist the orders of their puppet government, help Jews to escape across the borders and "watch and remember those who are accessories to murder and those who extend mercy until the approaching time when guilt and innocence will be weighed."*

*The statement was broadcast by the Office of War Information in Hungarian, French, German and the Balkan languages from New York for relay to the Continent.*

*The Committee's declaration was based on measures applied to the Jewish population of Hungary since the German occupation on March 19. These included the confiscation of Jewish shops and industries, the transportation of Jews into the interior of the country, away from the war zone, and the establishment of ghettos, into which, according to Laszlo Baky of the Hungarian Nazi party, 320,000 Jews have been sent.*

*TEXT OF STATEMENT*

*The people of the United States and all freedom-loving people are horrified by the news that Hitler has designated the 800,000 Jews in Hungary for death.*

*That the people of Hungary should countenance the cold-blooded murder of innocent men, women and children is unthinkable. Once Hungary was the haven of tens of thousands who fled the Nazi terror in other lands. Once*

*Hungary protected the helpless who sought refuge within its borders. Once Hungarians shielded their Jewish fellow citizens. But now the Hungarian puppet government has joined the Nazis in their ruthless determination to do away with the Jews.*

*While there is yet time the people of Hungary can demonstrate to the world that this unholy scheme is a betrayal of the true Hungarian spirit. They can hide the Jews until such time as they may help them to safety across the borders. They can refuse to purchase property stolen from the Jews. They can use every means to obstruct the Nazis and those Hungarians who are in league with the Nazis. They could keep watching to remember those who are accessories to murder and those who extend mercy, until the time when guilt and innocence will weigh heavily in the balance. That time is near.*

*The Foreign Relations Committee's statement was signed by Senators Tom Connally, Texas, chairman; Walter F. George, Georgia; Robert F. Wagner, New York; Joseph F. Guffey, Pennsylvania; Bennett Champ Clark, Missouri; Robert R. Reynolds, North Carolina; G.M. Gillette, Iowa; Theodore Francis Green, Rhode Island; James M. Tunnell, Delaware; Alben W. Barkley, Kentucky; Arthur Capper, Kansas; Robert La Follette Jr., Wisconsin; Arthur H. Vandenberg, Michigan; James J. Davis, Pennsylvania; and James E. Murray, Montana.*

**The New York Times. "Hungary Policy Assailed: Group Meeting Here Denounces the Extermination of Jews." June 18, 1944. ProQuest.com.**

*Hungarian American organizations and Christian churches, said to represent 500,000 of their countrymen now in this country, convened at the Hotel Biltmore yesterday morning to denounce the extermination campaign being directed against the Jews in Hungary.*

*The conference, sponsored by the Emergency Committee to Save the Jewish People of Europe, was attended by 40 representatives of Hungarian societies, who unanimously adopted a resolution to be short-waved by the Office of War Information to Hungary. It sharply condemned recent statements made by the Hungarian premier, Doeme Sztojay, that Jews were being exterminated to provide "room for American Hungarians to return to their native country after the war period."*

*The reply to the premier asserted that Hungarian Americans do not wish to return, since "we came to the United States of our own free will, in search of a better land in which to make our homes and raise our children."*

*The New York Times.* "Hungary Warned by Congressmen—House Foreign Affairs Body Demands Halt to 'Inhumane Conduct' Toward Jews." June 22, 1944. ProQuest.com.

> *WASHINGTON, June 21 (AP) — The House Foreign Affairs Committee, in a highly unusual action, called on Hungary today to halt the mistreatment of Jews, reminding the German satellite that the perpetrators of "inhumane conduct" would be punished. Chairman Sol Bloom, Democrat of New York, issued a statement for the committee, which seldom addresses the nation directly concerning a matter usually left to the diplomats.*
>
> *"Our concern and our determination are now addressed particularly to Hungary where the lives of almost a million Jews hang in the balance," it said. "Events show that the tide of military battle has now turned in favor of the United Nations. Let Hungary at this historic moment stem the tide of inhumanity toward the helpless people within her borders."*
>
> *The committee said that it was not content merely to speak with "horror at the barbarism of the governments involved—we are determined that the criminals who are guilty of this inhumane conduct shall be brought to justice."*
>
> *The statement followed the appearance of John Pehle before the committee. Mr. Pehle is Executive Director of the War Refugee Board, an agency created by President Roosevelt to deal with the refugee problem.*
>
> *In another statement today, Representative Emanuel Celler, Democrat of New York, contended that Dr. Carleton J. H. Hayes, American Ambassador to Spain, had refused to cooperate with the War Refugee Board and that Madrid was a "a lonely island" as far as refugees were concerned. He said Spain might follow the example of other neutrals and set up a "free port" for refugees if Dr. Hayes would so much as approach the Spanish government. "It is time to put the screws on the Francophile. Hayes should be recalled," Mr. Celler asserted.*

*The New York Times.* "Hull Backs Move to Warn Hungary: House Protest on Abuse of Jews Called For, He Says, Stressing Allied Policy." June 27, 1944. ProQuest.com.

> *WASHINGTON, June 26 — Secretary of State Cordell Hull again raised his voice against the mistreatment of Jews by Axis countries in commenting today about the resolution of the House Committee on Foreign Affairs calling upon Hungary to halt her mistreatment of Jews.*

*Individuals and groups and organizations, private and public, and officials of all kinds, he stated, had been vainly protesting and seeking to express their indignatian at the outrageous, unspeakable conduct of the German government and its puppets, and we cannot have too many persons or officials or groups joining in such strong and indignant protest.*

*Mr. Hull declared that the guilty persons would be punished for those crimes. He pointed to the statement on atrocities perpetrated by Hitlerite forces signed by President Roosevelt, Prime Minister Churchill and Premier Stalin, which was issued at the Moscow conference last November 1, and suggested that a paragraph in it pertinent to the situation was worth republishing at this time.*

*"At the time of granting of any armistice to any government which may be set up in Germany," the statement said, "those German officers and men and members of the Nazi party who have been responsible for or have taken a consenting part in the above atrocities, massacres and executions will be sent back to the countries in which their abominable deeds were done in order that they may be judged and punished according to the laws of these liberated countries and of the free governments which will be erected therein."*

## The New York Times. "350,000 More Jews believed Doomed: 400,000 Sent to Poland from Hungary Up to June 17." July 02, 1944. ProQuest.com.

*JERUSALEM, June 30 (Delayed) — Authoritative information indicating that the final stage in the tragedy of Hungarian Jews has begun has reached here.*

*Hungarian sources in Turkey reported that the 350,000 Jews at the mercy of the Nazis were being rounded up for deportation to death camps in Poland. By June 17, 400,000 had been sent to Poland; the remaining 350,000 are expected to be put to death by July 24.*

*These figures were given today by Isaac Gruenbaum, Chairman of the United Palestine Committee for the Rescue of European Jews. He said there were 800,000 Jews in Hungary in 1940.*

*The New York Times.* **"Hungary Deports Jews, Eden Says—He Confirms Massacres—Says Country Ignores Protests by Allies and Pope." July 6, 1944. ProQuest.com.**

*LONDON, July 5 — Widespread deportations and massacres of Hungarian Jews, despite repeated warnings by the United Nations that the German and Hungarian instigators would be punished, were regretfully confirmed by Foreign Secretary Anthony Eden in the House of Commons today.*

*Asked by S.S. Silverman, Chairman of the British Section of the World Jewish Congress, whether 400,000 had been deported and 100,000 had already been slain, Mr. Eden said he was not in a position to give figures but he feared that "there can be little doubt, in the main of what is going on."*

*[The Jewish population of Hungary at the outbreak of the war was 444,567, according to the latest edition of the American Jewish yearbook.]*

*Mr. Silverman pointed out that the last remaining organized Jewish community in Europe had been in Hungary. He asked whether a further appeal could be made, not to the Germans, but to the Hungarian government. Mr. Eden said that the British Broadcasting Corporation would be used for this purpose.*

### Cites Popes Representatives

*He added that a direct appeal had been made to the Hungarian people to defend the Jews, and that the Pope and the King of Sweden had made representations, but he concluded, "the principle hope of terminating this tragic state of affairs must remain the speedy victory of the Allied nations."*

*Information received by the World Jewish Congress leaves little doubt that the Germans are waging two wars—one against the enemies of Germany, the other against the Jews—and that, with Germany's defeat imminent, they are preparing to wipe out European Jewry. It is estimated conservatively that they have already massacred 4,000,000 of Europe's seven million Jews.*

*The Congress was notified more than two weeks ago that 100,000 Jews recently deported from Hungary to Poland had been gassed in the notorious German death camp at Oswiecim. Between May 15 and 27 sixty-two railroad cars laden with Jewish children between the ages of two and eight, and six cars laden with Jewish adults, passed daily through the Plaszow station near Cracow. Mass deportations have also begun from Thepsienstadt, Czechoslovakia, where the Jews had heretofore been unmolested.*

*Since the invasion of France the Germans have intensified their anti-semitic propaganda. On D Day the Brussels radio announced that if the Allies advanced, the Germans would wipe out every Jew on whom they could lay their hands. As a cover for their crimes German official spokesmen have announced that the Jews are regarded as "belligerents."*

**The New York Times. "Massacre of Jews in Hungary Scored: Special Services of Protest Held by 2,000 in Bronx and Manhattan." July 10, 1944. ProQuest.com.**

*In protest against the persecution of Jews in Hungary, Americans of Hungarian descent held yesterday special services. At Castle Hill Garden Park, the Bronx, 2,000 gathered at 5:00 PM for a ceremony sponsored by the New Light Temple of Yorkville and the American Hungarian Federation of Washington. The First Hungarian Reformed Church of New York held a service at 11:00 AM.*

*At the church 344 E 69th St, members of the Christian congregation received yellow Star of David arm bands to be worn for 24 hours as a symbol of sympathy with the persecuted Jews. The occasion held added significance because of the announcement on Thursday by Foreign Secretary Anthony Eden in the House of Commons that there had been widespread deportations and massacres of Hungarian Jews despite repeated warnings by the United Nations. The church service had been planned by the Reverend Geza Takaro in advance of this news.*

*"The Nazi massacre of Jews in Hungary is an outrage against all humanity," declared Governor Dewey in a telegram sent to the church. "Every American, Christian and Jew alike, is stirred with a deep abhorrence of this barbarism. the voice and the heart of America are with you in your special service of intercession for Jews in Hungary.*

*"You bespeak the views of all of us when you broadcast to the people of Hungary a plea to resist this criminality to the utmost. You speak for all of us when you tell the Nazis they shall pay more dearly for the consequences of their inhumanity."*

### Message from Mayor

*Mayor LaGuardia in the message asserted that the "brutality practiced by the Nazis in Hungary outrages all decent people of the world" and expressed hope that "the Magyars will take an active part in liberating their homeland from these beasts."*

*Senator Robert F Wagner wrote, "the people of the United States and all freedom-loving peoples have been horrified by the news that the present puppet government of Hungary was joined with the Nazis in their ruthless determination to do away with hundreds of thousands of innocent men, women and children. It is particularly appropriate that your congregation should, as Americans of Hungarian descent, demonstrate to the world that this unholy scheme is a betrayal of the true Hungarian spirit."*

*Mr Takaro explained that "we want to demonstrate that the persecution of Jews is abhorrent to the Christian sons and daughters of Hungary who can freely express their feelings and opinions in a free land."*

*Lewis Toth, chairman of the board of trustees of the church, declared that "we are profoundly shocked and dismayed that in the land of our birth men could be found to serve as accomplices of Hitler's murderous gang" and urged "the punishment of common ordinary murderers" on the men "who are now besmirching the good name of the Hungarian people."*

## Hurd, Charles. "U.S. and Britain Aid Jews of Hungary—Accept Budapest Proposals to Offer 'Temporary' Haven to Persecuted People." Special to *The New York Times*. August 18, 1944. ProQuest.com.

*WASHINGTON, Aug. 17 — The United States and Great Britain will give "temporary" refuge to any Jews able to leave Hungary by virtue of regulations set up by this enemy country authorizing the immigration of Jews, the State Department announced here tonight.*

*The two governments have notified Hungary, through the Red Cross, that it will give haven to these refugees, and has requested neutral countries to facilitate the passage of such Jews as reached their borders.*

*The State Department's announcement made clear that the plan did not involve preparation for permanent immigration. It spoke specifically of "temporary havens of safety" using the same term that has been applied to refugee camps set up throughout the Mediterranean area for refugees from Yugoslavia, Greece and France.*

*There was no comment on a question of whether the agreement would mean that Great Britain would admit Hungarian Jews to Palestine in the same manner that refugees already have been admitted to a refugee camp at Oswego, New York, but the commitments left this as an open question. It appeared probable that details of the refugee program would be worked out to accord with the numbers of persons involved.*

*While accepting the arrangement, the official announcement severely castigated the Hungarian government for invoking regulations that make necessary the flight of Hungarian Jews.*

TEXT OF STATEMENT
*The State Department's announcement follows:*

*The International Committee of the Red Cross has communicated to the governments of the United Kingdom and the United States an offer of the Hungarian government regarding immigration and treatment of Jews. Because of the desperate plight of the Jews in Hungary and the overwhelming humanitarian considerations involved, the two governments are informing the government of Hungary through the International Committee of the Red Cross that, despite the heavy difficulties and responsibilities involved, they have accepted the offer of the Hungarian government for the release of Jews, and will make arrangements for the care of such Jews leaving Hungary who reach neutral or United Nations territory, and also that they will find temporary havens of refuge where such people may live in safety.*

*Notification of these assurances is being given to the neutral countries, who are being requested to permit entry of Jews to reach their frontiers from Hungary.*

*The governments of the United Kingdom and the United States emphasize that in accepting the offer which has been made they do not in any way condone the action of the Hungarian government enforcing immigration of Jews as an alternative to persecution and death.*

**The New York Times. "Concessions to Jews Reported by Hungary." August 5, 1944. Proquest.com.**

*An improvement in the situation of an estimated 600,000 Hungarian Jews who have so far escaped deportation, and worse, to Germany under energetic anti-semitic decrees was reported today to the Swiss minister in Budapest by the Hungarian foreign minister. This official assurance was forthcoming only five days after negotiations by the international Red Cross delegate to Budapest had rung official permission from the Magyar authorities to visit and assist interned refugees.*

*In an official communique from the Berne government issued to the press tonight after announcing the report from its minister to Hungary he added, "assurances have also been given to our minister that further deportations of Jews to Germany for labor detail had been temporarily suspended. This Swiss legation in Budapest has moreover been authorized to facilitate the immigration of several thousand Jews to Palestine (one of the concessions won by the International Red Cross was the promise to grant exit visas to all Jews possessing visas for Palestine or other countries of asylum) while at the same time the International Red Cross has been granted the faculty of bringing immediate material relief to refugees at present interned in concentration camps."*

**The New York Times. "Hungary Threatens More Jews." December 4, 1944. Proquest.com.**

*The Szalasi Government in Hungary has informed the Swedish Government that it will apply Hungary's new and severe Jewish laws to 500 Hungarian Jews holding Swedish "protection" passports unless Sweden recognizes the Szalasi Government, it was learned tonight.*

**The New York Times. "Jews' Death March In Hungary Bared: 100,000 Driven from Budapest, 75,000 Reached Austria, A Witness Reports." December 29, 1944. ProQuest.com.**

*GENEVA, Dec. 28 (Jewish Telegraphic Agency) — How tens of thousands of Hungarian Jews perished last month in an epic "March of Death" from Budapest to the Austrian frontier has been revealed here by one of the "marchers" who escaped to Switzerland. His eyewitness story, as published in the Swiss press says:*

*"In the early days of November thousands of Jews—men, women and children—were herded together in Budapest and driven afoot toward the Austrian border. For seven or eight days we've launched an average of 30 kilometres daily, sometimes under heavy, cold rain. Before we set out Hungarian Nazis searched us to prevent us from taking along any valuables. Our identity documents were taken away from us."*

*"The road leading from Budapest, via Komaron to the Hungarian border town of Hegyshalom is more than 120 kilometers long. We were accompanied by members of the anti-semitic Arrow Cross Party. Anyone who showed signs of a breakdown was immediately shot. Wet through and through, our clothes torn to pieces, we had to spend nights sleeping along the*

*roadside. Every two days we received a plate of watery soup and this was all."*

*"Of 100,000 Jews who started from Budapest, only 75,000 reached the Austrian frontier. We were sent across the border in groups of 500. The Germans, however selected only those who were fit for hard labor. The others were returned and driven into the woods, where many died of disease, exposure and starvation."*

*Meanwhile the first authentic report of what has happened to the Jews in Budapest and other sections of Hungary since last March when the German army occupied the country reached here today.*

*"The Germans," the report says, "immediately started segregating Jews in ghettos. This was followed by mass deportations, so that by the middle of July not a single Jew remained in the Hungarian part of Transylvania, the Carpathian section of the country and southern Hungary. More than 600,000 Jews were deported within two months, most of them to the extermination camp of Oswiecim in German-occupied Poland."*

*"From Budapest only about 10,000 were deported at that time, while more than 250,000 were herded into special 'Jewish buildings.' It was hoped that these Jews would not be molested, but the situation took a new turn in October soon after the pro Nazi Szalasi Government came to power."*

*Acting upon the orders of Premier Ferenc Szalasi and supported by German troops, Arrow Cross units carried out a pogram on October 15 during which many thousands of Jews were massacred in the Budapest streets, the report continues. On the pretext that Jews were hiding arms, Arrow Cross units invaded Jewish homes, dragged residents into the streets and killed them. German tanks and armored cars fired at buildings that Jewish residents refused to leave.*

*The next day an order was issued prohibiting Jews to leave their dwellings. For five days they could get no food. This was followed by segregation of all Jews in a ghetto around Taback Street.*

# APPENDIX D:

## Lt. Col. Paul West Criticizes Ferko's Recruits for Kay Project*

From:   Lt. Col. Paul West
To:     J.M. Scribner
Date:   November 27, 1943

1. On November 21st the following five men arrived in Cairo: [names of five Yugoslavs]

2. These constitute what has been termed "Kay" force and from a consultation of our records here were apparently recruited some seven months ago for work in Italy and also on targets in Albania. Upon questioning, however, these men did not appear very clear in their minds as to their duties, nor in what localities the were to perform. They seemed at first somewhat alarmed at the prospect of being parachuted into any enemy-occupied territory for extremely hazardous duties.

3. As they are native born Yug subjects, and as Tito has definitely ruled against accepting any civilian or enlisted personnel for guerrilla work in his controlled territories, we obviously cannot use them in that part of Yugoslavia. The situation in Mihailovitch's territory is such that it would be extremely unwise to send any more personnel to him at this moment, and incidentally, these men being Partisans, would not survive very long in those areas.

4. At the same time, they are well trained personnel, and as we are anxious to use them out here, we have had them screened by S.I. and turned them over to that branch for action. S.I. can use them as undercover men for their type of operations are often outside of Tito's military zone and hence this type of civilian personnel, out of uniform, could probably operate on the fringes of Tito's territory, as information gatherers.

---

* J.M. Scribner, Assistant Chief to the Special Operations Branch, Washington, DC, to Paul West, Lt. Col., Nov. 27, 1943; Box 260, Entry 105, RG 226. National Archives, College Park, MD.

# APPENDIX E:

## Head of OSS Secret Counterintelligence Unit Z James J. Angleton Questions Ferko's Reports on Balkans*

MEMORANDUM

From:   From JJ Angleton SCI unit Z Rome
To:      Francis Kalnay, Chief of X-2 Venice
Date:    October 31, 1945

Dear Francis,

1. I am in receipt of several interesting reports from your unit, but wish to call your attention to the following, which will greatly facilitate coordinating your operations into our general program in Italy.

2. It would be appreciated if intelligence involving personalities physically in Italy were transmitted to this office direct. Here it will be edited under the Jay ZX number and disseminated in accordance with our usual practices.

    Where information is of interest to X-2 core you should transmit such information to them direct, with an information copy to this office where it is of interest to either Milan, San Remo, Turin, or Trieste. All other dissemination will be made solely through Sci Unit Z, Rome.

3. I have discussed the general situation with Steve, and believe that future operations on Balkanites in Italy must follow the well-established pattern which in our experience has been to interrogate and break a person of considerable stature, who in turn, throws out undeveloped leads which are followed up; all such information being continually incorporated into a schematical or diagrammatical presentation and analysis of the intelligence network uncovered. Otherwise it is quite impossible to control or take action on penetration agents reports.

4. Our present difficulty is mainly that of evaluating the various reports which have been produced by yourself, No. 5 SCI Unit and the SIM/CS (Italian CE), and SCI Unit Z, Trieste. I feel that the time must come to carefully examine and control the Balkan information obtained in Italy during the past four months, and, therefore we would appreciate your comments

---

*  James A. Angleton, Chief, SCI Unit Z Rome, to Francis Kalnay, Chief of X-2 Venice, Oct. 31, 1945; Box 260, Entry 108A, RG 226. National Archives, College Park, MD.

# ENDNOTES

## I. Introduction

1. "Live births, total fertility rate," Hungarian Central Statistical Office, accessed on October 16, 2022, https://www.ksh.hu/stadat_files/nep/en/nep0006.html.
2. Dates of birth and death provided by Esteban Kálnay, September, 1, 2018.
3. Marsha L. Rozenblit, *The Jews of Vienna, 1867-1914: Assimilation and Identity* (SUNY Press, 1984) 63.
4. Donna Gabaccia, personal communication with the author, March 17, 2022.
5. Esteban Kalnay, personal communication with the author, March 28, 2022.
6. Gonzague Corbin de Mangoux and others, History of ECT in Schizophrenia: From Discovery to Current Use, Schizophrenia Bulletin Open, Volume 3, Issue 1, January 2022, sgac053, https://doi.org/10.1093/schizbullopen/sgac053.
7. Professor Tamas Farkas, personal communication with the author, March 2020.
8. Tara Zahra, *The Great Departure: Mass Migration from Eastern Europe and the Making of the Free World* (New York: W.W. Norton & Company, 2016) 14.
9. Zahra, 38-39.
10. Zahra, 14.
11. Zahra, 18.
12. Cited in Farkas, Tamás. "Jewish Name Magyarization in Hungary." AHEA: E-Journal of the American Hungarian Educators Association 5 (2012): 1-16.
13. László J. Kulcsár, «Something Old, Something New: Hungarian Marriage Patterns in Historical Perspective,» *Journal of Family History* 32, no. 3 (July 2007): 329.
14. Philip J. Adler, "The Introduction of Public Schooling for The Jews of Hungary (1849-1860)," *Jewish Social Studies* 36, no. 2 (1974): 122.
15. Esteban Kalnay, personal communication with the author, January 6, 2022.
16. Donna Gabaccia, personal communication with the author, March 17, 2022.
17. Christiane Scheffler, Michael Hermanussen, and Alan Rogol, "Stunting: historical lessons that catch-up growth tells us for mapping growth restoration." *Archives of Disease in Childhood* 106, no. 8 (August 2021): 819-820.
18. Kovacs, András. "Jewish assimilation and Jewish politics in Modern Hungary." *Jewish Studies at the Central European University: Public Lectures 1996-1999* (2000): 109-33. http://web.ceu.hu/jewishstudies/pdf/01_kovacs.pdf
19. James W. Oberly, "Love at First Sight and an Arrangement for Life: Investigating and Interpreting a 1910 Hungarian Migrant Marriage," *Journal of Austrian-American History* 1, no. 1 (January 2017): 82.
20. *Sunshine* directed by István Szabó (Abbey Road Studios), 1999.
21. Silber, Michael K. 2010. Hungary: Hungary before 1918. YIVO Encyclopedia of Jews in Eastern Europe. https://yivoencyclopedia.org/article.aspx/Hungary/Hungary_before_1918 (accessed March 22, 2022).
22. Braham, *Politics of Genocide*, 8.
23. Annemarie Steidl, Wladimir Fischer-Nebmaier, and James W. Oberly, *From a Multiethnic Empire to a Nation of Nations: Austro-Hungarian Migrants in the US, 1870–1940* (Innsbruck: StudienVerlag, 2017) 131.
24. Steidl, 22.
25. Steidl, Fischer-Nebmaier, and Oberly, 8.

26. Braham, *Politics of Genocide*, 18.
27. Robert Rozett, "Hungary and the Jews: From Golden Age to Destruction, 1895-1945," *Mass Violence & Résistance*, published on: September, 21 2015, accessed on May, 17, 2021, https://www.sciencespo.fr/mass-violence-war-massacre-resistance/en/document/hungary-and-jews-golden-age-destruction-1895-1945.html, ISSN 1961-9898.
28. Braham, 95.
29. Braham, 918.
30. Braham, 29.
31. Ezra Mendelsohn, "Trianon Hungary, Jews and Politics," in *Hostages of Modernization*, ed. Herbert A. Strauss, vol. 2, *Austria - Hungary - Poland - Russia* (Boston: De Gruyter, 2011) https://doi.org/10.1515/9783110883299.893, 893.
32. Steidl, 22.
33. The count comes from a special "IPUMS" file of individual-level census data created by Annemarie Steidl, Wladimir Fischer-Nebmaier, and James W. Oberly (*From a Multiethnic Empire*, 36) who used the file to code the birthplaces of Central Americans as told to census enumerators in the 1920 Census. This permitted them to count the number of individuals who were born in Austria-Hungary or one of the post-1918 successor states, or whose parents met those criteria.
34. "History," The Lofts at Neilson Crossing, accessed on October 8, 2022, https://www.theloftsnb.com/about-3.
35. Steven Béla Vardy, *The Hungarian-Americans* (Boston: Twayne Publishers, 1985) 77.
36. Anonymous Announcement, *Amerikai Magyar Hirlap (American Magyar Journal)*, January 22, 1920, vol XI: 1, Youngstown, Ohio.
37. I have more details about Andrés than about Jorge because of a published biography about him. Centro de Documentación de Arquitectura Latinoaméricana (CEDODAL), *Andrés Kalnay: un húngaro para la renovación arquitectónica* (Buenos Aires: CEDODAL, 2002). A biography of Jorge Kálnay has subsequently been published by CEDODAL but was not available at the time of this writing.
38. In Hungary, by 1925, about a fifth of marriages involving Jews were intermarriages. However, the percentages were much lower in New York City. In 1912 only two percent of marriages involving Jews were religious intermarriages. German and French Jews had the highest intermarriage rates, followed by Jews from Hungary. Milton L. Barron, "The Incidence of Jewish Intermarriage in Europe and America," *American Sociological Review* 11, no. 1 (1946): 9.
39. Kulcsar, "Something Old, Something New," 329.
40. Ferenc Kálnay and Alejandro Low. *Intérprete húngaro español: El diccionario para principiantes. Charlas prácticas.* Second edition. Publication date unknown. Mention found in: Obras de escritores emigrantes húngaros.
41. Francis Kalnay, *Feltámadás elött* (Budapest: Globus Nyomdai Müintézet R Publishing House, 1922).
42. Thanks to Veronika Szente Goldston for reading and summarizing the poems and dedication. October 13, 2022.
43. Veronika Szente Goldston, personal communication with the author, October 13, 2022
44. Willem S. Nyland. *Gurdjieff Club.* https://gurdjieffclub.com/en/willem-a-nyland/
45. Helen Langa, "'At Least Half the Pages Will Consist of Pictures': 'New Masses' and Politicized Visual Art," *American Periodicals* 21, no. 1 (2011): 37.
46. Christine Stansell, *American Moderns: Bohemian New York and the Creation of a New Century* (Princeton: Princeton University Press, 2021) 8.
47. Stansell, 8.

48. "Sexual Practices," Gurdjieff and The Fourth Way: A Critical Appraisal, updated on updated February 3, 2017, accessed on October 8, 2022, http://gurdjiefffourthway.org/pdf/sexual.pdf.

49. Stansell, *American Moderns*, 226.

50. Kulcsar, "Something Old, Something New," 332.

51. István Deák, "Hungary," *The European Right: A Historical Profile*, Hans Roger and Egon Weber, eds., (Berkley: University of California Press, 1963) 364.

52. Braham, *Politics of Genocide*, 41.

53. Rozett, "Hungary and the Jews."

54. In the nineteenth century and into the beginning of the twentieth century family disputes over the burial of loved ones were not uncommon. Courts heard a number of cases in which family members battled one another for custody of a corpse. Elizabeth Searcy, "The Dead Belong to the Living: Disinterment and Custody of Dead Bodies in Nineteenth-Century America." *Journal of Social History* 48, no. 1 (2014): 114.

55. Clare White (Director of Education, The Mob Museum), personal communication with the author, September 9, 2020.

56. J. Anne Funderburg (author of *Bootleggers and Beer Barons of the Prohibition Era* [McFarland, 2014]), personal communication with the author, September 10, 2020.

57. Mark Thornton (author of *Economics of Prohibition* [University of Utah Press, 1991]), personal communication with the author, September 8, 2020.

## II. How to Become a Spy

1. Francis Kalnay, *Foglalj helyet Péter* (New York: Europa Books, 1936).

2. Summary by Veronika Szente Goldston, personal communication with the author, October 13, 2022.

3. Leyzer Burko, "What sort of Yiddish did Jews in Hungary speak?" *Forward*, July 26, 2022, https://forward.com/forverts-in english/512097/what-sort-of-yiddish-did-jews-in-hungary-speak/.

4. Richard Collins and Francis Kalnay, *A Handbook of Seasickness* (New York: Transatlantic Publishers, 1937).

5. John Whiteclay Chambers, "Training for War and Espionage: Office of Strategic Services Training During World War II," *Studies in Intelligence* 54, no. 2 (June 2010) 21.

6. Peter Finn, *A Guest of the Reich: The Story of American Heiress Gertrude Legendre's Dramatic Captivity and Escape from Nazi Germany* (New York: Pantheon Books, 2019) 55.

7. Walter Wolf, "Secret Agents, Secret Armies: The Spy Who Captured an Army," The National WWII Museum, April 16, 2020, https://www.nationalww2museum.org/war/articles/wwii-spy-allen-dulles.

8. Roger Hall, *You're Stepping on My Cloak and Dagger* (Annapolis: Naval Institute Press, 1957) 3.

9. The project, with the code name "George," was inherited by Dulles from Donovan. Waller, Douglas. *Disciples: The World War II Missions of the CIA Directors Who Fought for Bill Donovan*. Simon and Schuster, 2015, page 121.

10. Francis Kalnay. Memorandum to Col. Buxton, December 12, 1942. NARA Record Group 226, Entry 105; National Archives Building, Washington, DC. National Archives, College Park MD. Accessed August 20, 2019.

11. John Chambers, personal communication with the author, January 7, 2020.

12. Francis Kalnay. Memorandum to Col. Buxton, December 12, 1942. NARA Record Group 226, Entry 105; National Archives Building, Washington, DC. National Archives, College Park MD. Accessed August 20, 2019.

13. Unsigned "Minute Sheet" Personnel Form for Francis Kalnay. October 23, 1943. NARA Record Group 226, Entry 105; The KAY Project. National Archives Building, Washington, DC. National Archives, College Park MD. Accessed August 20, 2019.

14. Letter from Huntington to Amoss. April, 29, 1943. NARA Record Group 226, Entry 105; The KAY Project. National Archives Building, Washington, DC. National Archives, College Park MD. Accessed August 20, 2019.

15. Wayne Nelson, *A Spy's Diary of World War II: Inside the OSS with an American Agent in Europe* (Jefferson: McFarland & Company, Inc., Publishers, 2009).

16. Patrick J. Chaisson. "OSS Agents: Kill or Be Killed." *Warfare History Network*. Volume 16, no. 5, August, 2017. https://warfarehistorynetwork.com/article/kill-or-be-killed/.

17. Chambers, John Whiteclay. *OSS Training in the National Parks and Service Abroad in World War II*. Washington D.C.: U.S. National Park Service, 2008.

18. Lisle, John. *The Dirty Tricks Department* (pp. 161-162). St. Martin's Publishing Group. Kindle Edition.

19. Susan H. Allen, *Classical Spies: American Archaeologists with the OSS in World War II Greece* (Ann Arbor: University of Michigan Press, 2011) 104.

20. Kirk Ford, personal communication with the author, February 2022.

21. Braham, *Politics of Genocide*, xxv.

22. Franklin Lindsay, *Beacons in the Night: With the OSS and Tito's Partisans in Wartime Yugoslavia* (Stanford: Stanford University Press, 1993) 1-2.

23. Lisle, John. *The Dirty Tricks Department: Stanley Lovell, the OSS, and the Masterminds of World War II Secret Warfare*. New York: St. Martin's Press. Kindle Edition, 2023, page 163.

24. T.J. Naftali, *X-2 and the Apprenticeship of American Counterespionage, 1942-1944. (volumes I and II)* Order No. 9330996. ProQuest Dissertations & Theses A&I, 1993, page 562.

25. Chief of X-2, Cairo. Bi-monthly Report . September 16, 1944. NARA Record Group 226, Entry 105; The KAY Project. National Archives Building, Washington, DC. National Archives, College Park MD. Accessed August 21, 2019.

## III. Family Secrets

1. Esteban Kalnay, personal communication with the author, January 6, 2022.

2. Duncan Bare, "Hungarian Affairs of the US-Office of Strategic Services in the Mediterranean Theater of Operations from June 1944 until September 1945" (master's thesis, Universität Graz, 2015).

3. United States Holocaust Memorial Memorial Museum, Anti-Jewish Laws in Hungary. https://encyclopedia.ushmm.org/content/en/timeline-event/holocaust/1933-1938/anti-jewish-laws-in-hungary. Accessed April 8, 2022.

4. Jason Dawsey, "Organizing Genocide: Theodor Dannecker, Eichmann's Deportation Specialist," United States Holocaust Memorial Museum, January 13, 2022, https://www.nationalww2museum.org/war/articles/organizing-genocide-theodor-dannecker-eichmanns-deportation-specialist.

5. "The Holocaust in Hungary: Frequently Asked Questions," United States Holocaust Memorial Museum, accessed July, 6, 2022, https://www.ushmm.org/information/exhibitions/online-exhibitions/special-focus/the-holocaust-in-hungary/the-holocaust-in-hungary-frequently-asked-questions#primo.

6. Fritz, Regina. "Inside the Ghetto: Everyday Life in Hungarian Ghettos." *The Hungarian historical review: new series of Acta Historica Academiae Scientiarum Hungaricae* 4, no. 3 (2015: 623.

7. Fritz. "Inside the Ghetto", 621

8. RG-50.030*0056, Oral History interview with Eva Brust Cooper conducted by Linda Kuzmack, United States Holocaust Memorial December 9, 199, interview transcript, https://collections.ushmm.org/oh_findingaids/RG-50.030.0056_trs_en.pdf.

9. Accession Number: 2015.160.2, Gibor Weinberger, "My Story: Another Holocaust Survivor," typescript memoir, United States Holocaust Memorial Museum, https://collections.ushmm.org/search/catalog/irn601759#?rsc=131679&cv=0&c=0&m=0&s=0&xywh=-1206%2C-193%2C5119%2C3855.

10. Tim Cole, *Holocaust City: The Making of a Jewish Ghetto* (New York: Routledge, 2013) 30.

11. Joanna Kakissis, "Hungary's New Holocaust Museum Isn't Open Yet, But It's Already Causing Concern," *National Public Radio*, February 8, 2019, World, https://www.npr.org/2019/02/08/690647054/hungarys-new-holocaust-museum-isn-t-open-yet-but-it-s-already-causing-worry.

12. Mádi, Mária. *Budapest Blackout: A Holocaust Diary*. Edited by James W. Oberly. University of Wisconsin Press, 2023. https://doi.org/10.2307/jj.2667630.

13. Borhi, László. "More than Victims? Popular Responses to national Socialist and Stalinist Dictatorships - the Case of Hungary." Rough draft, Indiana University. ostromworkshop.indiana.edu/pdf/seriespapers/2016s_c/Borhi%20paper.pdf

14. Personal communication from Esteban Kalnay who visited the museum and viewed public records certifying his aunt's death there on December 2, 1944.

15. "Holocaust (Shoah) Records (Jewish)," GenGuide, accessed on October 16, 2022, https://www.genguide.co.uk/source/holocaust-shoah-records-jewish/.

16. Zahra, *Great Departure*, 234.

17. Sarah Wildman, *Paper Love: Searching for the Girl My Grandfather Left Behind* (New York: Penguin, 2014) 214-216.

18. Wildman, 216.

19. Kalotay, Daphne. A New Generation of Storytellers. Opinion Section, *New York Times*, Monday, April 17, 2023.

20. The term was used by geographer Tim Cole in his book *Holocaust City: The Making of a Jewish Ghetto*.

21. Rozett, "Hungary and the Jews."

22. Yeshayahu Jelinek, "Self-identification of First Generation Hungarian Jewish Immigrants," *American Jewish Historical Quarterly* 61, no. 3 (1972): 217.

23. Cooper, RG-50.030*0056, USHMM.

24. Braham, *Politics of Genocide*, xxv.

25. United States Holocaust Memorial Museum, "Jewish Badge During the Nazi Era," Holocaust Encyclopedia, accessed on July, 21, 2022, https://encyclopedia.ushmm.org/content/en/article/jewish-badge-during-the-nazi-era.

26. Braham, *Politics of Genocide*, xxvi.

27. Wildman, *Paper Love*, 50-52.

28. Mádi, Mária. *Budapest Blackout*, 38-41.

29. Braham, Randolph L. *The Politics of Genocide: The Holocaust in Hungary* (volumes 1 and 2), (New York: Columbia University Press, 1981)

30. Zahra, *Great Departure*, 144-158.

31. Andrew Meier, "'The God-Damnedest Thing': The Antisemitic Plot to Thwart U.S. Aid to Europe's Jews and the Man Who Exposed It," *Politico*, September 23, 2022, The Friday Read, https://www.politico.com/news/magazine/2022/09/23/henry-morgenthau-roosevelt-government-europes-jews-00058206.

32. Friedman, Dan. "If the U.S. had acted, Anne Frank might still be alive—Ken Burns on the Holocaust." The Forward.com. 9/14/22. https://forward.com/culture/517837/interview-

with-ken-burns-holocaust-pbs-documentary-anne-frank/?utm_source=Iterable&utm_medium=email&utm_campaign=sundayedition_5110253.

33. PJ Grisar, "A new book explains Pope Pius XII's silence during the Shoah—but does not excuse it," *Forward*, June 07, 2022, Culture, https://forward.com/culture/504773/pope-pius-xii-the-pope-at-war-david-kertzer-mussolini-hitler-vatican-archive/.

34. István Deák, "Bucharest, Budapest, Vienna: Three Capitals on the Itinerary of the Soviet Red Army, 1944-194" (Presentation, Munk Centre for International Studies, November 10, 2004).

35. Cole, *Holocaust* City, 192.

36. Cole, 204.

37. Cole, 207.

38. Personal Files of Prime Minister László Bárdossy. EHRI. https://portal.ehri-project.eu/units/hu-002739-mnl_ol_k_38. Acccessed April 8, 2022.

39. Wildman, *Paper Love*, 231.

40. Freedland, Jonathan. 2022. *The Escape Artist: The Man Who Broke Out of Auschwitz to Warn the World.* (New York: Harper Collins).

41. Wildman, 257-8.

42. Richard Breitman, *Official Secrets: What the Nazis Planned, What the British and Americans Knew* (New York: Hill and Wang, 1998) 137.

43. Zahra, *Great Departure*, 178.

44. National Archives, OSS Official Dispatch # 1597 Bern, March 10, 1943.

45. United States Holocaust Memorial Museum, "Deportation of Hungarian Jews," Timeline of Events, accessed on October 9, 2022, https://www.ushmm.org/learn/timeline-of-events/1942-1945/deportation-of-hungarian-jews.

46. Breitman, *Official Secrets*, 204.

47. Peter Black (Contract historian and consultant to the United States Holocaust Memorial Museum), personal communication with the author, March, 21, 2022.

48. Wildman, *Paper Love*, 14.

49. Victoria Aarons and Alan Berger, *Third-Generation Holocaust Representation: Trauma, History, and Memory* (Evanston: Northwestern University Press, 2017) 46.

50. Wildman, *Paper Love* 50-52.

51. Gerson, Stéphane. "A History from Within: When Historians Write about Their Own Kin." *The Journal of Modern History* 94, no. 4 (2022) 924.

52. Susan Rubin Suleiman, "Crises of Memory and the Second World War," (Cambridge: Harvard University Press, 2006) 107.

53. Neumann, Ariana. *When Time Stopped: A Memoir of My Father's War and what Remains.* Simon and Schuster, 2020.

54. Adorján, Johanna. *An Exclusive Love: A Memoir.* WW Norton & Company, 2011.

55. Rom-Rymer, Symi. "People of the Book: Interview with Julie Orringer." *The Moment.* February 11, 2011. https://momentmagazine.wordpress.com/2011/02/11/people-of-the-book-interview-with-julie-orringer/.

56. Joachim J. Savelsberg, *Knowing about Genocide: Armenian Suffering and Epistemic Struggles* (Oakland: University of California Press, 2021).

57. Levine, Deborah. "I Shared My Father's Letters About Nazi Horrors with the High School Class." Forward.com. March 21, 2023.

58. Joseph Skibell, *A Blessing on the Moon: A Novel* (Chapel Hill, N.C.: Algonquin Books, 1997), cited in Aarons and Berger, *Third-Generation Holocaust Representation* 109.

59. Michael Frank, "What It Took for Stella Levi to Talk About the Holocaust," *The New York Times*, September 14, 2022.

60. Wildman, *Paper Love*, 206-7.
61. Adam Biro, *One Must Also Be Hungarian*, trans. Catherine Tihanyi (Chicago: University of Chicago Press, 2006) 42.
62. Vajda, Júlia, and Éva Kovacs. "I Have a Certificate of Not Being an Anti-Semite." *East Central Europe* 24, no. 1 (1997): 181-204.
63. John Temple, "How I Finally Learned My Name," *The Atlantic*, September 24, 2022, https://www.theatlantic.com/family/archive/2022/09/how-i-finally-learned-my-name/671548/?utm_source=copy-link&utm_medium=social&utm_campaign=share.
64. Fritz, "Inside the Ghetto," 624.
65. Aarons and Berger *Third-Generation Holocaust Representation*, 175.
66. Misha Berson, "Tom Stoppard's early genius and late reckoning with Jewish identity," *Forward*, March 31, 2021, Culture, https://forward.com/culture/466777/tom-stoppards-early-genius-and-late-reckoning-with-jewish-identity/.
67. Reader Comments, "Speaking of the War at Long Last," *The New York Times*. May 7, 2023.
68. Ronald C. Newton, "The United States, the German-Argentines, and the Myth of the Fourth Reich, 1943-47," *Hispanic American Historical Review* 64, no. 1 (1984): 95.
69. Sergio Kiernan, "La memoria de Kálnay," *Página 12*, June 29, 2002, https://www.pagina12.com.ar/diario/suplementos/m2/10-70-2002-06-29.html.
70. "Nazi rally in Buenos Aires through rare photographs, 1938," Rare Historical Photos, accessed on September 20, 2021, https://rarehistoricalphotos.com/nazi-rally-argentina-1938/.
71. "Argentina Virtual Jewish History Tour," Jewish Virtual Library, accessed on August 8, 2022, https://www.jewishvirtuallibrary.org/argentina-virtual-jewish-history-tour.
72. Joachim J. Savelsberg, *Knowing about Genocide: Armenian Suffering and Epistemic Struggles* (Oakland: University of California Press, 2021).
73. Victor A. Mirelman, "The Semana Trágica of 1919 and the Jews in Argentina," *Jewish Social Studies* (Winter 1975) 66.
74. Mirelman, 73.
75. WNYC-FM. "Dani Shapiro's First Novel in 15 Years." All of It, WNYC-FM. October 24, 2022, https://www.wnyc.org/story/dani-shapiros-first-novel-15-years/.
76. Central Intelligence Agency, Memorandum to the Assistant Director of Special Operations, August 8, 1949, Appendix A, page 38, https://www.cia.gov/readingroom/docs/BISHOP,%20ROBERT%20%20VOL.%202_0030.pdf, accessed October 14, 2022.

## IV. End of the War and Leaving the OSS

1. Nelson, *Spy's Diary*, 168.
2. Map of OSS Missions and Bases in 1945, in Michael Warner, "The Office of Strategic Services: America's First Intelligence Agency," Central Intelligence Agency, May 2000, https://www.cia.gov/static/7851e16f9e100b6f9cc4ef002028ce2f/Office-of-Strategic-Services.pdf.
3. Map scanned from https://catalog.library.cornell.edu/catalog/4821910.
4. Duncan Bare, personal communication with the author, April 2015.
5. John Whiteclay Chambers, *OSS Training in the National Parks and Service Abroad in World War II* (Washington D.C.: National Park Service, 2008), https://irma.nps.gov/DataStore/DownloadFile/486417, 297.
6. USC Shoah Foundation, "War Crimes Trial Participant Nicholas Doman Testimony," interview conducted by Dan Danieli, January 30, 1998, YouTube, accessed on October 9, 2022, https://www.youtube.com/watch?v=NW8KPA3Qz3I.
7. Peter M.F. Sichel, communication on the OSS Society Discussion Group (https://www.osssociety.org/discussion.html) with the author, January 20, 2020. Also see Scott Anderson,

*The Quiet Americans: Four CIA Spies at the Dawn of the Cold War—a Tragedy in Three Acts*
(New York: Doubleday, 2020) 65.

8.  Michael G. Seidel, Section Chief Record/Information Dissemination Section, Information
    Management Division, Federal Bureau of Investigation, US Department of Justice, January
    21, 2002.

9.  Kalnay Personnel File. Confidential notice, "Security". July 31, 1945. NARA Record Group
    226, Entry 105; The KAY Project. National Archives Building, Washington, DC. National
    Archives, College Park MD. Accessed August 21, 2019.

10. Stansell, *American Moderns*, 314.

11. Zoltán Deák, ed., *This Noble Flame: An Anthology of a Hungarian Newspaper in America
    1902-1982* (New York: Heritage Press, 1982) 125.

12. Michael Holzman, personal communication with the author, April 27, 2017.

13. Michael Warner, "The Office of Strategic Services: America's First Intelligence Agency,"
    Central Intelligence Agency, May 2000, https://www.cia.gov/static/7851e16f9e100b6f9cc4
    ef002028ce2f/Office-of-Strategic-Services.pdf. See especially the section titled "X-2."

14. R. Dunlop, R. "Donovan: America's Master Spy." *NY: Rand McNally* 562 (1982): 467.

15. Director of National Intelligence CI Reader, Vol2. June, 1939. https://www.dni.gov/files/
    NCSC/documents/ci/CI_Reader_Vol2.pdf, p.2.

16. David P. Mowry. "Cryptologic aspects of German intelligence activities in South America
    during World War II." *National Security Agency, United States Cryptologic History, Series IV
    World War II*, 2011: 11.

17. Savage, Charlie. Reports Accuse Credit Suisse of Impeding Hunt for Accounts Linked to
    Nazis. *The New York Times*.

18. Torkar, Blaz. *Mission Yugoslavia: The OSS and the Chetnik and Partisan Resistance Movements*,
    1943-1945. Jefferson, North Carolina: McFarland Press, 2020:163

19. Enyeart, John P. *Death to Fascism: Louis Adamic's Fight for Democracy*. University of Illinois
    Press. Page 128.

20. Enyeart, Death to Fascism.

21. Enyeart, Death to Fascism.

22. Enyeart, Death to Fascism, 108.

23. Fernando Hernández Rebollar, personal communication with the author, September 17,
    2016.

24. Francis Kalnay, Curtis E. Avery, and Harry Behn, *I Am the Cat* (New York: Houghton
    Mifflin Harcourt, Date unknown).

## V. Impact

1.  Fernando Hernández Rebollar, personal communication with the author, October 2017.

2.  John Chambers, personal communication with the author, January 7, 2020.

3.  Patrick K. O'Donnell, *Operatives, Spies, and Saboteurs: The Unknown Story of the Men and
    Women of World War II's OSS* (New York: Free Press, 2014) XI.

4.  O'Donnell, *Operatives, Spies, and Saboteurs*.

5.  Jane Coaston, "Trump's new defense of his Charlottesville comments is incredibly false,"
    *Vox*, April 26, 2019, https://www.vox.com/2019/4/26/18517980/trump-unite-the-right-
    racism-defense-charlottesville.

6.  Andres Marantz, "The Illiberal Order," *The New Yorker*, July 4, 2022, 39.

7.  Bennett Muraskin, "Secular Jews and Pacifism," The Cultural and Secular Jewish
    Organization (CSJO), accessed on October 15, 2022, https://www.csjo.org/resources/
    essays/secular-jews-and-pacifism-by-bennett-muraskin.

8.   Hippo Taatila, "A history of violence: The concrete and metaphorical wars in the life narrative of GI Gurdjieff," *Scripta Instituti Donneriani Aboensis* 29 (2020): 98.

9.   "P.D. Ouspensky (1878-1947)," The Gurdjieff Legacy Foundation Archives, accessed on October 9, 2022, https://gurdjiefflegacy.org/archives/pdouspensky.htm.

10.  Peter Kalnay, personal communication with the author, October 9, 2018.

11.  OSS Society (@osssociety), "In one newly discovered letter from the summer of 1945, Hemingway writes to Bruce about his son Jack [who served in OSS] nicknamed Bumby, who had recently been released from a German prisoner of war camp during World War II," Twitter, September 21, 2022, 6:59 A.M., https://mobile.twitter.com/osssociety/status/1572556028109111297. Steve Newman, "Ernest Hemingway's son, Jack," Medium, July 3, 2018, https://stevenewmanwriter.medium.com/ernest-hemingways-son-jack-285b3e3d69bb.

12.  Daniel Mendelsohn, *The Lost: A Search for Six of Six Million* (New York: Harper Perennial, 2006) 73.

13.  Pogrebin, Letty Cottin. *Shanda: A Memoir of Shame and Secrecy*. Brentwood, TN: Post Hill Press. 2022.

14.  András Kovacs, "Jewish Assimilation and Jewish Politics in Modern Hungary," in *Jewish Studies at the Central European University*, ed. András Kovacs, vol. 1, *Yearbook 1996-1999* (Budapest: Central European University, 2011), https://jewishstudies.ceu.edu/sites/jewishstudies.ceu.edu/files/attachment/basicpage/45/01kovacs.pdf.

15.  Susan Faludi, *In the Darkroom* (New York: Metropolitan Books, 2016) 214.

16.  Aarons and Berger *Third-Generation Holocaust Representation*, 8.

17.  Aarons and Berger, 6-8.

18.  Yivo Institute for Jewish Research. "After the End of the World: Displaced Persons and Disiplaced Persons Camps. https://yivo.org/Displaced-Persons. Accessed April 19, 2022.

19.  *The Flat,* directed by Arnon Goldfinger (IFC Films), 20ll.

20.  Aarons and Berger, 64.

21.  Aarons and Berger, 202.

22.  Cited by Aarons and Berger, 151.

23.  Stiggers, Ken. "Like A Tree Without Roots." *Jackson Free Press*, 4 Feb. 2015, www.jacksonfreepress.com/news/2015/feb/04/tree-without-roots/.

24.  Rosner, Elizabeth. *Survivor café: The legacy of trauma and the labyrinth of memory*. Catapult, 2017:252.

# RESEARCH METHODS AND ACKNOWLEDGMENTS

I spent several days at the National Archives in College Park, Maryland, before they closed during the COVID-19 pandemic. There, skilled archivists helped me locate hundreds of documents from among 400,000 pages of declassified OSS records released by the CIA in 2000. I spent three days perusing original memos, reports, and letters and photographed relevant documents with my iPhone to later import into a database for coding and analysis.

Because only a small portion of the WWII documents in the National Archives are digitized, researching my grandfather's life entailed searching indexes to identify the location of documents related to his OSS work in various cities of Italy, checking out the boxes a few at a time, and searching through hundreds of pages of onion skin memoranda and reports. The process reminded me of the library research I conducted when I was writing my dissertation at Columbia in 1979 before Google searches or online journal articles were widely available.

I was fortunate to have access to hundreds of books and articles on Hungary and World War II via the internet and local and academic libraries. In addition to the writings of authors whom I contacted personally, certain classic works were especially useful. In particular, Randolph Braham's *The Politics of Genocide* is an invaluable guide to Hungarian history and politics.

Two contemporary family members were especially helpful to my search. My cousin Wendy Brown shared her personal memories of years spent living close to our grandfather and caring for Ferko at the end of his life, as well as her expert political interpretation of his children's books. In May 2018, I traveled to Spain to meet my mother's cousin Esteban Kalnay, who helped with his extensive knowledge of Kalnay family history.

Once back in New York, quarantining during the pandemic afforded me time to review the photographed records and to explore academic databases, online archives, immigration records, ship passenger lists, and declassified personnel materials retrieved from the CIA. Scrivener was an invaluable software program for writing notes and sorting hundreds of documents. I also used Aeon Timeline software to create timelines for the Kalnay family, Ferko's career, and historical events from the 1800s to my grandfather's death in 1992.

As the descendant of an OSS officer, I was able to join the OSS Society. I also benefitted from the assistance of reference librarians at the University of Minnesota and the New York Public Library.

Several online databases were helpful. Questions posted to NARA's crowd-sourced platform, History Hub, are answered by NARA archivists or interested members of the public who register with the site. JewishGen is an international online database of records, resources, and research advice. They provide a link to the Holocaust Database, as does The United States Holocaust Memorial Museum which also has an extensive list of tools for researchers. The CIA maintains a search tool called CREST, which is available via a FOIA search.

To research family events in New York State, I searched Putnam County newspaper archives, records in the New York Genealogical and Biographical Society, and the New York State Archives. I purchased court transcripts related to the disposition of charges of bootlegging against my mother's stepfather, Dan Steinbeck, and corresponded with a researcher at the Mob Museum about Prohibition.

I was greatly aided in my investigation by personal communications with scholars and Kalnay enthusiasts doing their own research. I describe several of them below because personal communication with academic experts is an untapped resource that many authors may not think to utilize.

Before writing this book I never knew there was a field called onomastics that covers the history of name changes. For Jews in central Europe in the nineteenth and twentieth centuries, name changes reflect important political and cultural changes. I learned from the work of Hungarian scholar Tamas Farkas and benefitted from his assistance researching Kalnay family name changes in the nineteenth and twentieth centuries.

Research on my grandparents introduced me to other quite unexpected fields of research such as nudist and artists' camps in rural America and bootlegging during Prohibition. Staff at county historical societies and libraries helped me find resources and newspaper archives on both of these topics. Other individuals with whom I corresponded were authors of books on bootlegging and even the director of education at The Mob Museum.

To better understand my great-grandmother Rózsa's fate, I corresponded with Professor Emese Lafferton at Central European University. Professor Lafferton answered several questions and shared some of her work on the history of psychiatric hospitals in the Austro-Hungarian Empire.

I contacted Mississippi College military historian Kirk Ford after reading his books on the OSS and Yugoslav resistance in WWII. Professor Ford generously read an early draft of my manuscript and pointed out several needed corrections. I also learned about the history of the OSS in the Balkans from the work of David Robarge (Center for Security Studies at Georgetown University and chief historian of the CIA) and Blaz Torkar (political scientist and historian at the Military Schools Centre of the Slovenian Armed Forces). Historian, Jim Oberly (Professor Emeritus of History at University of Wisconsin-Eau Clair helped me to understand Hungarian marriage questions and answered several of my questions about translations from Hungarian to English.

At the beginning of this book, I mentioned Duncan Bare, the researcher who wrote to me describing his research into the life of my grandfather and other Hungarian OSS agents. Duncan motivated my interest in this topic and taught me much from a reading of his University of Graz, Austria, master's thesis on this topic. Duncan is currently an associate fellow at large for Deutsches Asienforschungszentrum and editor of *The Journal for Intelligence, Propaganda and Security Studies.*

One of the challenges of writing about the Holocaust is the sheer volume of relevant materials. Research on the fate of Kalnay family members during WWII was facilitated by Zvi Bernhardt at Yad Vashem, The World Holocaust Remembrance Center, and Peter Black at the US Holocaust Memorial Museum. I describe what I learned in that search in Chapter 10.

I was fortunate to be in touch with people who knew the Kalnay family first-hand. Ferko's nephew Esteban Kalnay provided feedback on the draft manuscript and extensive information on my grandfather's family life and his work designing homes under the tutelage of his Hungarian-Argentine brothers. Esteban himself is an architect in Spain. Fernando Hernández and Pedro Riveroll are two men who wrote about Ferko's influence on the town of Valle de Bravo Mexico. Finally, information on my grandfather's skill as a personal chef came from a book on great meals published by Minneapolis food writer Virginia Safford. My cousin Wendy Brown knew Ferko better than anyone else I spoke with. Her suggestions and additions to the book improved it greatly.

My daughter Soraya Darabi provided important suggestions regarding distribution and promotion of the book, as well as access to marketing and publicity resources.

Finally, anthropologist and Jewish scholar Riv-Ellen Prell and immigration historian Donna Gabaccia provided valuable feedback on the draft manuscript, as did Leila Darabi, Debra Kalmuss, Silvia Blitzer Golombek, and Ann Markusen.

# SELECTED BIBLIOGRAPHY

Adorjan, Johanna. *An Exclusive Love: A Memoir*. New York: W.W. Norton Company, 2011.

Albright, M. K., and Woodward, W. *Prague Winter: A Personal Story of Remembrance and War, 1937-1948*. New York: Harper, 2012.

Allen, Susan Hueck. *Classical Spies: American Archaeologists with the OSS in World War II Greece*. University of Michigan Press, 2011.

Alperin, Elijah, and Jeanne Batalova. "European Immigrants in the United States." *Migration Policy* (August 1, 2018). https://www.migrationpolicy.org/article/european-immigrants-united-states.

Anderson, Scott. "'With friends like these...': the OSS and the British in Yugoslavia." *Intelligence and National Security* 8, no. 2 (1993): 140-171.

Ansart, Severine, Camille Pelat, Pierre-Yves Boelle, Fabrice Carrat, Antoine Flahault, and Alain Jacques Valleron. "Mortality burden of the 1918–1919 influenza pandemic in Europe." *Influenza and Other Respiratory Viruses* 3, no. 3 (2009): 99-106.

Bács, Zoltán. "Desde Jasenovac hasta Buenos Aires: un destino de dos hermanos." *Act Hispanica* 23 (2018): 315-323.

Bailey, Roderick. "OSS-SOE relations, Albania 1943–44." *Intelligence and National Security* 15, no. 2 (2000): 20-35.

Bankier, David, ed. *Secret Intelligence and the Holocaust: Collected Essays from the Colloquium at the City University of New York*. New York: Enigma Books, 2006.

Bilger, Burkhard. *Fatherland: A Memoir of War, Conscience, and Family Secret*. New York: Random House, 2023.

Braham, Randolph L. (volumes 1 and 2), The Politics of Genocide: The Holocaust in Hungary (New York: Columbia University Press, 1981.

Braham, Randolph L., and András Kovács, eds. *The Holocaust in Hungary: Seventy Years Later*. Budapest: Central European University Press, 2016.

Chalou, George C., ed. *The Secrets War: The Office of Strategic Services in World War II*. Washington D.C.: National Archives and Record Administration, 1992.

Chambers, John Whiteclay. *OSS Training in the National Parks and Service Abroad in World War II*. Washington D.C.: U.S. National Park Service, 2008.

Ciniglio, Alexandra. *Los Papeles Secretos de Pape*. Madrid: Nagrela Editores, 2021.

Collins, Richard and Francis Kalnay. *A Handbook of Seasickness*. June 22, 1937.

Cramer, Gisela and Ursula Prutsch, editors. *¡Américas unidas! Nelson A. Rockefeller's Office of Inter-American Affairs (1940-46)*. Madrid/Frankfurt: Iberoamericana/Vervuert, 2012.

Enyeart, John P. *Death to Fascism: Louis Adamic's Fight for Democracy*. Urbana: University of Illinois Press, 2019.

Fairweather, Jack. *The Volunteer: The True Story of the Resistance Hero Who Infiltrated Auschwitz*. London: WH Allen, 2019.

Faludi, Susan. *In the Darkroom*. Macmillan, 2016

Finchelstein, Federico. *Transatlantic Fascism: Ideology, Violence, and the Sacred in Argentina and Italy, 1919-1945*. Durham: Duke University Press, 2010.

Ford, Kirk. *OSS and the Yugoslav Resistance, 1943-1945*. (Texas A&M University Military History Series, number 28.) College Station: Texas A&M University Press, 1992.

Gerson, Stéphane. "A History from Within: When Historians Write about Their Own Kin." *The Journal of Modern History* 94, no. 4 (2022): 898-937.

Hall, Roger. *You're Stepping on my Cloak and Dagger*. Annapolis: Naval Institute Press, 2013.

Holzman, Michael. *James Jesus Angleton, the CIA, and the Craft of Counterintelligence*. Amherst: University of Massachusetts Press, 2008.

Jeffreys-Jones R. *American Espionage: From Secret Service to CIA*. New York: The Free Press, 1977.

Kalnay, Francis. *Feltámadás elött (Before Resurrection)*. Budapest: Globus Nyomdai Müintézet R Publishing House, 1922.

Kalnay, Francis. *Foglalj helyet Péter (Take a Seat, Peter)*. New York: Europa Books, 1936.

Kalnay, Francis and Richard Collins. *The New American: A Handbook of Necessary Information for Aliens, Refugees, and New Citizens*. New York: Greenberg Press, 1941.

Kalnay, Francis. *The Song of the Wooden Doll: A Play in Three Acts*. Listed in the Catalog of Copyright Entries, March 13, 1952. DU30319.

Kalnay, Francis. "Give Yourselves the New Thrill of Smoke Cookery," *House Beautiful Magazine*. December, 1953: 202-208.

Kalnay, Francis. *Chucaro: Wild Pony of the Pampa* (First edition). New York: Harcourt Brace, 1958.

Kalnay, Francis. "Enter the Wonderful World of Marinades," *House Beautiful Magazine*. November, 1959: 238-286.

Kalnay, Francis and Witold T. Mars. *The Richest Boy in the World* (First edition). New York: Harcourt, Brace, 1959.

Kalnay, Francis. "What! Flowers in Cooking?" *House Beautiful Magazine*. April, 1960: 161-194.

Kalnay, Francis. *It Happened in Chichipica*. New York: Harcourt Brace Jovanovich, 1971.

Kalnay, Ferenc and Alejandro Low. (Second edition). Publication date unknown. Intérprete húngaro español: El diccionario para principiantes. Charlas prácticas. (Hungarian Spanish dictionary) Database: Obras de escritores emigrantes húngaros (Publication date unknown.)

Katz, Barry M. *Foreign Intelligence: Research and Analysis in the Office of Strategic Services, 1942-1945*. Cambridge, MA: Harvard University Press, 1989.

Klein, Christopher. "How South America Became a Nazi Haven." History.com, 2014. https://www.history.com/news/how-south-america-became-a-nazi-haven

Lees, Lorraine M. *Yugoslav-Americans and National Security During World War II*. Urbana: University of Illinois Press, 2007.

Levine, Paul A. "Raoul Wallenberg in Budapest: Myth, History, and Holocaust." London and Portland, OR: Vallentine Mitchell, 2010.

Lindsay, Franklin. *Beacons in the Night: With the OSS and Tito's Partisans in Wartime Yugoslavia*. Stanford: Stanford University Press, 1993.

Liptak, Eugene. *Office of Strategic Services 1942–45: The World War II Origins of the CIA.* Oxford: Osprey Publishing, 2009.

Lisle, John. *The Dirty Tricks Department: Stanley Lovell, the OSS, and the Masterminds of World War II Secret Warfare.* New York: St. Martin's Press, 2023.

Macintyre, Ben. *Agent Zigzag: A True Story of Nazi Espionage, Love, and Betrayal.* Prince Georges County, Maryland: Crown Publishers, 2008.

Mádi, Mária. *Budapest Blackout: A Holocaust Diary.* Edited by James W. Oberly. University of Wisconsin Press, 2023. https://doi.org/10.2307/jj.2667630.

McIntosh, Elizabeth P., and Gabriella Cavallero. *Sisterhood of Spies: The Women of the OSS.* Annapolis: Naval Institute Press, 1998.

Mendelsohn, Daniel. *The Lost: A Search for Six of Six Million.* New York: Harper Perennial, 2006.

Moran, Christopher R. *Company Confessions: Secrets, Memoirs, and the CIA.* New York: Thomas Dunne Books/St. Martin's Press, 2016.

Naftali, Tim. *Blind Spot: The Secret History of American Counterterrorism.* New York: Basic Books, 2009.

Naftali, Tim. *X-2 and the Apprenticeship of American Counterespionage, 1942-1944.* Volumes I and II, Order No. 9330996. ProQuest Dissertations & Theses 1993.

Nelson, Wayne. *A Spy's Diary of World War II: Inside the OSS with an American Agent in Europe.* Jefferson, NC: McFarland & Company, Inc., Publishers, 2009.

Neumann, Ariana. *When Time Stopped: A Memoir of My Father's War and What Remains.* New York: Scribner, 2020.

O'Donnell, Patrick K. *Operatives, Spies, and Saboteurs: The Unknown Story of the Men and Women of World War II's OSS.* New York: The Free Press, 2004.

Packer, George. *Our Man: Richard Holbrooke and the End of the American Century.* New York: Alfred A. Knopf, 2019.

Perenyi, Eleanor. *More Was Lost: A Memoir.* New York: New York Review of Books, 2016.

Petersen, Neal H., ed. *From Hitler's Doorstep: The Wartime Intelligence Reports of Allen Dulles, 1942-1945.* University Park, PA: Pennsylvania State University Press, 2010.

Pogrebin, Letty Cottin. *Shanda: A Memoir of Shame and Secrecy.* Brentwood, TN: Post Hill Press. 2022.

Press, Sylvia. *In the Care of Devils.* New York: Bantam Books, 1966.

Rafalko, Frank J., ed. *A CounterintelligenceReader.* Washington D.C.: National Counterintelligence Center, 2004.

Ranki, Vera. *The Politics of Inclusion and Exclusion: Jews and Nationalism in Hungary.* New York: Holmes & Meier, 1999.

Rosner, Elizabeth. *Survivor Café: The Legacy of Labyrinth of Memory.* New York: Catapult, 2017.

Rozenblit, Marsha L. *The Jews of Vienna, 1867-1914: Assimilation and Identity.* Albany: State University of New York Press, 1983.

Rozenblit, Marsha L. *Reconstructing a National Identity: the Jews of Habsburg Austria during World War I.* New York: Oxford University Press, 2001.

Saunders, Frances Stonor. *The Cultural Cold War: The CIA and the World of Arts and Letters.* New York: New Press, 2013.

Savelsberg, Joachim J. *Knowing about Genocide: Armenian Suffering and Epistemic Struggles.* Oakland: University of California Press.

Schreiber, Rebecca Mina. *Cold War Exiles in Mexico: US Dissidents and the Culture of Critical Resistance.* Minneapolis: University of Minnesota Press, 2008.

Shandler, Jeffrey. *Holocaust Memory in the Digital Age.* Stanford: Stanford University Press, 2020.

Smith, Richard Harris. *OSS: the secret history of America's first central intelligence agency.* Rowman & Littlefield, 2005.

Smith, W. Thomas. *Encyclopedia of the Central Intelligence Agency.* New York: Facts on File, 2003.

Stansell, Christine. *American Moderns: Bohemian New York and the Creation of a New Century.* Princeton: Princeton University Press, 2021.

Steidl, Annemarie, Wladimir Fischer-Nebmaier, and James W. Oberly, eds. *From a Multiethnic Empire to a Nation of Nations: Austro-Hungarian Migrants in the US, 1870–1940.* Vol. 10 of *Transatlantica.* Innsbruck: StudienVerlag, 2017.

Suleiman, Susan Rubin. *Crises of Memory and the Second World War.* Cambridge: Harvard University Press, 2006.

Thomas, Gordon, and Greg Lewis. *Shadow Warriors of World War II: The Daring Women of the OSS and SOE.* Chicago: Chicago Review Press, 2017.

Torkar, Blaz. *Mission Yugoslavia: The OSS and the Chetnik and Partisan Resistance Movements, 1943-1945.* McFarland Press, 2020.

Troy, Thomas F. *Donovan and the CIA: A History of the Establishment of the Central Intelligence Agency.* Frederick, MD: University Publications of America, 1981.

Vági, Zoltán, László Csősz, and Gábor Kádár. *The Holocaust in Hungary: Evolution of a Genocide.* Lanham, MD: AltaMira Press in association with the United States Holocaust Memorial Museum, 2013.

Vardy, Steven Béla. *The Hungarian Americans.* Boston: Twayne Publishers, 1985.

Vital, David. *A People Apart: A Political History of the Jews in Europe 1789-1939.* New York: Oxford University Press, 2001.

Waller, Douglas. *Wild Bill Donovan: The Spymaster Who Created the OSS and Modern American Espionage.* New York: Free Press, 2011.

Weiner, Tim. *Legacy of Ashes: The History of the CIA.* New York: Anchor Books, 2008.

Wildman, Sarah. *Paper Love: Searching for the Girl My Grandfather Left Behind.* New York: Penguin, 2014.

Zahra, Tara. *The Great Departure: Mass Migration from Eastern Europe and the Making of the Free World.* New York: W.W. Norton & Company, 2016.

Zerubavel, Eviatar. *The Elephant in the Room: Silence and Denial in Everyday Life.* Oxford: Oxford University Press, 2006.

# INDEX

# ABOUT THE AUTHOR

KATHERINE FENNELLY is an emeritus professor of public policy at the Humphrey School of Public Affairs of the University of Minnesota, with a Ph.D. from Columbia University, where she was on the faculty in the School of Public Health early in her career. She is known for the breadth and quality of her social science research and for numerous academic publications. In this book, Fennelly applies her expertise in an investigation of the life of her maternal grandfather, a Jewish Hungarian immigrant who arrived in the US one hundred years ago and became the head of an elite espionage unit for the Allied Forces and an award-winning children's book author. Her strategies involved conducting genealogical research, accessing personnel files from the CIA, and reviewing hundreds of previously unpublished original documents at the National Archives. She read widely on each of the topics covered, and corresponded with scholars of World War II, Jewish history, and the Holocaust. She also interviewed surviving family members about her grandfather's life and accomplishments.

Made in the USA
Middletown, DE
31 August 2023

37688299R00149